Popular Culture, New Media and Digital Literacy in Early Childhood

This book offers a range of perspectives on children's multimodal experiences, providing a ground-breaking account of the ways in which children engage with popular, media and digital literacy practices from their earliest years. Many young children have extensive experience of film, television, print media, computer games, mobile phones and the internet from birth, yet their engagement with media texts is rarely acknowledged in the national curricula of any country.

This seminal text focuses on children from birth to eight years, addressing issues such as:

- Media and identity construction;
- Media literacy practices in the home;
- The changing nature of literacy in technologised societies;
- The place of popular and media texts in children's lives and the use of such texts in the curriculum.

In exploring children's engagement with popular culture, media and digital texts in the home, community and early years settings, the contributors look at empirical studies from around the world, and draw out vital new theoretical issues relating to children's emergent techno-literacy practices.

With an unmatchable team of international experts evaluating topics from text-messaging to *Teletubbies*, this book is a long-overdue, fascinating and illuminating read for educational researchers, practitioners and policy-makers.

Jackie Marsh is Senior Lecturer in Education at the University of Sheffield.

By Becky King, Gilbert Scott Infant Community School, Croydon

Popular Culture, New Media and Digital Literacy in Early Childhood

Edited by Jackie Marsh

 RoutledgeFalmer
Taylor & Francis Group

LONDON AND NEW YORK

First published 2005 by RoutledgeFalmer
2 Park Square, Milton Park, Abingdon, Oxon, OX14 4RN

Simultaneously published in the USA and Canada
by RoutledgeFalmer
270 Madison Avenue, New York, NY 10016

RoutledgeFalmer is an imprint of the Taylor & Francis Group

Typeset in 10.5/12pt Bembo by Graphicraft Ltd., Hong Kong
Printed and bound in Great Britain by TJ International Ltd,
Padstow, Cornwall

British Library Cataloguing in Publication Data
A catalogue record for this book is available from the British Library

Library of Congress Cataloging-in-Publication Data
Popular culture, new media and digital literacy in early childhood /
edited by Jackie Marsh.
       p. cm.
   Includes bibliographical references and index.
   ISBN 0–415–33572–8 (hardback : alk. paper) —
ISBN 0–415–33573–6 (pbk. : alk. paper)
   1. Mass media in education.   2. Media literacy.   3. Early childhood
education.   4. Popular culture.   5. Child development.   I. Marsh, Jackie.
   LB1043.P58   2004
   372.133—dc22
                                                      2004004144

Contents

Figures

Tables

Acknowledgements

First of all, I would like to thank all of the authors for their excellent contributions to this volume; their professional approach to the task ensured that editing this book has been a great pleasure. Secondly, I would like to express my gratitude to all of the participants in the ESRC-funded international research seminar series 'Children's Literacy and Popular Culture' which took place at the University of Sheffield, School of Education in the UK (2002– 2004), for their stimulating presentations and discussions. These were extremely rich and engaging and have contributed to a wide variety of outputs, including this book. I would also like to thank Alison Foyle and Priyanka Pathak at RoutledgeFalmer for their interest in, and commitment to, the project from the beginning and their expert guidance throughout. Eve Bearne and Guy Merchant were insightful 'critical friends' in their responses to my own chapter and I am most grateful to them for their helpful feedback – all the usual caveats about any shortcomings of the work being my own responsibility apply. Acknowledgement is also due to Lynda Graham for her generous work in tracking down the illustrator of the frontispiece (just one example of the wonderful work undertaken in Croydon LEA). Finally, my thanks, as always, to Julie and Angela for their unwavering support and patience.

Contributors

Leonie Arthur is a Lecturer at the University of Western Sydney, Australia where she teaches undergraduate and postgraduate courses in early literacy and new literacy studies. She has undertaken research studies which have explored the congruency between home and school cultures, particularly with regard to popular culture. These included a study from 1998 to 2001 which focused on early literacy learning in socio-economically disadvantaged areas. She has published papers and chapters relating to the field.

Catherine Ann Cameron is Honourary Professor of Psychology at the University of British Columbia, Emerita and Honourary Research Professor at the University of New Brunswick, and Adjunct Professor at the University of Victoria in Canada. She studies the cognitive and emotional development of children and adolescents, including early telephone communications and their relationship to emergent written expression, cross-cultural differences in truth telling and verbal deception and adolescent physiological responses to psychosocial stress. Her work appears in *Child Development*, *Discourse Processes*, *Educational Psychology Review*, *Applied Psycholinguistics*, and the *British Journal of Developmental Psychology*. She has recently co-edited *Understanding abuse: Partnering for change* (University of Toronto Press).

Victoria Carrington is a Reader in Education in the Faculty of Education at the University of Plymouth, UK. She is the author of numerous journal articles and book chapters related to early literacy across home and school contexts and has recently published *New Times: New Families* (2002) with Kluwer Academic Publishers. Her current research interests include the impact of new communications technologies and consumer culture on early literacy development and the emergence of new literacies.

Barbara Comber is Director of the Centre for Studies in Literacy, Policy and Learning Cultures, School of Education, University of South Australia. She is involved in projects that consider literacy teaching and learning from the perspectives of different groups and communities, who experience various forms of disadvantage. She has recently co-edited two books: *Look again: Longitudinal studies of children's literacy learning* (Comber and Barnett, 2003) and *Negotiating critical literacies in classrooms* (Comber and Simpson, 2001).

Beatrice Accorti Gamannossi participated in a research project in Italian kindergartens and schools investigating emergent literacy that involved 1,200 children over a period of five years. As a PhD student at the University of Florence, Italy, she is now working on her own study of links between kindergarten children's telephone discourse and the facilitation of the recontextualization skills demanded in processes of literacy.

Julia Gillen is director of the The Childphone Project (http://childphone.open.ac.uk). Her work has appeared in journals such as *Language and Education* and *Journal of Early Childhood Literacy* and as chapters in books including *Communication Research and Media Science in Europe* (eds Schorr, Campbell and Schenk, DeGruyter, 2003) and *The Articulate Classroom* (ed. Goodwin, David Fulton, 2001). She is a Lecturer in Applied Language Studies at the Open University, UK and the author of *The Language of Children* (Routledge, 2003).

Susan Howard is a Senior Lecturer in School of Education at The University of South Australia where she teaches courses at both undergraduate and postgraduate levels. She has published widely in the area of children and media, most notably the edited collection *Wired Up: Young People and the Electronic Media* (UCL Press, 1998). Since 1993 she has worked for the Australian Broadcasting Authority as a consultant advising on children's television programming. Other research interests include childhood and adolescent resilience, and children's perceptions of place, belonging and national identity.

Charmian Kenner is a researcher and consultant on bilingualism and family learning, based at Goldsmiths College, University of London, UK. She has recently directed an ESRC-funded project on children learning to write in different scripts, and is now directing another on intergenerational learning between children and grandparents in East London. Her publications include *Home Pages: Literacy Links for Bilingual Children* (Trentham Books, 2000).

Jackie Marsh is a Senior Lecturer in Education at the University of Sheffield, UK, where she co-directed, with Elaine Millard, the ESRC Research Seminar Series 'Children's Literacy and Popular Culture' (2002–2004). She recently edited, along with Nigel Hall and Joanne Larson, the *Handbook of Early Childhood Literacy* (Sage, 2003) and is an editor of the *Journal of Early Childhood Literacy*. Jackie is involved in research which examines the role and nature of popular culture and media in early childhood literacy both in- and out-of-school contexts.

Guy Merchant is Co-ordinator of the Language and Literacy Research Group at Sheffield Hallam University, UK. His current research focuses on children and young people's experience of popular digital literacy – particularly the use of synchronous chat and interactive communication through e-mail. He has published a number of research studies and produces a variety of curriculum materials in the area of primary literacy. As a founding editor of the *Journal of Early Childhood Literacy,* he has a strong interest in the changing nature of literacy and its impact on early childhood.

Helen Nixon is a Senior Lecturer in the Centre for Studies in Literacy, Policy and Learning Cultures in the School of Education at the University of South Australia. Her research is undertaken at the intersection of cultural studies and education and focuses on children, young people and the pedagogies of global media culture. With colleagues she has undertaken several large school- and classroom-based studies of English/literacy education and ICTs. A key research interest is how the widespread introduction of ICTs is interconnected with changing socio-cultural constructions of literacy and educational disadvantage.

Kate Pahl is based at the University of Sheffield, UK, where she teaches on the MA Literacy and Language in Education. Her research is focused on ethnographic studies which examine children's texts as traces of social practices and explore the role of multimodal and visual literacies in the home. Her publications include *Transformations: Children's Meaning Making in a Nursery* (Trentham, 1999), and she has a chapter in C. Jewitt and G. Kress (eds), *Multimodal Literacy* (New York: Peter Lang, 2003).

Susan Roberts is a Senior Lecturer in Media Studies with the Institute of Early Childhood at Macquarie University, Sydney, Australia. She teaches undergraduate and postgraduate courses and has published a number of articles on children and the media. Since 1991 she has worked for the Australian Broadcasting Authority as one of a small group of consultants advising on children's television programming. She is also a registered Psychologist. Her current research is in the area of young children's use of CD-ROM technology.

Muriel Robinson has been exploring questions related to popular culture and children's literacy development since her PhD, published as *Children Reading Print and Television* (Falmer, 1997), which found that children use narrative in similar ways across media to make meaning from the texts they encounter. In recent years she has become increasingly interested in the ways in which younger children use film, television and other media texts before school. She is currently working in higher education in Lincoln, UK.

Cynthia Smith is an Assistant Professor of Literacy Studies at the University of North Carolina at Chapel Hill, USA. She has published her research on young children and computer literacy in *Reading Research Quarterly* and the *Journal of Early Childhood Literacy*. She teaches graduate and undergraduate courses throughout the School of Education, ranging from emergent literacy to middle grades language arts. Her current research interests include an effort to engage in collaborative research with practitioners that seeks to inform the field of evidence-based practices in literacy research.

Bernardo Turnbull is a Social Psychologist and a full-time researcher at the National Institute of Social Security, the largest health organisation in Mexico. Ever since his early work as school counsellor he has been interested in the process of knowledge construction through human interaction and the media used in this process. His DPhil work findings show the importance of meaning negotiation in education and the interweaving of knowledge and power in these processes, using a case study with street children. His present work concentrates on learning processes using an actor-oriented approach.

Vivian Vasquez is an Assistant Professor in the School of Education at American University in Washington, DC, where she teaches undergraduate and graduate literacy courses. Previous to this she taught pre-school and primary school in Canada. Her research is focused on critical literacy, early literacy, inquiry and social justice. Her latest publications include two books, *Negotiating Critical Literacies with Young Children* (Lawrence Erlbaum, 2004) and *Getting Beyond I Like the Book – Creating Spaces for Critical Literacy in K-6 Settings* (International Reading Association, 2003). Other publications include book chapters and articles published in *Language Arts, Phi Delta Kappa, UKRA Reading, Journal of Adolescent and Adult Literacy, Reading Teacher* and *Reading Today*. Vivian has held appointive and elective offices in scholarly organizations including, The National Council of Teachers of English, The American Educational Research Association, The International Reading Association and The Whole Language Umbrella.

Chapter 1

Introduction

Children of the digital age

Jackie Marsh

Several of the chapters in this book are based on contributions to an international research seminar series titled *Children's Literacy and Popular Culture*,[1] which was funded by the Economic and Social Research Council[2] in the UK. One of the aims of the seminar series was to develop further the emergent work on popular culture and literacy and contribute to the development of a theoretical framework for this research. In addition to some of the participants in the seminar series, additional authors have been invited to contribute to the current volume because of their internationally renowned work in the early childhood literacy field. This book focuses on research pertaining to children aged from birth to eight years, with a predominant emphasis on children in the first five years of life. The reason for this narrow focus is simple; there is very little work in the international arena which examines the role of popular culture and new technologies in young children's literacy lives. All of the chapters in this book report on research which illuminates the ways in which contemporary childhoods are shaped by and, in turn, shape the changing communicative practices of the twenty-first century. Much has been written about the technological transformations taking place in the new millennium and their impact on literacy education, but, as yet, there has been little empirical data to support some of the claims made, particularly within the early childhood field. One of the main purposes of this book, therefore, is to share research in this area in order to develop understanding of the paradigm shift that has taken place in relation to young children's contemporary communicative practices. The chapters report on research studies undertaken in a number of countries including Australia, Canada, England, Italy, Mexico and the United States. In addition to the emphasis on international empirical studies, the chapters develop new theoretical models for analysing the relationship between popular culture, media and new technologies and children's literacy development. Drawing from a range of disciplines in addition to educational studies, this theoretical work makes an important contribution to the task of developing an understanding of children's literacy practices in a new media age and building an informed pedagogy which offers opportunities for re-appropriation (Stein, 2001) and transformation (Dyson, 1997). Before I move on to outline the content of this book, it would be appropriate to begin by exploring the terms used in the title of the text – popular culture, new media and digital literacy – given the indeterminacy of some of these concepts in the field.

Popular culture

Insofar as it would appear impossible to determine the exact meaning of the concept of 'culture' (Jenks, 1993), it is a fruitless task to attempt to provide a precise definition of 'popular culture'. For some, popular culture is the culture of the 'masses', culture which is consumed or created (usually consumed) on a large scale and often in opposition to 'high culture' (Adorno and Horkenheimer, 1979 [1947]). For others (Levine, 1988), the boundaries between 'high' and popular culture are contested and constantly shifting – opera and the work of Shakespeare are two examples of cultural forms which have crossed such borders over time.[3] The term 'popular culture' in relation to young children usually refers to those cultural texts, artefacts and practices which are attractive to large numbers of children and which are often mass produced on a global scale (Kenway and Bullen, 2001). These goods are frequently linked by common themes, so that 'tie-in' goods are related to popular television or film characters and narratives. However, it is becoming increasingly difficult to identify the origins of themes, given the multiplicity of platforms on which they occur. Indeed, it is this 'transmedia intertextuality' (Kinder, 1991: 3) which is particularly appealing to children, as meeting the same narrative in different forms can enable them to integrate varied aspects of their experiences and enhance their 'narrative satisfaction' (Hilton, 1996: 42).

Although it is often these meta-narratives which are seen as forming children's popular culture, it is important to recognise that particular groups of children will adopt more localised themes and texts that are specific to their cultural practices. Some of these popular cultural narratives will be exclusive to particular cultural groups and some will be adaptations of globalised narratives. *Pokémon*, for example, was a worldwide phenomenon, but was adapted in different ways by children in communities across the globe so that, for example, playing with *Pokémon* in Aboriginal communities in Australia looked very different to *Pokémon* mania in Canada (Vasquez, 2003). This process also happens in relation to adolescents' and adults' practices. For instance, MacDougall (2003) analyses the adaptation of Barbie dolls for initiation rites in a Mexican Indian community. This revision of globalised commercial merchandise in ways which ensure that these texts and artefacts reflect localised social practices creates a popular cultural 'third space' (Wilson, 2000). Furthermore, children's popular culture is often considered to be subject to the 'McDonalidisation' effect (Ritzer, 1998) in that it is assumed that US-based themes dominate the global market. However, this is often not the case, as the worldwide popularity of the *Teletubbies* (of UK origin) and *Pokémon* (of Japanese origin) attest. In short, this is a complex area in which assumptions made are often erroneous and the dynamic interplay between globalising and localising effects overlooked. In addition, it is important to note that culture is also produced, not simply consumed. Although children's culture is often shaped by adults and taken up by children (or not, as the case may be) in various ways, children also create their own, child-centred cultural practices. Ultimately, definitions of children's popular culture depend on a sensitive reading of socio-cultural practices in specific contexts, as is the case with the chapters throughout this book.

New media

In some ways, the term 'new media' is a little misleading because some of the media referred to by this phrase, such as television and radio, have been around for decades. What is new about these media is the impact of digitised technologies on the production and consumption of them. In addition, 'new media' refers to a wide range of technologies and communication media which have developed more recently. Since the 1980s, rapid developments in technology have led to a range of communicative practices which were simply not possible previously. However, the immense developments in technology should not cloud the fact that some things remain relatively unchanged; as Jewitt (2002: 194) suggests, 'old technologies always occupy new technologies (as witnessed by the running boards on cars, the keyboards on computers)'. Although it is important to acknowledge the immense changes new media have generated, over-emphasis of the impact of these technological developments should be avoided.

The use of the term 'new media' also provides a means of referring to a wide range of techno-cultural practices which each have specialised modes of operating, some of which may be common across media but others of which may be very specific to particular media. It is, as Lister *et al.* (2003) indicate, an inclusive term because:

> It avoids the emphasis on a purely technical and formal definition, as in 'digital' or 'electronic media'; the stress on a single, ill-defined and contentious quality as in 'interactive media', or the limitation to one set of machines and practices as in 'computer-mediated communication.'
>
> (Lister *et al.*, 2003: 11)

'New media', then, might benefit from a lack of specificity, but this might also limit the term's usefulness in the long term as the proliferation of media and related practices continues at such a rapid pace. For now, however, the term is useful in signalling fundamental shifts in contemporary communicative practices, for example one of the key changes in recent years which underpins much of the analysis in this book is the move from page to screen. The new media texts and practices which are considered in the chapters here include computer games, text-messaging on mobile phones and use of interactive television, all of which signal the current emphasis on screen-based technologies and all of which demand analysis in terms of young children's meaning-making practices. In this analysis, the terminology relating to children's engagement with these technologies is an important consideration and so, in the next section, the concept of 'literacy' itself is considered.

Digital literacy

The nature of 'literacy' is highly contested in the new media age (Bearne, 2003; Kress, 2003; Marsh, 2003). The plural form, 'literacies', has become widely adopted since the ground-breaking work of the New Literacy Studies emphasised the diversity of literacy practices in contemporary lives (Barton and Hamilton, 1998; Cope and Kalantzis, 2000; Lankshear and Knobel, 2003; New London Group, 1996). In addition, the term 'literacy' has become synonymous with the concept of competence in the encoding and decoding of a range of semiotic discourses (e.g. computer literacy, media literacy). A clear analysis of this rather confusing field is provided by Kress (2003) who insists that 'literacy' refers to 'lettered representation' and argues that we need to find other ways of describing the encoding and decoding processes used with other media. For this, the phrase 'communicative practices' offered by Street (1997) appears to be the most appropriate. The adoption of the term 'digital literacy' (Glister, 1997) for the title of this book both acknowledges Kress's definition of literacy and points towards the way in which lettered representation is being transformed and shaped by digitised technologies. Thus, the book examines the literacy practices which are related to digital technologies such as computer, television and mobile phone, and explores the 'digitextual practices' (Everett, 2003: 5) of children's everyday lives. The chapters also look at the wider range of communicative practices which are mediated through new technologies and acknowledge the multimodal nature of young children's meaning-making. Throughout, there is a concern to explore the complex relationship between these different modes of representation and to examine the affordances of (the possibilities offered by) each of the media featured.

Such an insistence on the inter-relationship between literacy and other communicative practices is essential in the current social, economic and technological climate. Much has been written about the changing technology of literacy and the impact this has on the epistemological and ontological foundations of contemporary communicative practices (Lankshear and Knobel, 2003; Kress, 2003). However, this discourse has yet to permeate widely the field of early childhood literacy. Much of the research in the area is focused on rather traditional models in which 'emergent literacy' is concerned primarily with pen, paper and phonics (Whitehurst and Lonigan, 2001). In this book, such a narrow discourse is challenged by authors who explore the ways in which young children's communicative practices are embedded in a range of technologies. Digital literacy practices share some of the features of more traditional literacy practices, but there are distinct aspects of text analysis and production using new media and these are explored throughout the chapters collected here, as outlined below.

Outline of the book

The book has three distinct parts: Changing Childhood Cultures, Children and Technologies and Transformative Pedagogies.

The first part of the book, Changing Childhood Cultures, explores the nature of children's everyday textual practices and the ways in which recent social, political, economic and technological changes have impacted upon these practices. These are chapters which take a broad perspective on the role of literacy in contemporary childhoods. In Chapter 2, Victoria Carrington provides a complex map of the changing textual landscapes of contemporary childhoods. She describes how the term 'Shi Jinrui', a term coined by Japanese parents meaning 'new humankind', is used to depict a younger generation which is forging ahead in terms of their technological practices. Carrington outlines some of these practices, such as text-messaging and computer game-playing, and provides a textual analysis of some of the online and offline magazines which shape children's 'Shi Jinrui' identities. Carrington offers a direct challenge to literacy educators who base their curriculum and pedagogy on traditional models of childhood and literacy and, in doing so, raises a number of theoretical and ideological concerns which are picked up throughout the rest of the book.

My own chapter follows and is focused on the way in which popular culture and media are deeply inscribed in the ritualised play and materiality of childhood. This chapter examines the dialectic between literacy and identities and suggests that new media texts play a central role in the construction of young children's social identities. Drawing from data arising from two studies of the media-related literacy practices of children aged two to four in the home, the analysis draws attention to the way in which families mediate children's communicative practices and support the development of identities which signal competency in the navigation of multimodal worlds. This scaffolding and guided participation of communicative practices is also a focus of Chapter 4. Muriel Robinson and Bernado Turnbull trace the development of Verónica in the first five years of her life and draw attention to the way in which she confidently moves across media, thus demonstrating the porosity of the texts encountered and questioning those who might try to separate out these various textual practices and examine them in isolation.

Robinson and Turnbull argue for an asset model of media education, rather than the more habitual deficit model, and they analyse the affordances of a range of categories of texts in order to demonstrate how this asset model might operate.

Despite the growing attention paid to the place of popular culture and media in children's lives, there is still relatively little analysis of the way in which young bilingual children draw on different elements of their popular cultural worlds to create hybrid textual spaces in which the various threads of their identities collide and merge. In Chapter 5, Charmian Kenner draws on two studies of multilingual children's literacy practices to illustrate how globalised and localised popular cultural discourses inflect children's literate identities and she presents a range of examples which demonstrate the way in which children recontextualise the stuff of home and community to create texts which bear traces of their cultural and social histories (cf. Dyson, 2002). This chapter draws the first section of the book to a close and thus, in these first four chapters, issues which underpin much of the work of the remaining chapters have been introduced. These chapters have focused on the broader social and cultural themes which emerge from any study of the changing textual landscapes of childhood; in the next part, specific aspects of these landscapes are examined in turn.

In the second part of the book, Children and Technologies, the place of specific media in children's communicative practices is explored and the affordances of each media examined in terms of its contribution to language and literacy development. In Chapter 6, Roberts and Howard challenge the traditional deficit discourse associated with television and young children. Outlining the findings of a study in which children under two years of age were observed watching the programme *Teletubbies*, they suggest that these children were not 'couch potatoes', but were in fact active meaning-makers in relation to televisual texts. In contrast to much of the research on young children and television which has ignored the affective aspects of their experiences, Roberts and Howard detail the ways in which children delight in the characters, the music and the action, responding both verbally and physically to a rich range of stimuli. The way in which the responses of young children to media artefacts are more significant than has been acknowledged previously is also the theme of Chapter 7. Cynthia Smith conducted a longitudinal observational study of her own child, James, in the first years of his life, as he interacted with the computer in the home. She details his play, which incorporated aspects of his emergent understanding of the computer and its affordances. Smith analyses James' responses in the light of research on children's book-related play behaviour and concludes that there are a number of key similarities, arguing that such play is an important contributor to young children's literacy development. In addition, computer-related dramatic play promoted symbol use related to computers which arose from James' engagement with the technology.

Although television and computers have featured largely in the recurrent 'moral panics' (Cohen, 1987) with regard to young children's media consumption, they have not met with the same level of anxiety engendered by games consoles, such as PlayStation2. Visions of zombie-like addicts who leave the consoles to engage in violent and anti-social behaviour have haunted the public imaginary for some years. In Chapter 8, Kate Pahl takes a close look at PlayStation2 and analyses the opportunities it provides for children to engage in a range of creative and dynamic meaning-making activities. Drawing from a longitudinal, ethnographic study of young boys' communicative practices in their homes, she suggests that games consoles provide opportunities for identity construction, multimodal text production and playful responses to texts. These media artefacts are highly potent and desirable popular cultural texts for young children and are an integral part of the media-related 'communities of practice' (Lave and Wenger, 1991) developed by children and their peers. This is also the case with mobile phones, of course. In Chapter 9, the final chapter in this part of the book, Julia Gillen, Beatrice Accorti Gamannossi and Catherine Ann Cameron draw on their comparative study of young children's telephone use in three countries (Canada, Italy and the UK) to explore the role and function of telephones in young children's socio-cultural practices. They illustrate how these devices not only enable children to develop a range of competences in relation to spoken language from birth, but also how children quickly adopt the wider social practices related to telephone use. As with all of the chapters in this part, the work of Gillen, Gamannossi and Cameron provides a strong challenge to deficit discourses in relation to young children's engagement with media artefacts and offers a more balanced account of the way in which technology impacts on children's cognitive, linguistic and socio-cultural development.

The final part of the book, Transformative Pedagogies, moves our attention towards the implications of the research outlined so far for the education of young children. If early years settings, nurseries and schools are to utilise media artefacts and popular culture effectively, they need to develop a clear understanding of the media-related 'funds of knowledge' (Moll et al., 1992) children bring with them to the site of learning. This could not occur without meaningful dialogue with parents, carers and families and, in Chapter 10, Leonie Arthur assesses how far this is possible, given the apparent differences in attitudes of parents and teachers towards popular and media texts. Arthur outlines data from an Australian study in which educators and parents across 79 early years settings were interviewed about their attitudes towards children's engagement with popular and media texts. The dissonance between home and school perceptions of the role of popular culture and media texts is explored and Arthur suggests that more extensive discussions need to take place between teachers and families if shared understandings are to emerge.

In Chapter 11, Guy Merchant focuses on young children's text production on screen. Observations undertaken in an early years setting in England are analysed in order to determine the principles which underpin early writing on computers and Merchant explores the materiality of digital print production. A comparison with Clay's (1975) principles of early writing development is undertaken and, in doing so, Merchant draws attention to the similarities and differences in writing on screen and paper. This kind of understanding is important if early years educators are to develop a curriculum which supports children's engagement with digital technologies and to offer learning opportunities which are meaningful and engaging. This is the focus of Vivian Vasquez's chapter, Chapter 12. Vasquez outlines a pedagogy which provides young children (aged three to eight years) opportunities to engage critically with texts, in this case, texts related to the popular cultural phenomenon, *Pokémon*. Although much has been written about the need to facilitate the development of children's critical literacy skills, there are few accounts of classroom practice in which young children are encouraged to question issues of power and ideology in texts; it is often assumed that children of this age lack the critical capacities required for such work, or need to develop traditional literacy skills first. Vasquez's chapter outlines data which challenge this assumption. This theme is also taken up in the final chapter of the book, Chapter 13, written by Helen Nixon and Barbara Comber. Nixon and Comber focus on detailing the curricula and pedagogies of two early years teachers as they engage children in media production. Drawing on Green's model of 3D literacy practices (Green, 1988), Nixon and Comber trace the operational, cultural and critical dimensions of literacy which are embedded in the classroom practices of these two teachers. Such accounts are crucially important for, as Nixon and Comber argue, they provide a strong counter to the conventional framing of early years classrooms which marginalises children's agency in relation to media texts and presents a normalising account of a technology-free childhood, more akin to educators' own life experiences than current socio-cultural practices (Luke and Luke, 2001). In this final chapter of the book, we see how the 'Shi Junrui' generation, discussed by Victoria Carrington in Chapter 2, can be offered a curriculum which provides fitting recognition of their expertise and acknowledges the complexities inherent in contemporary educational practices.

The chapters in this book do not provide a 'tool-kit' for this work, nor do they suggest that there are straightforward answers to questions relating to young children's popular cultural and media-related literacy practices. What they do offer is an extension of the theoretical framework in which children's engagement with such texts can be analysed and a reflective account of 'hybrid pedagogies' (Hicks, 2001) which provide young children with meaningful encounters with literacy in the new media age.

Notes

1 For further details of the series, including papers and bibliography, see http://www.shef.ac.uk/literacy/ESRC/seminar_series.html.

2 Gant number: R451265240.
3 For a more detailed discussion of the nature of popular culture, see Chapter 1 of
Marsh and Millard (2000).

References

Adorno, T. and Horkenheimer, M. (1979 [1947]) *Dialectic of Enlightenment*, London:
Verso.

Barton, D. and Hamilton, M. (1998) *Local Literacies: Reading and Writing in One
Community*, London: Routledge.

Bearne, E. (2003) Playing with possibilities: Children's multi-dimensional texts, in
E. Bearne, H. Dombey and T. Grainger (eds) *Classroom Interactions in Literacy*,
Buckingham: Open University Press.

Clay, M. (1975) *What Did I Write?* London: Heinemann Educational.

Cohen, S. (1987) *Folk Devils and Moral Panics: The Creation of the Mods and Rockers*
(2nd edn), Oxford: Blackwell.

Cope, B. and Kalantzis, M. (2000) *Multiliteracies: Literacy Learning and the Design of
Social Futures*, London: Routledge.

Dyson, A. H. (1997) *Writing Superheroes: Contemporary Childhood, Popular Culture, and
Classroom Literacy*, New York: Teachers College Press.

Dyson, A. H. (2002) *Brothers and Sisters Learn to Write: Popular Literacies in Childhood
and School Cultures*, New York: Teachers College Press.

Everett, A. (2003) Digitextuality and click theory: theses on convergence media
in the digital age, in A. Everett and Jon T. Caldwell (eds) *New Media: Theories and
Practices of Digitextuality*, New York: Routledge.

Glister, P. (1997) *Digital Literacy*, New York: John Wiley & Sons.

Green, B. (1988) Subject-specific literacy and school learning: a focus on writing,
Australian Journal of Education, 32 (2): 156–179.

Hicks, D. (2001) Literacies and masculinities in the life of a young working-class boy,
Language Arts, 78 (3): 217–226.

Hilton, M. (ed.) (1996) *Potent Fictions: Children's Literacy and the Challenge of Popular
Culture*, London: Routledge.

Jenks, C. (1993) *Culture*, London: Routledge.

Jewitt, C. (2002) The move from page to screen: the multimodal reshaping of school
English, *Visual Communication*, 1 (2): 171–195.

Kenway, J. and Bullen, E. (2001) *Consuming Children: Education – Entertainment –
Advertising*, Buckingham: Open University Press.

Kinder, M. (1991) *Playing with Power in Movies: Television and Video Games from
Muppet Babies to Teenage Mutant Ninja Turtles*, Berkeley, CA: University of Berkeley
Press.

Kress, G. (2003) *Literacy in the New Media Age*, London: Routledge.

Lankshear, C. and Knobel, M. (2003) *New Literacies: Changing Knowledge and Classroom Learning*, Milton Keynes: Open University Press.

Lave, J. and Wenger, E. (1991) *Situated Learning: Legitimate Peripheral Participation*,
Cambridge: Cambridge University Press.

Levine, L. W. (1988) *Highbrow/Lowbrow: The Emergence of Cultural Hierarchy in America*,
Cambridge, MA: Harvard University Press.

Lister, M., Dovey, J., Giddings, S., Grant, I. and Kelly, K. (2003) *New Media: A
Critical Introduction*, London: Routledge.

Luke, A. and Luke, C. (2001) Adolescence lost/childhood regained: on early intervention and the emergence of the techno-subject, *Journal of Early Childhood Literacy*, 1 (1): 91–120.

MacDougall, J. P. (2003) Transnational commodities as local cultural icons: Barbie dolls in Mexico, *Journal of Popular Culture*, 37 (2): 257–275.

Marsh, J. (2003) One-way traffic? Connections between literacy practices at home and in the nursery, *British Educational Research Journal*, 29 (3): 369–382.

Marsh, J. and Millard, E. (2000) *Literacy and Popular Culture: Using Children's Culture in the Classroom*, London: Paul Chapman.

Moll, L., Amanti, C., Neff, D. and Gonzalez, N. (1992) Funds of knowledge for teaching: using a qualitative approach to connect homes and classrooms, *Theory into Practice*, 31 (2): 132–141.

New London Group (1996) A pedagogy of multiliteracies: designing social futures, *Harvard Educational Review*, 66 (1): 60–92.

Ritzer, G. (1998) *The McDonaldization Thesis: Explorations and Extensions*, London: Sage.

Stein, P. (2001) Classrooms as sites of textual, cultural and linguistic reappropriation, in B. Comber and A. Simpson (eds) *Negotiating Critical Literacies in Classrooms*, Mawah, NJ: Lawrence Erlbaum.

Street, B. (1997) The implications of the new literacy studies for education, *English in Education*, 31 (3): 45–59.

Vasquez, V. (2003) What *Pokémon* can teach us about learning and literacy, *Language Arts*, 81 (2): 118–125.

Whitehurst, G. J. and Lonigan, C. J. (2001) Emergent literacy: development from prereaders to readers, in S. Neuman and D. K. Dickinson (eds) *Handbook of Early Literacy Research*, New York: Guilford Press.

Wilson, A. (2000) There's no escape from third-space theory – borderland discourse and the in-between literacies of prison, in D. Barton, M. Hamilton and R. Ivanic (eds) *Situated Literacies*, London: Routledge.

Part I

Changing Childhood Cultures

Chapter 2

New textual landscapes, information and early literacy

Victoria Carrington

Introduction

In the 1950s, Harold Innes (1950, 1951) noted that changes in communications technologies alter the structure of thoughts, the character of symbols and the nature of community. That is, changes in the ways in which we are able to communicate impact upon what we think about, the tools we use to think, and the context in which we do this thinking. This, in turn, changes how we see ourselves in the world and the ways in which that world operates. Importantly, Innes (1951) also described a link between the emergence of new communications technologies and the capacity for individuals and groups to engage with and potentially reshape dominant discourses. In this chapter, I suggest that these shifts and the challenges created by them are not the exclusive domain of adults. In fact, the more far-reaching consequences of changes in communications technologies are to be seen in their impact on children.

If we accept that changes in communications are embedded in larger shifts around technology, social structure and culture then there can be little doubt that there are implications for young children and, consequently, for those who are charged with their education. In terms of early literacy, a range of changes are taking place that can be directly associated with shifting and evolving communications technologies and the social practices associated with them. First, young people are immersed in textual landscapes that are no longer print dominated – this has implications for the skills and knowledge they bring with them to literacy instruction and for the worlds of work and leisure in which they will live out their lives. Second, many of these textual landscapes originate outside school or family, the traditional access point for children's texts. Instead, much of the textual landscape in which children are developing their literate habitus bubbles up and flows around popular and consumer culture and emergent electronic texts, often outmanoeuvring or subverting the supervisory gaze and control of adults. This is the changed and changing context in which children are being naturalised to particular forms of text and uses of communications technologies.

Third, there are implications for the ways in which we construct childhood in contemporary Western society. A particular view of childhood has underwritten the scope and direction of early literacy instruction and the design of texts for children. In industrialised Western societies, much of this instruction has pivoted around control of the flow of information to, and about, children (Postman 1994). Particular sets of interconnected and mutually reinforcing discourses around the nature of childhood have drawn upon, and fed into, this flow of information (Buckingham 2000). Children's increasing access to and mastery of new texts and literacies such as weblogs, e-zines, computer games, internet and txting gives them unprecedented, and often, independent, access to the same pool of information as adults. But, more interestingly, these texts and technologies allow children to be producers and disseminators of information. This is a departure from the more passive relationship with information posited by Postman (1994) who argued particularly that television's generic broadcast of information has acted to destroy the barriers between adult and child. It is inevitable that children will bring this changing skill and knowledge base and the different identities it enables to bear on other contexts. This chapter addresses these currents and briefly considers their implications for early literacy.

New textual landscapes

SMS txting

I recently observed an eight-year-old girl txting a message on a (non-predictive) mobile phone. She – Alex – picked up the phone, asked permission to send a message, asked where the 'message maker' was, and talked herself through the various sections of the message: 'Where is that space thing?', 'O . . . where's o? Oh, there you are!' Using her thumbs, she moved back and forth through the various key combinations to create her txt message. At one point, without raising her eyes from the keypad, she asked, 'How do you spell "today"?' When her message was complete Alex asked how to find the number and was told – once – how to key in the three initial letters of the person's name in order to scroll through the available listings. The presence of the recipient's name and number in the phone's memory indicated that this was someone known to the girl. She then confirmed that 'OK' was the button to press 'to send' and immediately sent her message. In the eight or nine minutes that it took to compose and send, at no time did Alex consult around the nature of her message, firm in the knowledge that this was her personal communication with the recipient. She then waited around five minutes before wondering aloud when the reply would arrive.

In the course of her everyday life, Alex does not have her own phone or unrestricted access to one; however in the instance described, she was able to navigate successfully and to great effect. Not only is she able to create and disseminate a text of her own creation, but she does this sure in the knowledge that this is a highly legitimate social practice. This knowledge comes from mass media and popular culture as she sees mobile phone advertising, used on television, in movies and pictured in magazines and receives them as toys.[1] Additionally, her own inner circle of family and friends are seen to possess, use and value this form of communications technology.[2] Alex is learning to engage in culturally valued textual practices.

This same scene is being played out around the world. Children everywhere are accessing mobile phone and other communications technologies. By mid 2003, 400,000 children in the United Kingdom under the age of ten years had their own mobile phone (Wireless World Forum 2003). For Alex, mobile phones and txting are part of the textual and social landscape. It is in this landscape that she and others like her are developing particular identities, literate skills and expectations of text. This young girl demonstrated a strong awareness of the nature of this textual form and the power of sending her newly created communication into the world to do work on her behalf. Her awareness of its instantaneous nature and its power as a social practice was evidenced in her assumption that this was a personal communication over which she had control, and in her expectation of a rapid response. Of far-reaching significance is her capacity to produce and transmit information in her own right. This makes her an active player in global flows of information. For a young child, this is a powerful and authentic textual activity. It is also an activity that demonstrates a particular sense of identity and awareness of the world outside her immediate locale. Identity construction is an ongoing process of 'self' construction and reconstruction.

The global reach of popular and consumer culture made possible by new communications technologies brings new discursive and identity resources within reach. The following section outlines one such resource.

Catazines and magalogues

Expanded access to communications technologies makes new kinds of texts available to children in new ways. Limited Too[3] is one of the first of a new genre of consumer text developing online – a site directly linked to a printed 'catazine' (sometimes also called a 'magalogue'). This textual form blends catalogue and magazine and is, in effect, one step further evolved as a consumer text than the smooth positioning of advertising and competitions found in the more traditionally formatted magazines described in the following sections. Limited Too is an online site and catazine directed at young girls from around the age of six or seven years. It shares the same sassy chick discourse and aspirational values of magazines such as Chick and Dolly, directed at preteens. Limited Too bridges the early childhood–preteen divide in a number of ways. It talks directly to the 'chicklette' reader who, it presumes, is adept at navigating internet sites and the associated communications technologies.

The consumers of these sites and magazines are young girls and they and their power as consumers are treated seriously. There is no differentiation of information for adults and children and there is no segregation according to intent – advertising is totally embedded in the text rather than situated in the margins. In this text, child-as-consumer is a serious category of life with as much legitimacy as any other and the decision-making capacities of children are fully integrated into the discourse. The catazine offers access to grown-up clothing selections along with displays of complete looks for reference and purchase. The site and the clothing are clearly directed at the young girls who will wear the clothing and decorate their bedrooms with 'girl stuff'. The clothing and lifestyle accessories are themselves aspirational as they translate clothing and design trends for older young women for the child and pre-teen market – from monogrammed luggage and inflatable furniture through to angora caps. Different ensemble identities are modelled via the text, graphics and consumer items depicted. These ensembles overlap across the printed and online versions of the catazine. Entire discourses (Gee 1991), each holding out the promise of a particular identity, can be read and/or purchased online or instore and their consumption, either visually or materially, allows young girls to build cultural capital for deployment in peer-oriented fields. Sites such as *Limited Too* and the emergence of niche texts such as catazines targeted at aspirational young girls immersed in 'girl power' make available discourses and identities that have currency in fields outside the family.

Not all emergent texts address themselves directly to an information-rich childhood. Many texts continue to reflect a more traditional, naïve childhood. Many of the more recent of these, however, manage to blend this view of childhood and family with quite strong consumer messages.

Children's magazines: Bananas in Pyjamas and Bob the Builder

A rapidly expanding range of children's magazines, of which *Bananas in Pyjamas* and *Bob the Builder* are only two examples, are gracing supermarket and newsagent shelves. Highly colourful, disposable and highly intertextual, these magazines build directly upon pre- and early school aged children's knowledge and enjoyment of children's television produced by the British Broadcasting Corporation (BBC) (United Kingdom) and Australian Broadcasting Corporation (ABC) (Australia). Available by subscription or in a range of outlets, the magazines are merchandising offshoots of these popular programmes. They build directly upon the characters and story lines evident in the television series, depicting humorous cartoon stories along with screen shots from various episodes. A variety of textual formats, layouts and fonts are used throughout, ensuring that these texts are vibrant and enticing. However, the more interesting aspect of these texts lies beneath the surface.

These texts are a colourful blend of advertising, illustrated story panels, recipes and school-readiness activities such as musical games, colouring, counting, spelling, tracing, writing numerals and letters, and joining-the-dots. The discourse of these activities is very 'school-like' and speaks with adult authority

– 'Use your stamper pen to go over Bob's name below' (*Bob the Builder*, ABC and BBC Worldwide 2003: 7) – in the full knowledge that the only way that very young children will access the information contained within the pages is through the mediation of an adult. While the text addresses itself to the child, it is written in adult language and is quite directive:

> Carefully go over the words with a pencil to spell out what the Teddies are dressed up as. (*Bananas in Pyjamas*, ABC and BBC Worldwide 2003: 19)

> Read the rhymes under the pictures. Colour the things that should be purple. (*Bananas in Pyjamas*, ABC and BBC Worldwide 2003: 18)

> Make munchy honey cakes with Morgan. Ask an adult to help you and follow the instructions below. (*Bananas in Pyjamas*, ABC and BBC Worldwide 2003: 23)

At the bottom of each activity, there is an informational panel for adults/ parents. One such panel notes, 'This is a great way for children to learn about repeating patterns (do give them clues if they get stuck). Older children could try drawing their own patterns' (*Bananas in Pyjamas*, ABC and BBC Worldwide 2003: 10). At the same time as the adult is positioned as information mediator, s/he is also being schooled in how to be more school-like, how to more closely approximate the idealised parent of middle-class pedagogy and curriculum. Not only is this text reflecting, and in fact teaching, a particular kind of childhood, it is also very powerfully constructing a particular adult presence. A highly particularised child and childhood are represented here, along with highly school-like printed text formats. There is a strong pedagogic aspect to these texts – they implicitly and explicitly construct particular roles and relationships. Running through both magazines is a strong normative model of childhood and the unproblematically homogeneous cultural and social perspectives that often accompany family and early literacy (Carrington and Luke 2003; Gregory 1997; Gregory and Williams 2000).

These texts speak to and of a childhood where parents are child-focused and not time-poor, where print-based literacy forms a core family concern and where children are passive information recipients. The themes of the stories reflect a protected childhood of make-believe characters and happy endings where childhood sits outside the flows and vicissitudes of everyday life.

And yet, there is a free themed gift attached to the front cover (in this case, it's a *Bananas in Pyjamas* Snap Card Game and a *Bob the Builder* stamper pen). There are competitions to win ('Win one of 10 fantastic "Can we fix it?" CD-ROMs worth $29.95 each!') skilfully interspersed with advertising and other content. It is, in fact, very difficult to tell the competitions and the advertising apart – the characters, text, colours, styles are the same. As well, these texts rely very much on children's prior interactions with popular and consumer culture – the videos, video games, television programmes, bedspreads, pyjamas, lunch boxes, lampshades, shampoo and other printed texts. At the same time, while the text conveys the impression of an uncomplicated childhood, it renders oblique recognition of changed technological and literate landscapes in its explicit links to DVDs, toys and computer games.

A brief reading of these texts tells us much about the power of text to construct particular views of childhood, adulthood and family. However, what is more interesting in this context is their capacity for blending advertising and consumer messages into this discourse and recognising the increasing participation of young children in consumer decision-making and purchasing. While, on the surface, these texts are not particularly new and exciting, they tell us much about changes in the textual landscape in which young children are immersed.

The references to computer games are important. Deeply entrenched in popular culture, computer games are increasingly complex interactional texts which have much to tell us about the literate practices and identities of the children entering our classrooms. Computer games enable insight into the implications of reading and interacting with new textual forms and the kinds of conceptualisations of child-as-reader and as participant in broader contexts embedded within them.

Computer games

Rugrats in Paris is a popular PlayStation game marketed at young children. Interaction with this game tells us much about the emergence of new texts and new literacies (Carrington, 2004). It also allows us the opportunity to focus on the assumptions about the reader/player, and hence 'childhood', reflected in the game's construction. *Rugrats* draws heavily on intertextual knowledge of the television series, children's books, clothing, toys and movies. It is assumed that even very young children will recognise the characters outside the television or toy context and translate their knowledge to a new medium. This assumption positions young children as sophisticated readers of popular cultural texts which are, by their nature, heavily intertextual. There is no assumption that children must be scaffolded or led to this transfer of knowledge – it is an inherent aspect of interaction with the game.

To engage with this text, you choose an avatar – one of the well-known *Rugrats* characters such as Tommy or Angelica – and operate with the particular skills assigned to that character. The game's primary goal is to reach the Raptar roller coaster ride at the centre of the theme park and along the way characters must complete various activities such as mini-golf or target throwing. While seemingly trivial, each of these challenges requires cumulative mastery of a range of skills, along with the demonstration of problem-solving and persistence. My personal experience of these small challenges has been fraught with frustration and difficulty, as has navigating successfully in a three-dimensional dynamically generating world. Quite different cognitive processing and spatial skills are called into play (Gunter 1998; Hogle 1996; Prensky 2001). At the same time as children are developing particular physical and cognitive learning styles in their interactions with computer games, they are also developing social learning skills and a particular relationship with the text itself. Recent research identifies the very social nature of interactions around these games and the technology that enables gaming (Vered 1998). It is also now acknowledged that gaming cuts across racial, cultural and demographic boundaries (Fromm, Meder and Vollmer 2000).

The assumption made by many of those who have never given computer games serious consideration is that printed text has been replaced with colour, music, mindless pushing of buttons and some hand-eye coordination. Even a brief experience of gaming challenges this belief. There is, in fact, an abundance of printed text, but its relevance to successful interaction is less direct. Regardless of the amount of printed text, there is never enough textual information or audio to play the game without experimenting, guessing, taking risks and being prepared to lose. As Hoestetter (2002) noted, in this form of text, the print is downgraded to an auxiliary source of information. Of particular relevance is the tendency noted by Oyen and Bebko (1996) to foreground graphical information over printed text. This is a distinct change from the pattern of interaction associated with traditional print text, where successful readers were trained to attend to the text first, using graphical information as supplementary and where this information was made available only via the mediation of adults.

Computer games are a prime popular culture multimodal text for children young and old. Mastery with, and knowledge of, these texts are highly valued commodities in peer cultures. It is becoming apparent, also, that there are implications for literacy in this engagement (Carrington, 2004). Many of these texts have quite distinctive features – non-linear narrative structure, quite distinctive spatial layouts, ongoing and cumulative challenge levels, multiple and interactive cueing systems. As a result, quite different approaches to text and reading are encouraged and rewarded. Different literate habitus are developed via these readings.

In terms of this emerging literate habitus, the words of a young man in his mid-twenties, the editor of a computer game magazine, are quite informative. He writes of himself and his generation as 'Shi Jinrui':

> 'Shi Jinrui' is a term coined by our parent's generation in Japan to describe our generation. It means [roughly translated] New Humankind. A breed so different from what came before that comparing the two is like comparing chalk and cheese. We think different, dress different, spend our leisure time in different ways. We are the beginning of what

William Gibson envisaged as the future – electron surfers and keyboard jockeys eager for the next digital thrill. We are an evolution, a revolution and a force to be reckoned with. We are the Shi Jinrui and we're here to stay.

(Wilks 2002: 6)

With the term 'Shi Jinrui', Wilks self-identifies himself and his cultural cohort as new and different in terms of world-view as well as literate and technological skills. These changes are doubly significant for children who are even more unselfconsciously naturalised to this emergent textual and technological landscape than someone of Wilks' age.

Textual landscapes

The term 'landscape' has been understood to mean 'fashioned from a natural landscape by a cultural group' (Sauer 1925: 348 cited in Mitchell 2000: 102) and as 'an ongoing relationship between people and place' (Wilson 1991, cited in Mitchell 2000: 102). As Mitchell goes on to argue, landscapes are 'a work' and, via the transformation of landscapes, we transform ourselves. Textual landscapes, then, are the multidimensional and multimodal landscapes in and through which we conduct our lives in a text-rich society. Moving through daily life in a text-rich society requires conscious and unconscious interactions with a range of texts. To illustrate: a brief walk through an urban setting will involve passing through a landscape composed of layers of differing types of text – advertising billboards are everywhere and come in all sizes; the people passing you on the street are wearing branded clothing, and some have tattoos; there are posters, many of them arranged repetitively for maximum effect; there are tagging message trails; there are chalk marks on the pavement of various forms; there are community notice boards and newsstands; there are street signs; there are colourful friezes on buildings. At the same time, there are multiple layers of music emanating from cars, from Walkmans, from store doorways. This is the textual landscape. As we each pass through it, we acknowledge and engage with some of the texts – visual and aural – and not others, depending on our literate habitus. Inside homes, this landscape will be composed of many different layers of diverse forms of text working to create the context and tools with which young children learn about literacies and texts in their community and society. An increasing acceptance of literacy as a social practice (Freebody and Luke 1990) woven into and across our relationships with material sites, rather than as an individual psychological activity, requires that we acknowledge the ways in which we position children within these social practices and landscapes. For contemporary children, the textual landscapes in which they are developing and deploying particular skills, knowledge and sense of self increasingly comprise the texts of new technologies and popular culture.[4] The agentive child engages purposefully in these textual landscapes as a means of expressing her/his identity and place in the social world. Given that landscapes are created by individuals and groups, new texts and literacies provide new tools for conceptualising and transforming the textual landscape.

Longstanding middle-class views of childhood have, however, assumed an 'unworldly' child whose experience of childhood, including interactions with textual landscapes, are predictable and limited. This view has positioned childhood within the confined parameters of family and adult supervision where a selective tradition of knowledge and values are modelled and transmitted. Buckingham (2000) traces this increasing segregation to the second half of the nineteenth century when 'children were gradually moved out of the factories, off the streets and into the schools: and a whole range of new social institutions and agencies sought to oversee their welfare in line with a broadly middle-class domestic idea' (2000: 8). This became the 'protected' childhood (Steinberg and Kinchloe 1998: 16) where, as Postman (1994) would argue, children are relatively dependent upon adults for the kinds and volumes of information made available and where, we could add, risks, both to and from children, are minimised.

This child and childhood have been translated into classroom texts and curriculum practices that presume a limited experiential and knowledge base outside the family or that refer to disconnected fantasy worlds (Luke and Carrington 2002). The themes of many of these texts revolve around family – the adventures of siblings and friends, parents, grandparents – and the issues attached to the family such as new babies, missing pets and mealtimes. Established wisdom argues that these texts build bridges between literacy and children's lives; between school literacy practices and home literacy practices; between the everyday discourses of children's lives and the pedagogic discourses of school literacy instruction. These links are made explicit in the instructions to adults that accompanied many of the activities described earlier in relation to children's magazines. Other childhood texts construct fantasy worlds entirely disconnected from the temporal or material spaces in which children exist – these texts create new worlds and events, embedded spaces and times unconnected to the lived world of children. With these texts, children are invited to suspend their connection to the here and now and construct alternative, imaginary realities (e.g. the *Bananas in Pyjamas* magazine). These childhood texts – parochial and fantasy – are often silent on more complex issues such as diversity, conflict and poverty, issues with which even young children are confronted on a daily basis. These texts also remove children from participation in the currents of information flowing outside family and classroom, presupposing a future literate and citizen rather than a participant in the here and now.

However, as Kinchloe's (1998) descriptions of the *Home Alone* movies attest, in the face of changed access to information, enabled by the emergence of a range of new communications technologies, a more worldly 'postmodern childhood' has emerged, accompanied by the evolution of new texts and literacies. The central character of Kevin is depicted as a worldly wise child who is quite capable of using credit cards, making his way around unfamiliar cities and outwitting hardened criminals. The *Home Alone* series cleverly employs popular culture to reflect upon a range of the companion issues around parenting, adulthood and societal change that accompany the emergence of a 'postmodern' childhood. This is the 'worldly' agentive child who creates and distributes information and who has the capacity to independently access expanding sources of information. This is not to argue that there is an essential 'childhood' and that it is now postmodern. Nor am I arguing that children like Alex are a new generation of netizens with skills around technology that outstrip their elders (Tapscott 1998). I am mindful that the either/or of traditional versus postmodern childhoods is, as Buckingham (2000) noted, overly simplistic, as is the direct connection of print literacy with childhood (Luke 1989). My point is that new communications technologies and the associated emergence of new texts and literate practices have changed the way in which young people understand themselves and the world.

As Buckingham (2000) noted, conceptualisations of childhood are not freestanding. Like literacy crises (Green, Hodges and Luke 1994), constructions of childhood are a litmus test of broader social, economic and political change. In noting the emergence of the postmodern child as identified by Kinchloe (1998), we are in effect attending to a range of intersecting factors ranging from economic and ideological shift to changes in text and literacy. Thus, I use the term 'worldly' to indicate the of-the-world and participatory nature of contemporary children rather than to imply unruliness and/or threat. Alex is representative of the contemporary experience of childhood as she uses a new communications technology to send her txt message to do work on her behalf in the world, in effect contributing to the form of the textual landscape she inhabits. This is the child and the childhood reflected in *Limited Too* and less obviously in the slick advertising embedded in *Bob the Builder* and *Bananas in Pyjamas*. It is the childhood reflected in the complex problem-solving, intertexuality and non-linear pathways of the *Rugrats* computer game. These texts, and others like them, situate contemporary children in global flows of consumption, identity and information in ways unheard of in earlier generations and contribute to the construction of new discourses around childhood. Where once children grew into literate habitus within a relatively confined, predictable and supervised field of information and discourses, this is no longer the case.

Access to information has another facet. Ulrich Beck's (1992, 2000) theories of the 'risk society' note that the traditional narratives and structures that have acted to mediate individual risk are in the process of decay as industrial societies transition through globalisation. A consequence has been the emergence of more direct individual risk and a concomitant need to continuously make decisions and choices on a daily basis. Grounding this notion of 'reflexive biographies' in the everyday, individual risk assessment and decision-making are highly dependent on access to, and analysis of, information (Tullock and Lupton 2003: 29). In a culture increasingly characterised by risk taking as a 'practice of the self' (Foucault 1988; Tullock and Lupton 2003), the ways in which children construct their identities and, in turn, literate habitus, cannot but reflect this trend. This has relevance in terms of how we conceptualise childhood. According to Postman (1994):

> Childhood . . . was an outgrowth of an environment in which a particular form of information, exclusively controlled by adults, was made available in stages to children in what was judged to be psychologically assimilable ways. The maintenance of childhood depended on the principles of managed information and sequential learning.
>
> (Postman 1994: 72)

Here, Postman positions childhood as one of the narratives of industrial societies with control of information used as a technique to manage and minimise risk. He argued that the mass media and new communications technologies were destabilising this narrative by changing the patterns of information access. However, a decade ago, Postman (1994) was not in a position to recognise that the advent of the postmodern or worldly childhood is not just about the capacity of children to access increasingly desegregated information. The 'worldly' child not only has access to adult information as Postman (1994) suggested, but increasingly, this child is a creator and distributor of information, seeking to transform the textual and social landscapes in which s/he is located. The worldly child, who, like Alex, creates new information and uses new communications technologies and new forms of text to transmit it correctly views herself as skilful and of the world. Not the end of childhood, but the fading of a particular dominant discourse around childhood and the social and economic conditions that sustained it.

As the texts identified in this chapter indicate, the textual landscapes in which children are learning the practices, skills and knowledge that determine the kinds of literates and citizens they become are no longer confined to the parameters of family and school, nor are they print based. However, a more fundamental shift is taking place. While the passive, unworldly child was expected to merely inhabit the textual landscapes created by others, children developing literate habitus around new communications technologies, popular culture and expanding access to de-segregated information are already active participants.

Concluding thoughts: towards new landscapes

Changing views of childhood and changing patterns of access to both information and risk have, of course, implications for classroom literacy. Models of early literacy instruction, regardless of pedagogic or theoretical approach, have tended to unproblematically assume an 'unworldly' child. That is, regardless of arguments about whether reading should be a top-down or a bottom up process, whether phonics should be the focus of all reading and writing programmes, or which phonics programme is the 'best', there has always been a consensus on what kind of child is imagined and what needs around literacy s/he has. If the argument presented here is even partly true, there are children sitting in our classrooms who view themselves and the world in quite new ways and who have needs around text and literacy that cannot be met within these models of curriculum. Shifts in technology, society and access to information have, as both Postman (1994) and Innes (1950, 1951) quite rightly argued, altered the boundaries around information and the ways in which we understand the world. At the same time, new information communications technologies and forms of text enable contemporary children to participate in the creation of information as never before. Consequently, our classroom curricula and practices must also shift.

The next generation of instruction and theoretical models for early literacy instruction must take account of the pivotal nature of information. Each child's role as analyst of information from multiple sources must be focal, as well as serious attention paid to ensuring that s/he is scaffolded towards effective and ethical production and dissemination of information. This means that multiple forms of text from a range of sources – traditional, popular, electronic, consumer, fantasy, non-fiction, institutional – must be brought into classrooms for analysis and use. It also means that children should be producing and disseminating texts that engage meaningfully with the world outside the classroom, not via token gestures such as faux letters, brochures and the like, but as contributors to public debates both local and global. These textual contributions may range from the traditional 'letters-to-the-editor' through the construction of a weblog that engages with citizens around the world concerning a key issue, or through the creation of an animation for entry into a short film festival. The literacy curriculum may, for example, include the study of SMS txting, tracing its history, developing an understanding of the technologies enabling its spread, developing class-specific txting vocabularies, engaging in research around txting in their community.

While print must remain a central component of literacy curricula, it should be repositioned within a broader aim. The focus should always be on encouraging and scaffolding students to participate fully in the world outside the classroom in ethical and effective ways. Here, curricula could easily be built around Dewey's vision of collaborative, real-world projects where students and teachers actively work together in new power configurations and for new purposes, building specific textual mastery along the way. I believe this repositioning will also require a shift in temporal focus. Where more traditional models of literacy prepare children for a somewhat distant future, at which time they will participate in meaningful ways in the 'real' world, a model of literacy matching the needs of contemporary children must take as a first principle that children are already active participants and risk takers. As Kellner (2003: 2) notes, 'the demands of the new global economy, culture, and polity require a more informed, participatory, and active citizenship'. What better or more important place to begin than with early literacy instruction?

Becoming literate is, or should be, about developing the skills to transform the world. The spread of new communications technologies and the new forms of access to information and the emergent text forms associated with them open potential for socially critical and transformative literacy curricula. While the importance of print is not lessened by the emergence of new technologies and new forms of text, this shift may provide opportunities and gaps through which to challenge dominant discourses. The emergence of new forms of text, new access to information and the shifting importance of print within them may just open the door enough for indigenous, migrant, ESL, poor and rural/remote students – those who have traditionally struggled around traditional print-based literacies – to find a voice and the capacity to transform their textual and social landscapes. This was, after all, Innes' hope so long ago.

Notes

1 See Marsh (2002) for a discussion of the role of toys as miniature versions of adult consumer items.
2 There is a growing interest in the sociology of mobile phone use. See for example Geser 2002, Katz 2002, Katz and Aakhus 2002, Myerson 2001.
3 See http://www.limitedtoo.com/?WT.mc_n=LIMITED_TOO_HEADER.
4 See, for example, Hutchby and Moran-Ellis, 2001.

References

Australian Broadcasting Corporation and BBC Worldwide Ltd (2003) *Bananas in Pyjamas* (Funtime Special), August. Ultimo: NSW.
Australian Broadcasting Corporation and BBC Worldwide Ltd (2003) *Bob the Builder*, Issue 36. Ultimo: NSW.
Beck, U. (1992) *Risk Society: Towards a New Modernity*. London: Sage Publications.
Beck, U. (2000) *The Brave New World of Work*. London: Polity Press.
Buckingham, D. (2000) *After the Death of Childhood*. Cambridge: Polity Press.
Carrington, V. (2004) Texts and literacies of the Shi Jinrui. *British Journal of the Sociology of Education*: 215–228.
Carrington, V. and Luke, A. (2003) Reading, homes and families: from postmodern to modern? In A. van Kleeck, S. A. Stahl and E. B. Bauer (eds) *On Reading to Children: Parents and Teachers*. Mahwah, NJ: Erlbaum.
Foucault, M. (1988) Technologies of the self. In L. Martin, J. Gutman and P. Hutton (eds) *Technologies of the Self: A seminar with Michel Foucault* (pp. 16–49). London: Tavistock.

Freebody, P. and Luke, A. (1990) 'Literacies' programs: debates and demands in cultural context, *Prospect: The Journal of Adult Migrant Education Programs*, 5 (3): 7–16.

Fromm, J., Meder, N. and Vollmer, N. (2000) *Compterspiele in der kinderkultur* [*Computer Games in Children's Culture*]. Opladen: Leske & Budrich.

Gee, J. (1991) What is literacy? In C. Mitchell and K. Weiler (eds) *Rewriting Literacy: Culture and the Discourse of the Other* (pp. 3–13). New York: Bergin & Casey.

Geser, H. (2002) Towards a sociological theory of the mobile phone. University of Zurich, August 2002 (Release 2). Available at: http://socio.ch/mobile/t-geser1.htm. Accessed 18th August, 2003.

Green, B., Hodges, J. and Luke, A. (1994) *Debating Literacy in Australia: A Documentary History, 1945–1994*. Melbourne: Australian Literacy Foundation.

Gregory, E. (1997) *One Child, Many Worlds: Early Learning in Multicultural Communities*. New York: Teachers College Press.

Gregory, E. and Williams, A. (2000) *City Literacies*. London: Routledge.

Gunter, B. (1998) *The Effects of Video Games on Children: The myth unmasked*. Sheffield: Sheffield Academic Press.

Hoestetter, O. (2002) Video games – The necessity of incorporating video games as part of constructivist learning. Available at: http://game-research.com/art_games_contructivist.asp. Accessed 15 August 2003.

Hogle, J. (1996) Considering games as cognitive tools: in search of effective 'edutainment'. University of Georgia Department of Instructional Technology (ERIC Document Reproduction Service No. ED 425 737).

Hutchby, I. and Moran-Ellis, J. (2001) *Children, Technology and Culture: The Impacts of Technologies in Children's Everyday Lives*. London: Routledge/Falmer.

Innes, H. (1950) *Empire and Communications*. Toronto: University of Toronto Press.

Innes, H. (1951) *The Bias of Communication*. Toronto: University of Toronto Press.

Katz, J. (ed.) (2002) *Machines That Become Us: The Social Context of Personal Communication Technology*. New Jersey: Transaction Publishers.

Katz, J. and Aakhus, M. (eds) (2002) *Perpetual Contact: Communication, Private Talk, Public Performance*. Cambridge: Cambridge University Press.

Kellner, D. (2003) New media and new literacies: Reconstructing education for the new millennium. Accessed 27 October 2003 at: http://www.gseis.ucla.edu/courses/ed253a/kellner/newmedia.html.

Kinchloe, J. (1998) Home alone and 'bad to the bone': the advent of a postmodern childhood. In S. Steinberg and J. Kinchloe (eds) *Kinderculture: The corporate construction of childhood*. Boulder: Westview Press.

Luke, A. and Carrington, V. (2002) Globalisation, literacy, curriculum practice. In R. Fisher, G. Brooks and M. Lewis (eds) *Raising Standards in Literacy*. London, RoutledgeFalmer.

Luke, C. (1989) *Pedagogy, Printing and Protestantism: The Discourse on Childhood*. Albany, NY: SUNY Press.

Marsh, J. (2002) Colloquium: Electronic toys: why should we be concerned? A response to Levin and Rosenquest, *Contemporary Issues in Early Childhood*, 3 (1): 132–137.

Mitchell, D. (2000) *Cultural Geography: A Critical Introduction*. Oxford: Blackwell.

Myerson, G. (2001) *Heidegger, Habermas and the Mobile Phone*. Cambridge, UK: Icon Books.

Oyen, A. and Bebko, J. (1996) The effects of computer games and lesson contexts on children's mnemonic strategies, *Journal of Experimental Psychology*, 62 (2): 173–189.

Postman, N. (1994) *The Disappearance of Childhood*. New York: Vintage Books.

Prensky, M. (2001) *Digital Game-based Learning*. New York: McGraw Hill.

Steinberg, S. and Kinchloe, J. (eds) (1998) *Kinder-culture: The Corporate Construction of Childhood*. Colorado: Westview Press.

Tapscott, D. (1998) *Growing Up Digital: The Rise of The Net Generation*. New York: McGraw-Hill.

Tullock, J. and Lupton, D. (2003) *Risk and Everyday Life*. London: Sage Publications.

Vered, K. O. (1998) Blue group boys play incredible machine, girls play hopscotch: Social discourse and gendered play at the computer. In J. Sefton-Green (ed.) *Digital Diversions: Youth Culture in the Age of Multimedia* (pp. 43–61). London: UCL Press.

Wilks, D. (2002) Editorial, *PCGameZone,* Issue 1, October, p. 6, Redfern, NSW: Next Publishing Pty Ltd.

Wireless World Forum, Mobile Youth (2003) Accessed 23 October 2003 online at http://www.mobileyouth.org/news/mobileyouth957.html.

Chapter 3

Ritual, performance and identity construction

Young children's engagement with popular cultural and media texts

Jackie Marsh

Given the growing evidence of the central role that popular culture and media play in many young children's lives (Makin *et al.*, 1999; Marsh, 2003a; Marsh, 2004), it is, perhaps, timely to consider how these texts and artefacts contribute to children's literate identities and practices. This is, indeed, the central aim of many of the chapters in the current book; in this chapter, I intend to focus specifically on the relationship of the process of identity formation to children's communication, language and literacy practices. Drawing from data collected in two studies of two- to four-year-old children's popular cultural and media practices in the home (Marsh, 2004; Marsh and Thomson, 2001), the chapter will examine the nature of children's home communicative practices and consider the ways in which these practices are shaped by contemporary cultural 'mediascapes'[1] (Appadurai, 1996). I will focus on two aspects of children's experiences in particular, because these are central to young children's development: play, and the role of material objects in their communicative practices. I intend to explore these two themes in ways which draw together what are often distinct areas of analysis in the field of early childhood literacy studies: developmental psychology, anthropology, sociology and cultural studies.

The role of play in children's early communication, language and literacy development has been analysed predominantly from the perspective of developmental psychology, with some attention given to ecological and socio-cultural factors in terms of the relationship between children's play and their encounters with the wider environment and literacy in everyday life (Roskos and Christie, 2000). The work of play theorists who emphasise the necessity to integrate psychological analyses of play with socio-cultural aspects (Sutton-Smith, 1998) needs to inform further our understanding of the dynamic between literacy and play. In this chapter, cultural and social anthropologists' reflections on ritual and performance are drawn upon in an analysis of children's media-related play. In addition, I examine the inter-relationship between different theoretical explanations for the place of objects in children's lives, weaving together the threads relating to developmental psychology, with its emphasis on the role of transitional objects in children's development, the sociological analysis of the commodification of material artefacts and the work of anthropologists on the importance of fetishised objects to particular socio-cultural practices. This drawing together of disparate strands appears to me to be a necessary task in developing a fuller understanding of the role of popular culture and media in children's literacy practices. The developmental psychology tradition, while of fundamental importance to the field of early literacy education, is not sufficiently interested in wider cultural processes; the disciplines of anthropology, sociology and cultural studies, illuminating as they are on the role and nature of socio-cultural practices, say little about the particular function of such practices in very young children's literacy lives. First, however, I consider the nature of identity construction and its relationship to literacy learning.

Identities in practice

Giddens (1991) has suggested that, in late modernity, self-identity is an individual project in which people construct an ongoing sense of self through narrative:

> A person's identity is not to be found in behaviour, nor – important though this is – in the reactions of others, but in the capacity to keep a particular narrative going. The individual's biography, if she is to maintain regular interaction with others in the day-to-day world, cannot be wholly fictive. It must continually integrate events which occur in the external world, and sort them into the ongoing 'story' about the self.
>
> (Giddens, 1991: 54)

In such a framework, it is clear that a continuous, stable identity is a construct and that a constant concept of selfhood is indeed no more than a narrative creation, a drawing together of particular elements of the self and a minimisation, or dismissal, of other aspects (Jenkins, 1996). Fragmented and diverse in nature, facets of identity can be conflicting and transient and, indeed, some have argued that a sustained concept of self over time is a falsehood and that these multiple selves form the lived reality of personhood (see Jenkins, 1996 for a review). Identity, in a poststructuralist analysis, becomes a process rather than a concept (McCarthey, 2002).

Research which has concerned itself with children's identities has indicated that context is central to the discursive production of self. In a study of young children's identities in relation to 'race', gender and class, Connolly suggests that the identities of the children he studied were 'contingent and context-specific, dependent upon the particular field they were located in at any one time' (Connolly, 1998: 190). This draws from a theoretical framework in which the concept of an essentialist self can be construed as a modernist myth and such a position would lead one to assume that as multiple identities are constructed in context, there can be no sustained sense of self over time. However, Holland *et al.* (2001) argue instead for an emphasis on a 'self-in-practice', a selfhood that is constantly re-working and re-fashioning itself in context but which draws from a historical set of practices which are the interaction of context and the embodied self:

> This self-in-practice occupies the interface between intimate discourses, inner speaking, and bodily practices formed in the past and the discourses and practices to which people are exposed, willingly or not, in the present. It authors, or orchestrates the products of these sites of self.
>
> (Holland *et al.*, 2001: 32)

In this theoretical framework, behaviour is to be viewed not as an outward indicator of an essentialist self but as a sign of self-in-practice, a self in the process of constructing identities located within socio-historical contexts. Inevitably, this process is a social one and, for young children, family members play a crucial role in discursive identity formation (Alexander, Miller and Hengst, 2001). From Bowlby's early work on attachment theory (Bowlby, 1969) to more recent theories of childhood socialisation which centre on families' discursive practices (Miller *et al.*, 1990), the crucial role families play in shaping children's identities has been extensively discussed. Later in the chapter, I will consider the way in which family members in the studies reported here supported the development of children's identities as expert navigators of popular and media culture. First, however, the development of identity is, inevitably, linked with children's acquisition of skills, knowledge and understanding in relation to communication, language and literacy and thus the inter-relationship between these two aspects deserves particular analysis.

Literacy and identity

The literate identities of children, young people and adults have a significant impact on their orientation to literacy and their affective and cognitive relationship with it over the lifecourse (Gregory and Williams, 2001; Mahiri and Godley, 1998). In a study of students in Grades Three to Six at three different schools in the USA, McCarthey (2002) demonstrates how students' literate identities are crucial in determining whether children appropriate, contest or recontextualise curriculum tasks. She suggests that students who are able, when teachers allow, to transform their identities within classroom contexts can create a 'third space' (Gutierrez, Baquedano-Lopez and Turner, 1997) in which schooled norms and student lived experience can meet and ensure that children have agency and voice, much like the classroom spaces described by Dyson (1997; 2002). This ability to transform pedagogical spaces relies in part on a recognition by teachers of the 'cultural capital' (Bourdieu, 1977) which children bring with them to the site of literacy learning, a recognition which is not always apparent in educational discourses in early childhood (Brooker, 2002; Marsh, 2003b). As well as recognising and valuing children's cultural experiences, teachers need also to give permission for children to reflect on ways in which their subjectivities have been shaped by the literacy experiences encountered in school and out-of-school settings (McCarthey, 2002). Further, we need to recognise that the construction of literate identities is a complex, multi-faceted process in which the 'self-in-practice' shapes the literacy event at the same time as the social context, and mediated tools of such textual encounters frame the way in which these processes impact on subjectivites. In an attempt to trace in finer detail some of these processes, I want to consider four particular research studies that illuminate aspects of the way in which literacy practices and identities inter-relate. These four studies look, variously, at how children's, young people's and adults' literacy practices shape their identities, but also how their established identities shape their literacy practices. This continuum (literacy practices shape identities – identities shape literacy practices) is represented by the vertical arrow in Figure 3.1. In addition, these research studies have also explored how other people shape one's literate identities in explicit or implicit ways and have examined the role of the self in forming those literate identities. The self–other continuum is represented by the horizontal arrow in Figure 3.1.

An example of the dynamic presented by Quadrant 1 is the work of Elizabeth Birr Moje (2000), who demonstrates how important the 'self' is in shaping literacy practices, which in turn signal particular identities. In an

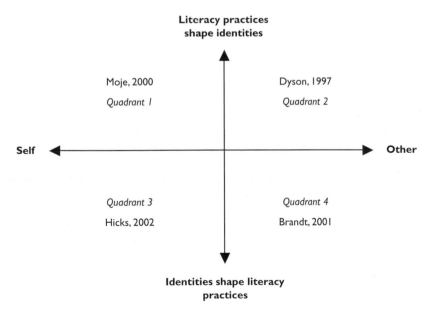

Figure 3.1 Literacy practices and identities

ethnographic study of young people who were involved in gangs, Moje out-lines how the gang members deliberately adopted particular literacy practices to signify membership of the group, such as 'tagging' (writing one's name in graffiti-style) or writing gang symbols on various physical spaces. Deliberate, individual choices are made by gang members about the kinds of literacy practices in which they engage in order to signal specific identities. Moje notes how:

> Once allowed into that social space, the young people used these differ-ent literacy practices to make sense of their everyday lives in and out of school, to maintain their membership in the gangs or other peer groups, and to move to new levels of membership within the groups.
>
> (Moje, 2000: 662)

Such purposeful choices signal agency within these particular socio-cultural spaces and the currency accrued by literacy practices in these spaces con-trasted strongly with the gang members' experiences of schooled literacy.

In Quadrant 2, the work of Anne Haas Dyson (1997) helps to develop understanding of the role of others in shaping literacy practices which in turn impact on identity construction. She looks at the dynamic of peer relation-ships in elementary classrooms and explores how children's individual literacy practices are influenced by others. Thus, children write superhero stories in which they cast themselves and their friends in starring roles, ensuring wide approval from classmates when they act out those stories in 'authors' theatre'. Writing becomes a means of forging literate *and* social identities as children negotiate with each other (and, in some cases, exert direct pressure) to gain key roles in their peers' stories. Social and ideological issues are traced by Dyson as she outlines how children used these writing episodes to marginalise or privilege other children in relation to issues of gender, 'race' and class and she notes how 'stories served to generate ideological tensions and, potentially, to mediate them as well' (1997: 173).

In Quadrant 3, the work of Deborah Hicks (2002) can be utilised to trace the way in which self-identity shapes literacy practices in an individualistic manner. She studied Jake, a four-year-old working-class boy who identified strongly with his father, a carpenter. Jake preferred to be physically active, like his father, and chose to engage in literacy practices which centred on movement, for example developing narratives which were 'rooted in physical action' (Hicks, 2002: 104). Jake's self-identity was a strong influence on how he engaged with schooled literacy practices on entry to kindergarten and, unsurprisingly, he struggled with some of the expectations of his teachers.

Finally, Quadrant 4 explores the role of others in shaping one's identity, which in turn influences the kinds of literacy practices in which one engages. To illustrate this process, I draw on the work of Deborah Brandt (2001), who studied the literacy histories of adults in the USA. Brandt interviewed 80 participants in order to identify the nature of, and influences on, their literacy practices over their lifecourses. In one interview, we hear how Johnny Ames, an African-American male born in 1959, lost his motivation to write because of the racism he faced. He described how the story of Little Black Sambo damaged his self-confidence and sense of identity, in addition to the way in which racist signs impacted upon his orientation to literacy:

> 'And then there were the signs [i.e. No Negroes Allowed], and they had to write those signs. In my mind I can see how that association took the drive out of me. It didn't motivate me to write'.
>
> (Brandt, 2001: 59)

Like all diagrams which privilege dualistic discourses, Figure 3.1 is limited in its ability to make transparent the complexities of the relationship between self, others, literacy and identity. While it could be argued that any one of the four studies considered could be placed in any one of the quadrants and other aspects of those studies drawn out for analysis, this way of examining the dynamic synergy between these four elements (self, others, literacy and identity) may contribute to an understanding of how multifaceted and contested this process can be. In the context of this chapter, what Figure 3.1 provides is a means of illuminating how the four quadrants each have something to say about the way in which young children's literacy practices shape their identities, the way in which already formed identities limit to some extent the kinds of literacy practices which they take up and the intense dialectic between the self and others – in this case, family members – which impacts on literacy practices and identities. If identity construction is, as the studies outlined above attest, a socio-cultural process, then children's development of identities in relation to literacy will inevitably be influenced by the communities of practice (Lave and Wenger, 1991) in which they participate. There are a range of influences on children's construction of literate identities, the family being one of the most salient in the early years (Hannon, 1995). However, most explorations of young children's literacy practices in the home have focused on mapping out those experiences which are based on print texts. Given the major changes to contemporary communicative practices in the new media age, it is essential that such a perspective is broadened to include a focus on popular cultural and media texts. In this chapter, I use data collected from two studies of young children's communicative practices in the home to illustrate some of the key theoretical themes discussed so far and, in the analysis, I focus in particular on the role of popular cultural and media texts in the construction of communicative practices. Before moving on to discuss the findings in greater depth, the methodologies adopted for both projects will be outlined briefly.

The studies

In the first study featured in this chapter, parents and carers of children who attended a nursery in a city in the north of England were asked to complete a 'literacy diary' which documented their children's reading and writing practices (of print-based and televisual[2] texts) over the period of one month. This was a predominantly white, working-class community, housed in pub-licly-owned buildings, with high levels of unemployment. The community was relatively stable, with young people often leaving the family home to live close to their parents, grandparents and other family members. In total, 18 parents of three- and four-year-old children in this community maintained a literacy diary for four weeks, during which time they documented their children's practices across a range of media including television, computers, books, comics, magazines and environmental print (see Marsh and Thompson, 2001). Fifteen of these parents were then interviewed about their children's communicative practices in the home and their views about the relationship of these practices to the nursery curriculum were determined (Marsh, 2003b).

In the second project, undertaken in the same city, 44 parents of children aged 2.5–3.11 years old completed questionnaires related to their children's media-related literacy practices and 26 of these parents were then interviewed at home. Again, this community was predominantly white and working-class and because of the high levels of economic deprivation in the area, the com-munity was part of the national Sure Start initiative, a government interven-tion project targeted at such communities. The questionnaire and interviews focused on children's literacy practices in the home in relation to a wide range of media such as books and comics, environmental print, television and film, computer games, mobile phones and music. Parents were asked about how children used these media, their own interactions with children using the media and their attitudes towards this media use in relation to home and nursery (see Marsh, 2004). Field notes were also taken during the home visits which focused on children's media use. Data from these two projects, with 62 families in total, have been used to inform the following analysis.

Data were analysed both quantitatively and qualitatively, as appropriate. Quantitative analysis included use of descriptive statistics. Qualitative analysis was undertaken using inductive coding techniques (Strauss and Corbin, 1990) in that interview transcripts and concept maps were analysed using open coding in order to allow patterns to emerge. Although the wider data sets are used to inform the general analysis of young children's popular culture and media-related communicative practices in this chapter, I will focus in parti-cular on five children from both studies: Carl, aged three, Dale, aged four, Emma, aged two, Jade, aged four and Keiran, aged three. These children have been identified because, in many ways, they exhibited fairly typical patterns in relation to the use of popular culture and media, but also because the interviews with their parents drew attention to some of the theoretical concepts outlined previously. All the children were white, from working-class families and all lived in publicly-owned housing.

Carl was a three-year-old boy whose parents both worked in a bread-making factory. He was an only child. His extended family lived in Scotland, so Carl's family spent a lot of their time travelling to and from Scotland. Carl owned a large number of videos, book and comics, toys and some computer games. Carl's mother, Sonia, was pregnant with her second child at the time of the interview.

Dale was a four-year-old boy who lived with his parents, five older brothers and a younger sister. Dale's father was disabled and unemployed and cared for full-time by Dale's mother. The family did not have very much money and Dale owned few toys of his own. He shared numerous popular cultural and media texts and artefacts with his brothers, the most prized of which was a games console, a Dreamcast.

Emma was aged two years, eleven months and lived with her mother. She had no siblings. Emma's mother, Gayle, was a single parent, unemployed and coping with a very stressful daily life, but Gayle did have a supportive mother and sister who bought Emma toys and books for birthdays and public holidays.

Jade was a four-year-old girl who lived with her parents quite near the nursery she attended. She was an only child. Jade's father was a computer technician for a local firm, her mother was unemployed. Jade's mother described the family as having little money, but this did not prevent them from spending what they could on Jade and, as a result, she owned a range of popular cultural and media products.

Keiran was a three-year-old boy, an only child, who lived with his parents. His father worked in a call-exchange and his mother was just about to start a job as a part-time worker with parents in a local community project. Keiran enjoyed a relatively higher degree of material wealth than the other children in the Sure Start project and owned a range of toys, texts and artefacts linked to popular cultural and media interests.

Exploring the patterns in media use by children in the two projects as a whole, it was clear that there were many similarities with data from surveys undertaken with older children. For example, in the Livingstone and Bovill (1999) survey of six- to seventeen-year-olds, television was the most prominent source of narrative pleasure; this was also the case for two- to four-year-old children in the 62 families featured in these studies. In the first project, children watched television programmes and films more than twice as often as engaging with any other kind of text (see Marsh and Thompson, 2001). In the second project, 65 per cent of the children watched television for three hours or more a day. However, related to the use of children's television across both projects was a wide range of communicative practices which involved computer games (PC and, predominantly, games consoles), comics, magazines and books (often related to popular culture and media interests), junk mail and environmental print which were often linked to popular cultural interests (e.g. food labels, computer game covers), mobile phones, toys and various other artefacts such as clothing, furniture and miscellaneous items (for a fuller discussion of the range of media incorporated in the children's communicative practices, see Marsh, in press). These children inhabited a rich, multimodal world and moved across the various textual platforms with ease. As Robinson and Turnbull in Chapter 4 indicate, it no longer makes sense to examine one aspect of children's meaning-making in isolation from others – they are integrated in complex and profound ways. Other chapters in this book deal with the specific relationship of some of the texts and artefacts outlined above to children's early language and literacy development. In this chapter, I will focus on the role of this media in children's identity formation, the construction of themselves as literate beings and the place of play and material objects within this.

Identities, popular culture, media and literacy

The children in both studies were most often engaged with those texts and artefacts which linked with their popular cultural and media interests. These were the texts that were most meaningful to them and which motivated them to participate in a wide range of communicative practices. For example, Jade loved the Winnie the Pooh[3] narrative. She collected a wide range of texts and artefacts which linked to this character, as indicated in Figure 3.2.

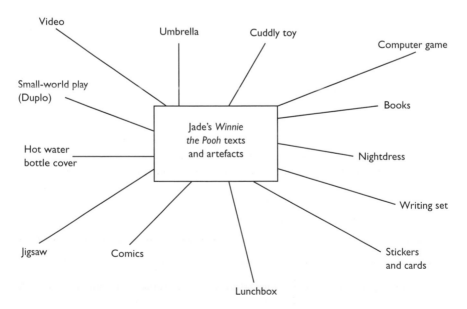

Figure 3.2 *Winnie the Pooh* texts and artefacts owned by Jade

This narrative web is significant in a number of ways. First, it provided a 'narrativised' (Fleming, 1996: 102) semiotic system in which Jade encountered the same narrative in a range of different modes and it enabled her to explore the affordances of the various modes (Bearne, 2003; Kress, 2003). In moving across modalities, children encounter key interruptions and questions which force them to reconsider perceptions and accommodate new learning about these semiotic systems (Dyson, 2002). Secondly, these texts and artefacts are central to the development of a sense of identity, or ontological security (Giddens, 1991). Parents, carers and wider family members in these projects all contributed to this synergy between popular texts and identities, buying children more and more items related to a particular favourite figure. Sonia had even taken her son, Carl, to a site which contained train engines based on the Thomas the Tank Engine narrative:

> He's been to see *Thomas the Tank Engine*, calls them by the proper names, he'll know every one of them. But he's been to the real place. Yeah, they've got big trains and he knows everyone of their names and he can sit and he's got most of the trains. He can tell you the names of every one of them. There must be about 40 trains and Thomas the Tank and he can tell you every one of the names . . . I would say Thomas the Tank is a big thing for him. He's got train tracks. He's got everything, you name it, Thomas the Tank and it's took . . . maybe in the last 6 months it's just been Thomas, Thomas, Thomas, Thomas. He always talks about Thomas the Tank Engine, always.

This was a consistent pattern across all of the parent interviews. Even though parents might at times be quite exasperated by their children's predilections – as could perhaps be detected in Sonia's interview ('. . . it's just been Thomas, Thomas, Thomas, Thomas'), they were fully supportive of this attachment to media icons and indeed contributed to extending it by buying goods across a wide range of categories. These narratives permeated all kinds of family practices, although somewhat disturbingly at times. For example, during the interview with Sonia, Carl started to shout loudly and his mother reprimanded him by saying, 'You're going to your bed if you don't stop it. That controller'll come and get you. Yes he will' – the 'controller' referring to the station manager in *Thomas the Tank Engine*. Fortunately, the use of these media characters to reprimand children was minimal, but this instance does indicate something of the intensity with which these narratives pervaded family life. (For more extensive discussion of the role of popular culture in family narratives, see Pahl, 2002).

The data from both studies did reveal the centrality of material objects in children's lives. Parents talked about popular cultural and media texts and objects that children played with, talked to, sat next to, slept with, bathed with, ate with and cuddled. Some of these objects became so precious that children would not sleep without them, or became distraught when they could not be found. There is much literature on the role of transitional objects in young children's development (Winnicott, 1965). Transitional objects have been identified as those soothing objects which are very important to young children because they serve the purpose of providing comfort at times of distress and they ease the transition between dependence and independence. In some ways, the use of popular cultural and media objects as soothers could be seen as the adaptation of these objects for transitional purposes. For example, Emma's mother reported the importance of a Barbie bedspread for her daughter:

> . . . we've got a Barbie bedspread and some days she's got Winnie the Pooh in her bedroom and some days she'll go to bed and she will have a real fit because she doesn't want to sleep with Pooh bear on her bed. She needs Barbie on her bed. And I'll have to change a complete bedspread just because of the point that she won't sleep in that bed if I don't. Or, if not, I end up with her in my bed.

However, the work of cultural anthropologists on fetishes could also be of interest in an analysis of this phenomenon (Spyer, 1998). Fetishes are objects which are presumed to have, or are given, a particular influence or power over people and, in an anthropological sense, are closely linked to animism. Marx adopted the concept in the development of his analysis of commodity fetishism (Marx, 1990 [1867]). In Marx's critique of the materialism of capitalism, he recognised that 'human passion – both of possessing and being possessed, of greed and fancy – emerges within a material dialectic between human sensory routines and material objects' (Pels, 1998). It is this aspect of contemporary childhood which has, perhaps, sparked more 'moral panics' (Cohen, 1987) than any other. Children's fascination with material objects has been the centre of concerns about the future of childhood itself, with nightmarish visions being presented of contemporary children surrounded by an array of potentially harmful and limiting electronic toys and gadgets (Levin and Rosenquest, 2001). While it was clear throughout the two studies discussed in this chapter that material cultural objects held a strong fascination for children, there was no evidence that they had developed harmful responses to such items, nor was there evidence of the existence of children for whom commodity fetishism was out of control. These items played similar functions to more traditional soothers (e.g. teddy bears); the key difference was that these contemporary 'transitional objects' were more directly linked to a whole array of cultural and material goods in children's lives. There was evidence of these material objects being the objects of desire on a number of levels, but work on the consumptive act as a cultural phenomenon has indicated the complex relationship between the acquisition of items, identities and agency (Humphery, 1998; Miller et al., 1998). There is obviously a

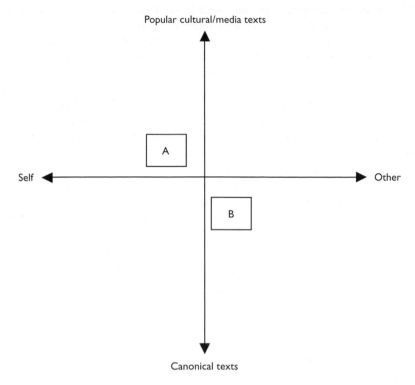

Figure 3.3 Popular culture and identity

balanced discussion of this aspect of contemporary childhood to be had, a discussion which acknowledges the pleasures and stimulation such objects bring at the same time as taking a long, cool look at their material nature and their place in the globalised practices of multinational companies (Kenway and Bullen, 2001).

Although the use of popular cultural and media texts in nurseries and schools has been advocated by a number of researchers (Dyson, 2002; Marsh, 2003b), there is still resistance to these discourses from many educators (Lambirth, 2003), perhaps because of the concerns surrounding consumerism, outlined above. It may be the case that this resistance would weaken if educators were clearer about the important role such narratives play in children's identity construction. Marginalising these texts, or banning them outright, serves only to ask of children that they cast off aspects of their identities as they move from home to school. Figure 3.3 attempts to demonstrate the centrality of these material objects to children's identity construction. The section labelled 'B' in Figure 3.3 is where many of the texts used in nurseries and school lie; they are often well-established titles for children and feature experiences and characters far removed from many working-class children's lives. In that sense, for many of the children in these two studies, the texts in section 'B' said more about the 'other' than the 'self'. Section 'A' of this diagram is where many of the textual experiences of children in the two studies reported in this paper lie. These texts were primarily rooted in popular culture and media and were part of the very fabric of children's daily lives; they reflected the 'self' in a myriad of ways. However, few of the books the children owned were titles found on nursery and school shelves (Marsh and Thompson, 2001). This is not to suggest that children should only have access in nurseries and schools to texts which merely reflect their current subject positions and experiences; of course it is important to introduce children to a world which is accessed and transformed through their imaginations. Figure 3.3 is merely a tool that points to the way in which popular culture and media are integral to the construction of many children's literate identities in complex and important ways (Dyson, 2002) and it is clear that lack of attention to these aspects is, in some senses, symptomatic of the dissonance between schooling and personal identity.

Also central to young children's construction of identity is play, and I will now move on to explore data from the studies which indicated the way in which popular culture and media impacted on play and, in turn, shaped children's literate identities.

Play, ritual, performance and media

Television was a fundamental aspect of children's play in these studies and this reflected its pivotal role in the space–time configurations of family life. As Tufte noted in his study of the place of Brazilian telenovelas in women's lives in South America:

> television, both as a material possession, as a centre in a field of ornaments and decorations and finally through the interaction of content and flow with the viewer, can contribute in multiple ways to the constitution of spaces in everyday life.
>
> (Tufte, 2000: 50)

Television-related play spaces were clearly provided by the majority of parents who were interviewed in their homes. The use of space in the living rooms of the 26 families visited in the Sure Start study indicated that the television was a primary text within the home. In many of the homes visited, the space around the television appeared to be demarcated as a space for celebrating and extending children's relationship with the screen. Often, children's dressing-up clothes, toys or books which were associated with television characters were situated there, ready for when children wished to incorporate them into their meaning-making practices. This playful response to televisual texts enabled children to re-enact narratives and engage with favourite characters. As Rowe (2000: 8) noted in a study of children's play-related responses to books, 'One of the most noticeable ways children connected books to play was through an active, physical search for book-related toys and props'. This pattern was also seen in relation to televisual texts in the studies featured here. Children were frequently observed playing with representations of favourite television characters as they watched the related programmes, and parents were supportive of their children's playful responses to television. For example, Keiran, aged three years and seven months, loved to wear his grandmother's high heel shoes as he watched *101 Dalmations*. The shoes were always kept next to the television. His mother stated:

> He re-enacts it. That's why we've got my mum's shoes over there. [*To child*] 'Cruella Deville, aren't you? You are Cruella Deville, aren't you?' [*To interviewer*] And he re-enacts everything that he watches in *101* and *102* all the time . . . and then we'll re-enact it but we'll re-enact it for about two weeks. Honestly, if he's really found it funny or something he can talk and talk and talk and talk. And he talks about the same thing over and over again.

This kind of response to moving images narratives is important because of the clear relationship between play and language and literacy development (Barrs, 1988; Roskos and Christie, 2000). For example, Pellegrini (1985) found that there was a positive correlation between children's use of decontextualised, 'literate' language and their level of engagement in socio-dramatic play. For young children in the study, play related to television and films was an integral part of their daily lives in the home and facilitated those 'text-to-life' (Cochran-Smith, 1984) responses which are key to the development of meaning-making.

The television-related play in which children engaged was often ritualistic in nature. Anthropologists have long been interested in ritual as a cultural practice. Once relegated to the sacred, it is now acknowledged as an important aspect of secular life and is closely related to performance: 'Ritualisation is best reconstructed in terms of social practices which are situated and performed' (Hughes-Freeland and Cain, 1998: 2). The boundary between ritual and performance is blurred, but ritual can be recognised as performance which is habitual (Rostas, 1998). There are obvious links here with the repetitive nature of children's media play in these studies. An early twentieth-century Dutch analyst of play and culture, Johan Huizinga, suggested that one of play's most important features is its 'spatial separation from ordinary life' (Huizanga, 1976: 60), realised either materially or ideationally. He proposed that play and ritual are similar in a number of ways. Rituals, for example, often draw on particular artefacts which play a specific role in the performance. In this study, parents contributed to children's television-related play through their provision of space and material objects which were used in ritualistic ways, as is the case with the shoes of Keiran's grandmother, described above. Part of the fascination with ritual is the appeal of repetition and, in an analysis of this aspect of the data, the integration of anthropology and psychology might throw meaningful light onto these children's practices. There has been extensive work on the role of schemas in young children's development (Athey, 1990; Nutbrown, 1999). A schema is 'a pattern of repeatable behaviour into which experiences are assimilated and that are gradually co-ordinated' (Athey, 1990: 37). Through the repetition of various physical and mental acts, children accommodate and assimilate new learning. Therefore, ritual practice has an important role to play in the development of schema and, indeed, it might be difficult to separate out these processes in the social practices of children's daily lives. Certainly, in relation to Keiran, particular schema may be relevant to his repetitive actions in this ritualised play and facilitate his cognitive development in relation to language and literacy.

One of the benefits of understanding these actions as ritualistic in some way is that we can begin to examine the way in which such recitals are used by children to create social performances in which they are the pivotal character. Many families described how children chose to be the central media character in a televisual narrative and then positioned other family members as minor characters in order to act out particular scenes or plots. This kind of performance is not only about re-telling the narrative as a multimodal form of reader-response, although that is, of course, an important aspect (Rowe, 2000); it is also about performing a particular kind of ritual which can be used to establish social practices and identities. These media rituals often included children, parents and siblings and the actions became part of family discourse. As Alexander et al. suggest:

> family life is embedded in recurring activities and mediated by particular discourse practices, and . . . young children come to orient themselves within particular systems of meaning by participating in these everyday social practices.
>
> (Alexander et al., 2001: 379)

As I have already indicated, space is an important element of ritual and in the homes of families in these studies, the space around the television set in the living room was a site for ritual performance and the family's social practices. Tufte describes the space surrounding television as a 'hybrid sphere of signification' (2000: 232) in which patterns of interaction with mass media become diffused into everyday social practices. In these spheres of signification, televisual narratives became embedded into family discourses and permeated many aspects of daily lives, including play (related to televisual narratives), shopping trips (in which children asked for items associated with characters, such as Bob the Builder pasta), visits to town (in which children pointed out texts and images relating to their favourite characters) and family celebrations (at which children would often be given further items which reinforced interest in these televisual discourses).

In addition to the role of ritual in children's playful engagement with media texts, we need also to consider the place of performance and its function in identity construction, given the close relationship between ritualisation and performance (Bell, 1992). Judith Butler has argued that the concept of 'performativity' is central to gender construction (Butler, 1999). Thus, she argues, gender does not have ontological status, but is constituted through purposive acts:

> Such acts, gestures, enactments, generally construed, are performative in the sense that the essence or identity that they otherwise purport to express are *fabrications* manufactured and sustained through corporeal signs and other discursive means.
>
> (Butler, 1999: 173)

Throughout the studies reported in this chapter, parents discussed how their children utilised media characters and narratives to perform aspects of their gendered identities – some boys were, for example, Bob the Builder, in action with hammers and chisels, and a number of girls were described as playing out Disney narratives dressed in Cinderella or Sleeping Beauty costumes. Media-related performativity was a crucial ingredient in the formation of these young children's identities and shaped their understanding of the constructed nature of masculinities and femininities. However, the media-related performances of children were not used simply to replicate stereotypical, hegemonic versions of gendered identities, although of course this was a predominant feature. At times, children resisted the normalisation process and presented contested and transgressive models of gendered practices, as we saw in the case of Keiran.

Gendered identity was not the only category of identity that children performed. During the home visits, observational field notes taken as well as interview data indicate that children also performed identities related to various aspects of popular culture and media, for example as 'media-savvy' consumers, knowledgeable experts in relation to a particular televisual narrative or as competent user of new technologies. Dale was one of the few four year-olds in the studies whose skills in using games consoles equalled, or surpassed, those of his older siblings. I asked his mother, Jean, about Dale's interest in computer games:

	Observational notes
Jean: Oh, he loves them. He's mad on them.	Dale moves over to
Jackie: Is it Playstation or Nintendo?	the Dreamcast console.
Jean: Dreamcast. We've had PlayStation. We had	One of his older
PlayStation but we've got Dreamcast now.	brothers is already
He's good at both of them . . .	playing on it. Dale
Jackie: And what games does he play?	looks at me and
Jean: Three wheeler thing and . . . driving games and that.	nudges his brother,
Jackie: Driving games. Can he operate them?	who ignores him for
Jean: Yeah, he does it all his self. He can turn it on,	a few seconds then
he can put, set it up and the lot his self . . .	passes the controls
Jackie: How long has he been playing this?	over.
Jean: Since he were about two for PlayStation but we've	
only just got Dreamcast so . . . If he had his way he'd	
stay on it all day but we have to take him off it for	Dale is using it to
meals and that for a start, and he screams place	navigate the screen.
down when we take him off it. And when we take	
him off it for bed and that. So now we have to limit	Dale looks at his mum,
it, like he's not going on it today, because he's	who hasn't noticed him
obsessed with it.	playing the machine,
Jackie: How long will he play on it?	despite her ruling. Dale
Jean: He'd play on it all day if he could. If he had chance	then looks across to
he'd be on it from getting up in a morning to going	me.
to bed at night and he wouldn't eat no meals in	
between.	

What was of interest in this interview was not so much what Jean, Dale's mother, said about Dale's skills, although the level of competence and interest in console games was surprising for a boy who had just turned four; what was of particular note was Dale's actions as we conducted the interview. It may have been the case, of course, that Dale felt that his mother was sufficiently distracted not to notice him transgressing the rule of the day in relation to his use of Dreamcast. However, another reading of the data is that Dale was performing the role of competent games console player for my benefit. This was a performance of competence, perhaps to illustrate that his mother's words were true. The role of performativity in identity construction thus had a wider significance in these studies than a focus on gender. Furthermore, parents provided a range of evidence that they supported their children's media-related performances and, in doing so, helped them to develop identities as competent media users. I have described elsewhere how, in the Sure Start study, parents and siblings scaffolded children's experiences in using games consoles by letting the children play alongside a skilled family player using a set of hand controls that were (unbeknown to the younger child) not plugged in (Marsh, 2004). Such support is essential in the learning process and has been recognised in relation to print-based literacy practices (Hannon,

1995); further studies are needed of the way in which families support young children's development as skilled users of a range of new technologies.

A final point to note in relation to questions of media and performativity is that a pattern emerged from a number of interviews with parents which indicated that media appeared to provide scripts for acts which then may or may not be materialised in everyday life. For example, Emma's mother felt that watching television helped children to learn:

> About other places. I think places they can't really go in. Do you know like she says if she's watching Tweenies, 'Oh Mommy, seaside!' and things like that. She actually sees them but it's not something you see every day is it? So you get to learn about new experiences without actually having to go and do them. And then when they do them at least they know a little something about them.

The phrase 'without actually having to go and do them' would ring alarm bells for some cultural theorists, who have warned that the media provide alternative 'realities' in which originals have been replaced by simulacra. Baudrillard (1983), for example, has written extensively about the way in which, because of developments in media and new technologies, we have created a 'hyper-reality' in which we can no longer distinguish between what is real and what is unreal. For example, 'Disneyland is presented as imaginary in order to make us believe that the rest is real, when in fact all of Los Angeles and the America surrounding it are no longer real, but of the order of the hyper-real and of simulation' (Baudrillard, 1983: 29). The current craze for 'reality TV' confirms to many that the media has become so mean-ingful in people's lives that they live vicariously through it. Built into this is often the assumption that as community and family ties have loosened in late modernity, television provides an alternative means of feeling as if one be-longs (Bauman, 2002). However, this is a rather pessimistic view which fails to take account of the way in which television and new technologies are enhancing already established communities of practice (Lave and Wenger, 1991) and helping to create new ones. In relation to the lives of the young children in these two studies, popular culture, media and new technologies were not providing a parallel reality but, rather, interacted with daily indivi-dual and social practices in complex and significant ways.

Self/other/media/identity

Figure 3.1 suggested that there is a dynamic interplay between self, other, literacy and identity. The data arising from these two studies indicate that this configuration was also prevalent in these young children's experiences. Chil-dren shaped their own media-related literacy practices in ways which allowed them to express or explore identities, but others were also powerful actors in this process. In particular, older siblings often influenced the kinds of new media communicative practices in which children engaged and thus helped to shape their young sisters' or brothers' identities as competent users of a range of technology. Furthermore, the data indicate how the children formed their own identities, or their identities were strongly influenced by the practices of others and these identities in turn impacted on the range of communicative practices in which they engaged. This explains, to some extent, the gendered patterns in media use, but also points to the way in which particular narratives and texts became important to individual children. The 'self-in-practice' develops 'figured worlds' (Holland *et al.*, 2001) of media-related literacy practices which reflect not only the wider socio-cultural context but also the intense and ever-changing dynamic between the individual child and other family members. What weaves its way throughout the data is a clear sense that the children were active agents in these processes of meaning-making, a useful counter to those who emphasise children's consumptive practices at the expense of their cultural production.

Conclusion

For all of the 62 children whose home communicative practices were the focus of these two studies, popular cultural and media texts were fundamental elements of their lifeworlds. The texts and artefacts rooted in popular discourses were pivotal to the development of a range of skills, knowledge and understanding which facilitated the encoding and decoding of a variety of multimodal texts and were an essential ingredient in the potent mix of play, ritual and performance of identities. Although the primary focus for many studies of children's early literacy development in the home has been printed texts (Cairney, 2003), we are beginning to develop an awareness of the limitations of this narrow interpretation of contemporary communicative practices. However, studies such as the ones reported in this chapter have barely touched the surface of this rich and complex field of study. What is needed are further extensive and detailed analyses of children's multimodal text-making and text-responses in the home and a critical review of the place of popular culture and media within these 'figured worlds' (Holland *et al.*, 2001). With such data, educators can begin to develop a pedagogy which is based on an informed account of children's 'funds of knowledge' (Moll *et al.*, 1992) and can build on the extensive expertise that children already have as media consumers and users of new technologies as they enter nurseries and kindergartens. Such a task is not a simple one for, as Dyson (2002) reminds us:

> Adopting an inclusive approach to the communicative arts, let alone to cultural art forms, involves more, however, than teacher agency. It involves a major ideological rethinking on the part of schools, educational

agencies and society as a whole about schooling, literacy, and the nature of chidhood itself . . .

(Dyson, 2002: 191)

This challenge cannot be ignored if early childhood education is to offer curricula and pedagogical practices which are relevant to the needs of children who navigate social and cultural worlds rooted in the economic, the technological and the globalised meta-narratives of late modernity.

Notes

1 Appadurai (1996) developed a framework for exploring disjunctures between economy, culture and politics in a globalised economy in which he identified 'five dimensions of global cultural flows that can be termed (a) ethnoscapes, (b) mediascapes, (c) technoscapes, (d) financescapes, and (e) ideoscapes' (1996: 33). Mediascapes refer to the global distribution of electronic media and images of the world created by media. These combine to create narratives in which commodities and ideology are combined in complex ways and Appadurai argues that these mediascapes offer scripts for imagined lives. Certainly within the studies reported in this chapter, the mediacsapes encountered by children permeated their fantasy lives in innumerable ways.
2 In this context, 'televisual texts' refer to texts which children access on screen, either still or moving image texts.
3 Winnie the Pooh is a character featured in a series of books by A. A. Milne. These stories have been adapted for screen by Disney and a wide range of spin-off merchandise is now available.

References

Alexander, K. J., Miller, P. J., Hengst, J. A. (2001) Young children's attachments to stories, *Social Development*, 10, 3: 374–398.

Appadurai, A. J. (1996) *Modernity at Large: Cultural Dimensions of Globalization*. Minneapolis: University of Minnesota Press.

Athey, C. (1990) *Extending Thought in Young Children: A Parent–Teacher Partnership*. London: Paul Chapman.

Barrs, M. (1988) Maps of play. In M. Meek and C. Mills (eds) *Language and Literacy in the Primary School*. London: Falmer Press.

Baudrillard, J. (1983) *Simulations*, trans. P. Foss, P. Patton and P. Beitchman. New York: Semiotext.

Bauman, Z. (2002) *Society Under Siege*, Cambridge: Polity Press.

Bearne, E. (2003) Playing with possibilities: Children's multi-dimensional texts. In E. Bearne, H. Dombey and T. Grainger (eds) *Classroom Interactions in Literacy*. Buckingham: Open University Press.

Bell, C. (1992) *Ritual Theory, Ritual Practice*. New York and Oxford: Oxford University Press.

Bourdieu, P. (1977) *Outline of a Theory of Practice*. Cambridge: Cambridge University Press.

Bowlby, J. (1969) *Attachment and Loss. Volume 1; Attachment*. New York: Basic Books.

Brandt, D. (2001) *Literacy in American Lives*. Cambridge: Cambridge University Press.

Brooker, L. (2002) *Starting School: Young Children Learning Cultures*. Buckingham: Open University Press.

Butler, J. (1999) *Gender Trouble*. London: Routledge.

Cairney, T. (2003) Literacy within family life. In N. Hall, J. Larson and J. Marsh (eds) *Handbook of Early Childhood Literacy*. London, New Dehli, Thousand Oaks, CA: Sage.

Cochran-Smith, M. (1984) *The Making of a Reader*. Norwood, NJ: Ablex.

Cohen, S. (1987) *Folk Devils and Moral Panics: The Creation of the Mods and Rockers* (2nd edn). Oxford: Blackwell.

Connolly, P. (1998) *Racism, Gender Identities and Young Children: Social Relations in a Multi-Ethnic, Inner-City Primary School*. London: Routledge.

Dyson, A. H. (1997) *Writing Superheroes: Contemporary Childhood, Popular Culture, and Classroom Literacy*. New York: Teachers College Press.

Dyson, A. H. (2002) *Brothers and Sisters Learn to Write: Popular Literacies in Childhood and School Cultures*. New York: Teachers College Press.

Fleming, D. (1996) *Powerplay: Toys as Popular Culture*. Manchester: Manchester University Press.

Giddens, A. (1991) *Modernity and Self-identity: Self and Society in the Late Modern Age*. Cambridge: Polity Press.

Gregory, E. and Williams, A. (2001) *City Literacies: Learning to Read across Generations and Cultures*. London: Routledge.

Gutierrez, K., Baquedano-Lopez, P. and Turner, M. G. (1997) Putting language back into language arts; When the radical middle meets the third space, *Language Arts*, 74: 368–378.

Hannon, P. (1995) *Literacy, Home and School: Research and Practice in Teaching Literacy with Parents*. London: Falmer Press.

Hicks, D. (2002) *Reading Lives: Working-Class Children and Literacy Learning*. New York: Teachers College Press.

Holland, D., Lachicotte, W., Skinner, D. and Cain, C. (2001) *Identity and Agency in Cultural Worlds*. Harvard: Harvard University Press.

Hughes-Freeland, F. and Cain, M. M. (1998) Introduction. In F. Hughes-Freeland and M. M. Cain (eds) *Recasting Ritual: Performance, Media, Identity*. London: Routledge.

Huizinga, J. (1976) Nature and significance of play as a cultural phenomenon. In R. Schechner and M. Schuman (eds) *Ritual, Play and Performance: Readings in the Social Sciences/Theatre*. New York: The Seabury Press, pp. 46–66.

Humphery, K. (1998) *Shelf Life: Supermarkets and the Changing Cultures of Consumption*. Cambridge: Cambridge University Press.

Jenkins, R. (1996) *Social Identity*. London: Routledge.

Kenway, J. and Bullen, E. (2001) *Consuming Children: Education–Entertainment–Advertising*. Buckingham: Open University Press.

Kress, G. (2003) *Literacy in the New Media Age*. London: Routledge.

Lambirth, A. (2003) 'They get enough of that at home': Understanding aversion to popular culture, *Reading*, 37 (1): 9–13.

Lave, J. and Wenger, E. (1991) *Situated Learning: Legitimate Peripheral Participation*. Cambridge: Cambridge University Press.

Levin, D. E. and Rosenquest, B. (2001) The increasing role of electronic toys in the lives of infants and toddlers: Should we be concerned? *Contemporary Issues in Early Childhood*, 2: 242–247.

Livingstone, S. and Bovill, M. (1999) *Young People, New Media: Report of the Research Project: Children, Young People and the Changing Media Environment*. London: London School of Economics and Political Science.

Mahiri, J. and Godley, A. (1998) Rewriting identity: Social meanings of literacy and 'revisions' of self, *Reading Research Quarterly*, 33 (4): 416–433.

Makin, L., Hayden, J., Holland, A., Arthur, L., Beecher, B., Jones Diaz, C. and McNaught, M. (1999) *Mapping Literacy Practices in Early Childhood Services*. Sydney: NSW Department of Education and Training and NSW Department of Community Services.

Marsh, J. (2003a) Early childhood literacy and popular culture. In N. Hall, J. Larson and J. Marsh (eds) *Handbook of Early Childhood Literacy*. London, New Dehli, Thousand Oaks, CA: Sage.

Marsh, J. (2003b) One-way traffic? Connections between literacy practices at home and in the nursery, *British Educational Research Journal*, 29 (3): 369–382.

Marsh, J. (2004) The techno-literacy practices of young children, *Journal of Early Childhood Research*, 2 (1): 51–66.

Marsh, J. (in press) Digikids: Young children, popular culture and media. In N. Yelland (ed.) *Contemporary Issues in Early Childhood*. Buckingham: Open University Press.

Marsh, J. and Thompson, P. (2001) Parental involvement in literacy development: Using media texts, *Journal of Research in Reading*, 24 (3): 266–278.

Marx, K. (1990 [1867]) *Capital: A Critique of Political Economy, Volume 1*. Harmondsworth: Penguin, in association with New Left Review.

McCarthey, S. (2002) *Students' Identities and Literacy Learning*. Newark, Delaware: IRA.

Miller, D., Jackson, P., Thrift, N., Holbrook, B. and Rowlands, M. (1998) *Shopping, Place and Identity*. London: Routledge.

Miller, P. J., Potts, R., Fung, H., Hoogstra, L. and Mintz, J. (1990) Narrative practices and the social construction of self in childhood, *American Ethnologist*, 17 (2): 292–311.

Moje, E. B. (2000) To be part of the story: The literacy practices of gangsta adolescents, *Teachers College Record*, 102 (3): 651–690.

Moll, L., Amanti, C., Neff, D. and Gonzalez, N. (1992) Funds of knowledge for teaching: Using a qualitative approach to connect homes and classrooms, *Theory into Practice*, 31 (2): 132–141.

Nutbrown, C. (1999) *Threads of Thinking: Young Children Learning and the Role of Early Education* (2nd edn). London: Paul Chapman.

Pahl, K. (2002) Ephemera, mess and miscellaneous piles: Texts and practices in families, *Journal of Early Childhood Literacy*, 2 (2): 145–165.

Pellegrini, A. (1985) The relations between symbolic play and literate behaviour: A review and critique of the empirical literature, *Review of Educational Research*, 55: 102–121.

Pels, P. (1998) The spirit of matter: On fetish, rarity, fact and fancy. In P. Spyer (ed.) *Border Fetishisms: Material Objects in Unstable Places*. London: Routledge.

Roskos, K. A. and Christie, J. F. (eds) (2000) *Play and Literacy in Early Childhood*. Mahwah, NJ: Lawrence Erlbaum.

Rostas, S. (1998) From ritualization to performativity: The Concheros of Mexico. In F. Hughes-Freeland (ed.) *Ritual, Performance, Media*. London: Routledge.

Rowe, D. W. (2000) Bringing books to life: The role of book-related dramatic play in young children's literacy learning. In K. A. Roskos and J. F. Christie (eds) *Play and Literacy in Early Childhood*. Mahwah, NJ: Lawrence Erlbaum.

Spyer, P. (ed.) (1998) *Border Fetishisms: Material Objects in Unstable Places*. London: Routledge.

Strauss, A. and Corbin, J. (1990) *Basics of Qualitative Research: Grounded Theory Procedures and Techniques*. London: Sage Press.

Sutton-Smith, B. (1998) *The Ambiguity of Play*. Harvard: Havard University Press.

Tufte, T. (2000) *Living with the Rubbish Queen: Telenovelas, Culture and Modernity in Brazil*. Luton: University of Luton Press.

Winnicott, D. (1965) *The Family and Individual Development*. London, Tavistock Publications.

Chapter 4

Verónica

An asset model of becoming literate

Muriel Robinson and Bernardo Turnbull

On a visit to Mexico City, Verónica's British godparents bring her a copy of Michael Foreman's book, *Dinosaurs and All That Rubbish*. The book provokes a strong negative reaction from Verónica when it is 'read' to her (translated by her mother into Spanish). This is despite the fact that, at the age of three years and six months, Verónica has an abiding and informed interest in all things to do with dinosaurs and a passion for stories. Why is this book so unpopular? On discussion with Verónica, we learn that it is because the story represents humans and dinosaurs as co-existing at the same point in history.

Early in her enthusiasm, around a year before this incident, Verónica had asked when she could go to see the dinosaurs and been heartbroken to discover they were extinct. After her disappointment at learning that dinosaurs are extinct, she is not prepared to tolerate a book which ignores the historical evidence for the sake of a good story. Over the period of the visit we return to the book a few times and gradually Verónica agrees to listen to the whole story; on several occasions she is observed looking at the book by herself as if trying to reconcile the book with her prior knowledge.

The incident described above is just one of a series of our encounters with the child in question which raised questions about the ways in which young children draw upon their experiences as they seek to understand the world they encounter and, more particularly, the texts of that world. Much of the existing literature which explores young children's literacy development and their related use of other media either sets out to demonstrate a deficit model, whereby the non-traditional, non-print media are seen as damaging the child's chances of becoming literate, or to compare the differences between the use of different media (Robinson and Mackey, 2003). However, there are clear indicators available in research that a more productive way of understanding children's media use might be to start from what Tyner (1998: 7) has called an asset model: 'An asset model for media teaching assumes that mass media and popular culture content can work as a benefit to literacy instead of as a social deficit.'

Tyner does not develop her argument – that we may increase our understanding by exploring what assets a person brings to bear on a literacy event – but this chapter will seek to use a case study of one child, Verónica, to test what might be meant by an asset model and what this might mean for those responsible for helping young children to become literate in today's world. The case study offers a starting point for an investigation of the role of popular culture in the literacy development of young children and the ways in which the situated practices a child encounters may act to help the child develop a set of competences on which to draw – an asset model.

An asset model would start by identifying the skills, competences and understandings that anyone needs to be able to make sense of print and media texts and by mapping the experiences which enable and support learning. This, as we suggest above, is in sharp contrast to the prevailing orthodoxy in much literature about media use in particular, which starts with a deficit model, assuming, for example, that TV viewing may be damaging or deleterious. Mackey (2002) has begun to outline a set of categories of literate experiences which might contribute to the development of such an asset model and in this chapter we will test these categories of asset as a way of describing Verónica's experiences and competences.

Different media – competing or co-existing?

A key factor in much research is competition. Different media are compared and contrasted; for example, the amount of time spent in using different media is measured and compared. This view of media use starts from an assumption of clear boundaries between the different interpretive situations, which does not seem to bear much relationship to the world of a modern child. One of us has argued elsewhere (Robinson and Mackey, 2003) that for young children the range of media experiences they encounter is a seamless continuum from the familiar characters on their baby wipes and plasters to the traditional books some may have in their bedrooms. The different texts leak into each other to create what has been described as a porous relationship:

> It would seem that the children know that stories do not merely *lean* on other stories; stories are so *porous* to each other that they can be combined, stitched, woven together, and fused into more all-encompassing imbrications and palimpsests.
>
> (Sipe, 2000: 85)

Such porosity is evident in the behaviour of the children studied by Dyson (1997) and others and has been a feature of Verónica's response to texts. The concept of literacy has, of course, been hotly debated for many years and there is an increasing criticism of the tendency to extend the term into media other than print. In this chapter, rather than attempting to enter into this debate, we will follow Barton (1994) by referring to that range of activities which involves a child in learning how to make sense of a wide range of texts in their environment as communicative practices and events. The case study here emphasises the ways in which one child draws on a range of textual and intertextual contexts which are not neatly categorised by the medium in which they are encountered and used.

A note about methodology

This chapter is largely concerned with exploring the communicative practices of one child through personal participant observation by the authors (the child's godmother and father) of the communicative events in which she participates. Much of this observation has been informally recorded in email or conversation but the chapter also draws on a more formal questionnaire completed by the father and an interview with Verónica conducted by her father when she was five and a half years old. The chapter covers the period from birth to Verónica's sixth birthday in November 2003, but the observations continue. This is not, of course, what would be seen by many as firm evidence of the kind that could be provided by a large-scale, triangulated study. The adults involved are intimately connected to the child subject and many of the observations draw on the deep knowledge thus acquired. However, as Mitchell (1984) has argued, case studies should not be seen as offering typical examples but rather as offering 'telling' cases, that is, cases in which the particular circumstances around the case make 'previously obscure theoretical relationships suddenly apparent . . . ; they are the means whereby general theory may be developed' (Mitchell, 1984: 239). It is in this spirit that we offer this pen portrait. There is a tradition of early literacy researchers using case studies of familiar children as a starting point for developing theoretical principles that can be more widely transferred, as can be seen in the work of Bissex (1980) and Crago and Crago (1976). The thickness of the description (Geertz, 1973) is increased by the two very different kinds of account that can be provided by the two authors. One of us has seen Verónica more or less daily for her whole life and brings to bear on these encounters a background as a psychotherapist turned social scientist and professional researcher. The other has had less frequent encounters but has brought to these a professional interest in literacy development and media education as well as the slightly more detached eye of a visitor to the family home.

We would want to stress from the start that Verónica is not an exceptional child, just one that we have been able to study relatively closely over time.

Verónica reveals herself to be a fairly conventional five-year-old in her interview comments in particular. Buckingham has warned us of the dangers of the 'wise child' model of media theory:

> The traditional view of children as passive and vulnerable has increasingly been challenged by the more recent view of them as 'media wise' and innately competent. Whilst my sympathies are evidently with the latter perspective, I have also argued that it can lead to a kind of sentimentality and an unwarranted optimism.
>
> (Buckingham, 2000: 192–193)

It would be as naïve to assume that children are all sophisticated self-taught interpreters of texts as to assume that they do not know how to make sense of anything until we teach them; it would be as foolish to build too much on a child's casual utterances as to assume a blank slate in the mind of the child who enters school. The interview with her, and her father's commentary on this, tell us as much about the limits of her willingness to tell it like it is as about her current understandings and interests:

> I must say a word about interviewing conditions. She was interested but bouncy and jumpy. . . . I tried my best not to put words into her mouth, but for some time I was sure she was not telling me all she was remembering. You can read me doubting her and breaking most of the interviewing rules to push her to 'remember better' and the like. I say this because we know that sometimes she repeats lines and describes details from films and books she has not seen in ages. Evidently this is not my field and maybe it is the selectivity of her memory and not a deliberate agenda I am getting from her.
>
> (Benny, commentary on transcript of interview)

Verónica in context

First, let us introduce Verónica in more detail and put her in context, through two snapshots from her life so far.

November 1997

Verónica, just one day old, is already at home in her parents' flat in a university residence in the South of England and has already heard her parents speaking Mexican Spanish to each other and English at the hospital and to visitors when her prospective godmother visits for the first time. She will spend the next eight months of her life in this flat, surrounded by visitors of a range of nationalities and hearing a mixture of Spanish and English. She will see her father reading and working on a laptop as he completes his thesis; she will see some television, both in the flat and when she visits friends, including at her English godparents' home; she will see a variety of other literacy practices including her mother reading and writing, cards and letters arriving and being read, and a range of language uses related to the chaplaincy. Her first visit to Sunday evening mass is at seven days old and she will be there most weeks after that. This will expose her to formal English and to other languages (including Spanish, French, Italian and Latin) being read and sung. After mass she will spend the time being held and entertained by almost every member of the community at some point and will be chatted to in several languages and in a variety of English accents.

Much of this environment is what might be viewed by any literacy expert as ideal. There is adult engagement with formal literacy and what Bourdieu (1984) would surely recognise as high culture. It would be easy from this description to assume that the significant events in Verónica's life on which she will draw in developing her communicative competences are these encounters with high culture. What part does popular culture play here in offering other significant experiences to add to her asset bank? As she develops, the influences of a wide range of popular texts become very clear, as the rest of this chapter will argue. But let's start by looking at what a more up-to-date snapshot would show:

April 2003

Verónica, now five and a half, is by now fully fluent in Spanish and using the grammar well. She has been at kindergarten for two years and has had half a year in formal schooling. She can write anything she wants to, albeit with misspellings and skipped letters, also 'flipped' or mirrored letters, as in 'b' instead of 'd' and vice versa, and her handwriting is already legible. She enjoys being read to and reading to her parents. She reads small books (even to her three-year-old brother) and prefers large print. She can also read short stories now, but gets tired soon. She demonstrates most concentration when using her hands and can draw, colour and paint for hours on end.

She can use the television and video recorder and is comfortable using the computer with some help. She could use these independently before she could read. She has a repertoire of well-known videos, many of them viewed repeatedly, as well as a collection of books. At the right time she can watch an entire film, but it is easy to distract her, while with books it is harder to interrupt a reading.

Among her current enthusiasms are the many and varied products of Disney and similar companies, which she possesses or covets in just about every form imaginable, from toys and clothes through to films and books – most of the forms of text arrayed around the outer perimeter of Figure 1 are to be found in her bedroom. She is also markedly enthusiastic about animals of many kinds. Pandas are favourites but she shows interest in many others. Some of her readings have provided her with interesting facts on animals and she occasionally asks trivia questions to her parents. Some other times, animals become 'characters' and behave like people, for example, when she draws a circle of female pandas wearing leotards and tutus.

Verónica is becoming competent, confident and enthusiastic in a wide range of communicative practices and events. She has considerable assets to draw on as she does so which, as we argue below, include not just the traditional high culture texts of children's literature but experiences across media. To begin to construct a thicker description of the ways in which Verónica has developed this set of assets, we shall start by using Mackey's categories to discuss a number of vignettes from our observations of Verónica's behaviour in different contexts, before considering an extended episode of Sipe's (2000) porosity of texts around a theme of dinosaurs.

Text on paper

Mackey (2002) locates in this category not just books, which would automatically escape being seen as contributing to a deficit, but a wide range of paper-based texts, including comics, graphic novels and manuals. We would redefine this for young children as including not only picture books, but also stickers and activity books, food packaging, advertisements both in newspapers and magazines and on billboards and posters, toy-related text on packaging and toys which include text such as alphabet games.

Verónica from her earliest days has been an avid enthusiast of books and printed material. Photos of her at nine months show her exploring with interest a colour supplement from a daily paper, enjoying the experience of turning pages. At the age of two she was happy to sit and 'read' for herself and was pointing to parts of the page as she did so, though with no clear one-to-one correspondence. As with many young children, Verónica frequently demonstrated reading-like behaviour, chanting the familiar words by heart as she turned the page or improvising stories inspired by the pictures.

Figure 4.1 Verónica exploring a newspaper colour supplement

She has long shown a clear interest in writing too, and even at the age of two would sit with drawing materials and draw/write for long stretches of time (45 minutes on one occasion captured on video in January 2000). The products were a mix of very early developmental writing and drawings which have a momentum (Barrs, 1988; Pahl and Marsh, 2003) – she would tell herself the story as she drew and try to draw the movement too.

All of this is very much the stuff of traditional early literacy studies and Verónica is in many ways a textbook example of developing interest in and exploration of print. However, whereas many such studies have assumed a model of childhood untainted by the wider world and isolated from other cultural experiences, here we want to emphasise that this early literate behaviour is inextricably interwoven with Verónica's other experiences in a wide range of textual contexts. As we shall demonstrate below with regard to her interest in dinosaurs, she uses all available textual sources to increase her awareness, and is as likely to use environmental print to help when the family is shopping or to demand a new purchase as she is to engage with a story-book. Her father reports:

> She tries to read signs and things on the street, but then we realise that such signs (like shop logos and things) are very often in another language, express made-up words and almost always come in weird fonts. But she often asks what something means when we are out there.

More significantly, although according to her father books are a major influence, she tends to operate not so much *within* as *across* media and within themes, a notion we will explore more fully below:

> Her enthusiasms are still very much in books and stories. She may scream out for a film but may also lose interest too soon. If there is a recurring theme it is princesses and, sorry to say, much in the Disney line. The links to books and films are evident, but I have no clue about how she chooses to pursue one theme over the other. I must say that school has a lot to do with it. For example, some time ago, still in the old school, she began asking me to put rabbits in her Noah's Ark stories on the way to school in the morning. That summer, her end-of-year presentation was all the different Cri-Cri[1] songs with rabbits in them. She was a baker rabbit herself. Last Halloween she played a bat girl (not Pfeiffer's though) and took a liking to the cuddly bat I gave her and to which she had given no attention before. Films and merchandise around them are definite influences but it is hard to tell which was first. I myself do not really know from among her interests and enthusiasms which ones were created by toys chosen by the adults in her life rather than directly by Verónica.

Now, at the age of five, Verónica is starting to spend significant amounts of time outside the home and the influences of a wider community are as much a part of the picture as the immediate family.[2] Books and other printed texts are significant in her developing asset model, but so are other media, as we shall now consider.

Audio-visual text

For Mackey (2002), this category includes television, film, video and DVD. An important point which she makes is that whereas a generation ago the production of such texts was nearly always outside the experience of young people, today many youngsters encounter at least simple home video from a very early age, and this is certainly the case for Verónica. At a simpler level, we need to include here such things as musical greetings cards and Advent calendars.

Figure 4.2 Verónica engaging with television

Just before she returned to Mexico City in July 1999, Verónica and her parents visited her godparents during the World Cup and we all watched one of the Mexico games. She displayed a clear interest in the screen (Figure 4.2). At the age of five, Verónica engages very actively with video and television, and has done so since she was a toddler. She has a repertoire of favourites which she asks for repeatedly and she will sit and watch these for long periods of time. The video and television set had to be placed within a playpen when she was younger to prevent her gaining access and pulling the television over onto her and she regularly attempted to scale this barrier to get her own way with regard to choice and frequency of viewing.

Her favourites change more rapidly now and she is reluctant to identify the earlier films as favourites although at the time they were viewed repeatedly, as this extract from the interview with her shows:

43	B	*Muy bien . . . Ahora dime ¿qué películas recuerdas de cuando eras chiquita?*	B	Very good . . . now tell me, which films do you remember from when you were little?
44	V	*Ninguna . . . ¡Bichos!*	V	None . . . *A Bug's Life*!
45	B	*Bichos . . . ¿te acuerdas de Bichos?*	B	*A Bug's Life*, you remember *A Bug's Life*?
46	V	*Bichos!*	V	*A Bug's Life*!

47	B	*Muy bien. Y ¿qué te acuerdas de* Bichos?	B	Very good. And what do you remember about *A Bug's Life*?
48	V	*Que tiene a Hopper, a Flick, a Ata, a Dot la chiquita.*	V	That there was Hopper, Flick, Ata and Dot, the little one
49	B	*Uhu. Muy bien*	B	Uh huh. Very good.
50	V	*Y . . . ya no me acuerdo más.*	V	I can't remember any more right now.

It is possible to differentiate between current and past persistently viewed films and favourites which infiltrated play, as this discussion around the interview reveals:

Muriel: It is interesting that now the favourites seem to last less long? And interesting too that she didn't mention *Teletubbies* or *Babe*, both of which we suffered repeat viewings of on our visits.

Benny: I think that favourites is a different category from 'persistents'. For example, these past few days they have watched *The Neverending Story I and II* every other day (they are off school now) but there is *absolutely no reference to it either in play or talk*. This could last for two weeks or maybe three if they do not get a new video before then. I do not remember if persistent exhibitions of *Teletubbies* or *Babe* were accompanied by any games or references, but the present persistent films are not. *Teletubbies* have been around but mainly as the computer game you sent them but *Babe* has been entirely absent, I would say, since then.

A Bug's Life was a text which did provoke a great deal of play and where the characters from the film, possessed in a variety of forms, spent much time with us each day, including on trips away from home. The story was frequently recounted and Verónica is still able to remember the characters. Favourites at the time of the interview included *Antz*, *Rapunzel* and *Treasure Planet*, and for these films Verónica is prepared to say a little more about the parts she likes:

63	B	*Y ¿qué me quieres platicar? ¿qué te gusta del* Planeta del Tesoro?	B	And what would you like to say? What do you like about *Treasure Planet*?
64	V	*Que salen bebés . . .*	V	That babies come out of it . . .
65	B	*¿Salen bebés?*	B	Babies come from it?
66	V	*Sí . . . al final . . .*	V	Yes, at the end . . .
67	B	*Ah . . . ¿qué más te gusta del* Planeta del Tesoro?	B	Ah . . . What else do you like about *Treasure Planet*?
68	V	*Que que que que. Morf, ese globito*	V	That, that, that, that Morf, that little balloon[3]

69	B	*Uhu*	B	Uh huh
70	V	*Globito rosa . . . globito . . . se come la sopa he he he he*	V	The little pink balloon, the little globe it eats the soup, (giggles)
71	B	*He y ¿qué más hace?*	B	And what else does it do?
72	V	*Globito, globito ese Morf?*	V	The little balloon, the little balloon, that Morf
73	B	*Uhu*	B	Uh huh
74	V	*Globito . . .*	V	The little balloon
75	B	*Otra cosa que te . . .*	B	Anything else you . . .
76	V	*Se lleva la bota del niño . . .*	V	It takes the boy's boot . . .
77	B	*Otra cosa que te guste del Planeta del Tesoro*	B	Another thing you like about *Treasure Planet*
78	V	*Este . . . que una ballena que vuela le echa una cosa horrorosa a la cámara del doctor*	V	That . . . that a whale which flies throws a dreadful thing at the doctor's camera
79	B	*A la ¿qué, a la cámara?*	B	At what, at the camera?
80	V	*Sí a la cámara*	V	Yes, at the camera
81	B	*Ah muy bien*	B	Ah, very good
82	V	*Y a la foto que no saca ninguna ballena*	V	And at the photo so that he can't take any whales

Here Verónica's responses include empathy and emotive responses and she is able to select salient features ('And at the photo so he can't take any whales', turn 82) as well as recalling events. This text affords opportunities to develop these key strategies just as much as her current favourite print-based text, an anthology of classic fairy tales and stories from history.

Verónica has also had opportunities to understand how audio-visual texts are produced. Not only has she seen herself and her family on home video tapes and watched as the cameras were used, but also for a while was able to see her uncle's then girlfriend on television acting in a TV soap. The current generation of children is increasingly likely to draw on knowledge of production as well as reception when learning how to interpret audio-visual texts. Even where the texts are from outside any canon of high culture, the assets gained are both considerable and transferable.

Audio

As Mackey (2002) reminds us, audio resources are traditionally classed into two categories: music and spoken word. Increasingly, young children encounter audio texts not just from radios or music recording (whether vinyl, cassette or CD) but as part of other artefacts such as baby toys – Verónica's collection included a toy telephone which 'talked' to her as well as a toy CD player, various toys which made noises and Christmas ornaments which played carols. The musical ornaments fascinated her and were repeatedly played. She was able to recognise and match the carol which was played by these and by her Advent calendar.

When Verónica was about three years old, she was given a CD of *Peter and the Wolf*. She asked for it a few times, but not very often and not for very long, but then, starting a few weeks after the first playing of the CD, she asked to be told the story every morning in the car on the way to school for at least three months. This would suggest there is no obvious correlation between the number of expositions to a text (in any medium) and its impact on Verónica's other activities.

From her experiences of audio and televisual texts, Verónica has already developed the ability to interpret background music accurately. In the car one night, going to see her grandmother, Verónica, then aged three, spontaneously announced that she didn't always like the music in *Dinosaur* – some of it was '*muy feo*' (very bad or ugly) and that the bad music indicated when bad things happened in the film. This unsolicited comment recalls similar findings in research carried out by one of us with eight- and nine-year-olds (Robinson, 1997).

Electronic, online and wireless texts

Mackey (2002) divides these texts into separate categories. She distinguishes between electronic images (digital video games, whether accessed through a computer or through specialised equipment (PlayStations, GameBoys) or arcades), electronic text (including CD-ROM information texts), online text (the many and varied uses of the internet, from official websites to chatrooms) and wireless text (mobile phones and the like). For the young adults working with Mackey in her research, there were clear distinctions between these; for Verónica, the distinctions are less clear or the texts less a part of her experience, and so here we group these categories under one heading.

Electronic and online texts are among the fastest developing at present, and recent work has drawn our attention to the very real differences between school versions of electronic text and those used in the real world. Mitchell and Reid-Walsh chart the ways in which children 'on the cyber-frontier' (2002: 141) are not just accessing but also creating websites in a way they are unlikely to do at school, at least in the UK. Lankshear (2003) has reported how students have moved beyond email, using it only to communicate with their tutors (who are just getting to grips with it), and for personal use rely more on Microsoft Network Messenger. For Verónica, however, the distinction between the CD-ROM and online texts is less clear than their shared characteristics – for her, they are both accessed via the computer.

At an early age, Verónica and her mother used to play with a CD-ROM called *Dangerous Creatures*, in which she could see pictures, read facts, and play mini video clips. With regard to the internet, her main interest so far has been specific pages with games, such as the Princess page and the Barbie site.

She has played *Teletubbies* games on their web page as well as on a CD-ROM. Recently, she has played most regularly and enthusiastically with the games on the Barbie page: dressing her like a paper doll, finding animals in a landscape, and so on. Verónica also likes drawing programmes, in particular *Paint*. As her reading and writing ability has increased, so she has shown an increased ability to manipulate sites for herself and to write simple texts, sometimes asking her father to enlarge the font. At an early stage she would use this large type to write simple signs, but now will send simple letters or chat online to her aunt in Spain using MSN Messenger.

The connections with other texts are clear here and in playing the games related to her videos, books and toys, Verónica has to use the knowledge gained in those contexts. She will also draw on added experiences from her computer experiences when she returns to the books or videos, just as adults are learning that websites related to favourite television programmes can add to the viewing experience in a dialectical relationship. What is also clear, though, is that for all these computer-accessed texts, the distinctions which we draw as adults are not those which are meaningful for Verónica. The porosity of texts also applies within this set of Mackey's categories as well as between these and other texts.

One of Mackey's categories has so far proved of little interest to Verónica. In the UK and in certain other countries (notably Scandinavia) many young people today use SMS texts to communicate via mobile phones. Even very young children are able to tell their parents or older siblings when a text message has been received, long before they can read the message, and play mobile phones are increasingly on offer as toys even for the very youngest. Research is showing how such technology changes the cultural mores of those using it, so that for mobile phone users, being late is less of a social solecism than forgetting your phone (and thus being unable to regroup and meet up with those you have missed) (Rheingold, 2002). This is one area where new technologies are having markedly different impacts in different countries (for example in the USA, where local telephone calls are free, and young people typically have their own conventional phone, cell phones have taken less of a hold than in Europe). Mobile phones are very common in Mexico, but Verónica's parents do not have one yet. As in the UK, youngsters sometimes carry a mobile but do not pay for the cards and only carry them about to be able to receive calls. Verónica's uncle, a frequent visitor, has a mobile but as yet she has paid little observable attention to this form of communication.

Toys and artefacts

A category not included by Mackey (2002), but very relevant for the study of young children's symbolic development, is that of toys. Vygotsky (1978) has shown us how the use of objects is a part of children's symbolic development and Meek (1982) has charted how this relates to a developing understanding of narrative and books. The vignette from Christmas 2000, when Verónica was just over two years old, gives some idea of the complexity of play and the way it relates to the specific context:

Christmas 2000

Her play includes an amount of fantasy play with small animals and dolls. She is particularly interested in the preparations for Christmas but repeatedly disrupts the nacimiento (crib scene) which her mother has begun to prepare. This at first consists only of the figures placed at child height on Verónica's own play table and she repeatedly knocks the figures over and pushes them off with some violence. Only once the nacimiento is fully decorated with background and lights added does she begin to engage with it as a source of pleasure to be respected, despite the earlier entreaties of her parents and godparents. She repeatedly returns to her English Advent calendar to listen to the carol that plays when the calendar, a pop-up crib scene, is opened. She can recognise this carol and identifies that the same carol plays on a musical Christmas ornament she has been bought by her grandmother. She can sing the same tune accurately and clearly has an interest and pleasure in music.

On Christmas Eve, around midnight, at the end of a family celebration meal, Verónica and her small cousin are asked to take the figure of the baby Jesus around to everyone to see before it is placed in the crib. As she realises the way this fits with the familiar story she has just heard her uncle read from the Bible, she rushes around the room excitedly shouting out, 'Ya nacio!' which can perhaps best be translated as 'He's born at last!'

What matters here to Verónica is not the medium but the message (to invert McLuhan, 1964) that it is Christmas, a time which as a two-year-old she was for the first time able to enjoy with understanding and which at the same time had the power to surprise her. The ornaments, the Advent calendar and the story were new to her that year and were returned to repeatedly as the Christmas season unfolded. The figures for the crib were not initially seen as part of this new pattern but as parental intrusion on her play space, but, once the full decoration was added, Verónica was able to make connections to the other elements of the experience (including the traditional Christmas tree in the same room) and adjusted her behaviour towards the figures. The story which had been read to her from a variety of books and which was represented in the Advent calendar formed a connecting thread, as did the theme of celebration (extra visitors, presents, special meals, staying up late) and she drew on every experience from any available medium to make sense of this aspect of her world. Toys, books, TV, music and personal experience all added to her asset bank about Christmas, which will be drawn upon as necessary in future.

Enrichment or distraction? Dinosaurs and all that rubbish

At the beginning of this chapter, we argued that the wide range of media experiences which young children have can offer a source for future situations and that previous arguments which privilege certain texts and label others as deleterious are flawed. We have shown how for one child the wide range of experiences she has had are all used as a way of understanding and re-interpreting the world. In particular, we have explored the encounters that Verónica has had with printed materials, with televisual and audio texts, with electronic and online texts and with toys and artefacts, and argued that the breadth of experience across media which Verónica has had has helped her learn how to make sense of new texts and new situations.

Nowhere was this blend of media more apparent than in Verónica's intense interest in dinosaurs, which lasted from the age of about two and a half for about eighteen months and which still lingers, as will be seen below, although she now repudiates this publicly.

181	B	*Y este . . . y ¿en la escuela ya no juegas a los dinosaurios?*	B	And, er, . . . in school you don't play at dinosaurs now?
182	V	*Nooo*	V	No-oo
183	B	*¿No?*	B	No?
184	V	*No me gustan . . . ya no me gustan*	V	I don't like them . . . I don't like them now

Her father commented on this exchange as follows:

> I would say that when she said 'I don't like them anymore' she was playing a role she adopted for the interview. I did not want to overinterpret her words but it is not consistent with behaviour. I would not even say 'less interested'; it is only that her interest is shared with other things. She still tells me dinosaur facts and does play dinosaurs with Miguel. Don't take it as a fact but, if she does not show further interest in dinosaurs in public, social repression may have to do with it because in her second year of kindergarten she complained that she was alone because nobody wanted to play dinosaurs with her and everyone wanted to play either

princesses or Power Rangers (you may guess who wanted what). Yes, it was gradual, not sudden at all and it is not as low as she claims.

In support of his view is the fact that Verónica's denial of interest comes after a longer exchange where she has demonstrated enthusiasm for the film *Dinosaur* and good recall of its characters and events. These contradictions demonstrate the complexity for children trying to be accepted by their peer groups and learning as they do so the differences between home practices and those of a wider society.

Our final series of encounters with Verónica tracks the different stages of her dinosaur enthusiasm and identifies the different media which contributed to her knowledge.

> The interest starts on a shopping expedition when Verónica, then about two and a half, as a reward for being good in the bookshop, is allowed to choose a book for herself. For no apparent reason, she chooses two small and not apparently very attractive remaindered books about dinosaurs. From this starting point her interest develops and she watches (in Spanish) the BBC series *Walking with Dinosaurs* with enthusiasm.

At this point, the texts (book and video) are both largely informational rather than narrative, although the BBC series blurs the distinction between documentary and drama as well as the time line – there are people in the series, which is filmed as though it is taking place now. For Verónica, the style of the documentary served as a source of confusion in this regard, and as already noted, an early disappointment came when Verónica had to be told that dinosaurs are extinct. It may be that in this respect television is slightly confusing for younger viewers: one of us has shown elsewhere (Robinson, 1997) that for eight- and nine-year-olds the one area of modality uncertainty with regard to televisual and printed narrative came with regard to *Grange Hill*, a fictional series set in a school. However, the amount of accurate information Verónica drew from the series easily outweighed this one rapidly corrected misunderstanding and it cannot in itself be seen as interfering with her future ability to make sense of other texts. As we reported at the beginning of the chapter, the co-existence of humans and dinosaurs in the Foreman book had easily as much potential for misinformation, although Verónica was able to use her own knowledge to challenge the book.

Over the subsequent two years, Verónica continued to demonstrate an intense enthusiasm for dinosaurs, which drew on dinosaur books ranging all the way from children's encyclopedias to stories in which the dinosaurs were used as metaphors, but her enthusiasm went well beyond printed texts.

In the summer of 2000, driving through Mexico City, the family pass a large billboard for the Disney film *Dinosaur* which has on it a picture of Bayleen the Brachiosaurus, a character in the film. Verónica is able to ask whether the billboard is advertising a film and when she learns that it is, she asks to go to see the film. Her parents discuss with her the length of time she would need to be still and quiet in a cinema and the possibility that she might find the film upsetting or scary. It is agreed that they will take her but that she can ask to leave at any time and that will be okay. The cinema visit happens and Verónica watches throughout with interest, emerging with an even stronger enthusiasm for dinosaurs focused in particular on the products related to the film.

Although her recognition of a brachiosaurus in the billboard did not respond to other advertisements but to the book she asked to have read to her several times a day, her awareness that this might be advertising a film was drawn from a wider set of experiences. Books, advertising and an embryonic awareness of cinema all came together to enable her to request a trip to see *Dinosaur*. Her prior enthusiasm for repeated readings of the Disney version of *The Jungle Book* (even before she owned the video) has much in common with later requests to view the *Dinosaur* video repeatedly. Watching the film, though her attention was held for the whole film, Verónica would sit very attentively for the slower scenes; when there was action on screen, she echoed this, charging about the room as the dinosaurs fled from peril. The film acted as a prompt for her play and in that play it was easy to discern her use of action to understand the narrative (Vygotsky, 1978).

Toys were an important part of Verónica's set of assets, and as she played there were clear signs of her use of the film narrative. This was not only the case with respect to toys marketed by Disney (such as the egg that hatches if you hold it and keep it warm, complete with baby dinosaur inside which has to be fed to stop it crying). Verónica was also able to make connections between the story of the film and her other toy dinosaurs:

When Verónica is about three and a half, her godparents give her an inflatable Tyrannosaurus Rex almost as tall as Verónica, a good 90 cms. What is notable is the kind of play which this toy provokes. At times he is treated like a doll – put to bed, has his teeth cleaned and so on. At other times, however, he becomes a substitute for Aladar and Chix, Verónica's toy zebra, has to stand in for the lemur whom Aladar befriends in the film, with Chix placed on Dino's head to emulate the scenes from the film, with Verónica retelling the relevant parts of the film as she acts out the scenes with the two toys.

Just as we have shown in the description of Verónica's eclectic use of a range of sources as she experienced Christmas, again we can see the wide variety of media she used to explore and recreate the world of dinosaurs. Books, films and toys all served to feed her exploration, and her play and storytelling drew on all the elements of her asset bank of dinosaur knowledge, as her father reports:

> I don't know if I told you about a Cri-Cri song titled 'Caminito de la escuela'. It features animals on their way to school, each of them doing something (the mouse wears spectacles, the peacock carries a notebook, the dog has an eraser in his mouth . . .). Well, I used to sing that when driving Verónica to kindergarten but later, when she got used to it, she asked me to replace the animals with dinosaurs. The exciting part (for me) was that, as I started plugging dinosaur names into the song by phonetic criteria (the ones that rhymed or had the right number of syllables) she complained and made me choose them by their relative roles: so, for example, I had to replace the lion with a Tyrannosaurus Rex (a predator), the giraffe with a Brachiosaurus (the tallest of all) and the mouse with a Gallinimus (a small dinosaur).
>
> (email from Benny, September 2003)

This series of glimpses into Verónica's life has shown how truly porous the different texts are in feeding her enthusiasm for dinosaurs. Her asset bank of experiences has in it a wide variety of texts to be drawn on in an equally wide range of communicative practices and events. What might in deficit models be rated as either irrelevant or damaging (the Disney film, the computer games) add to her overall awareness and understanding in a way which cannot be separated from the lessons she has learned from the traditionally respectable medium of print.

Mackey's categories – how useful are they?

One of the purposes of using the categories identified by Mackey (2002) has been to assess their usefulness in defining the territory. It is worth pausing for a moment to consider their effectiveness for use with a wider age group than that which she worked with to begin the task of exploration. Overall we would suggest that the set of categories is a good starting point for future work. We have combined certain categories and added one and it is probable that any future use of this model would need to make similar adjustments to allow for a best fit to the actual experiences of particular groups or individuals. Further work with larger groups of younger children would allow for a refinement and possibly extension to Mackey's original, which could make it even more helpful in identifying the potential asset value of childhood encounters within and across a range of texts.

It would be very easy to dismiss Verónica's situation as atypical; clearly Verónica's parents take an active interest in her and engage with her in a wide range of activities, and are aware of the wider consequences of their socialisation strategies. However, studies such as Marsh's (2004) observations of children learning about PlayStation from older siblings and fathers have shown how, for other families, the texts and the explicit articulation of what is going on may change but the engagement and scaffolding can be equally important. Nor are Verónica's parents privileging printed texts over other media, even where their personal views lead them to wish to do so:

> I do not know where Verónica's reading eagerness really comes from, but I can say we have not said: 'Get off the television and go read a book'. When we say no to a video it is usually because it is the third one in a row, or when showtime is 10 p.m. So, we have not marked one means as good and another one as bad although deep in my heart I'd rather see her reading than watching.
>
> (email from Benny, September 2003)

Why a connection? Why this text?

While it is relatively easy to see why certain texts have become significant to Verónica (peer influence and commercial astuteness, for example, render Barbie a desirable text despite her mother's reluctance to allow her to engage with this), it is much harder to see why others are so significant. Her current enthusiasm for pandas follows on from the dinosaurs, but before dinosaurs she was enthused by hippos, apparently as a result of one of her earliest picture books.

What could be referred to as thematic obsession intrigues us and is hard to track to any particular origin. On occasion these enthusiasms, common among young children, are not encouraged by parents but actively discouraged, but parental attitude seems to have little impact on the nature or duration of the interest. We have not tried to time these formally, but it is clear that such obsessions do not die but rather fade. Verónica's Dinosaur Age lasted much longer than most of her other episodes of thematic overfocusing, but was just as unpredictable.

So what can we learn from Verónica?

In this chapter we have sought to demonstrate how for one young child a wide range of communicative practices and events has formed the basis for a set of assets which is supporting her development. The cultural capital of the texts she has used ranges from very high to very low, yet all the texts have added to her understanding and experience and have been truly porous as she has moved between them with little need to recognise media boundaries.

There has not been space within this chapter to do more than pay cursory attention to the ways in which Verónica is influenced by and influences her social context. It is, however, a significant factor in the development of any child's range of assets. Verónica, throughout her interactions with others and with texts, is an active participant in negotiating meaning. In this sense, all human interactions can be seen as on-going negotiations of meaning. One of us has researched the situation of street children in Mexico City and the kinds of interventions most likely to have a positive outcome (Turnbull, 1998). The project workers were struggling to impose on the street children their meanings of such terms as 'aid', 'well-being', and 'childhood'. This research argued that our failure at 'helping' them starts with a haggled rather than negotiated meaning of 'help'; they defend their meaning as we try to impose ours because we think it is the only one around. In the case of a child being socialised within a family and the mainstream community, we are bombing her with meanings in the hope she will share with us enough of them to build a family culture, or metacontext (Hinds, Chaves and Cypess, 1992), that will enable us to live together. Although parents may be able to determine many shared meanings, children such as Verónica are constantly negotiating others. The meaning of 'bedtime' and 'too many films for today' may be overtly negotiated; other more submerged negotiations will become even more critical at adolescence because the meaning of meanings she will be negotiating is the meaning about herself: her identity. Every text which Verónica draws on as she builds up her set of assets also contributes to this deeper negotiated identity. Such negotiation is what moves the notion of an asset model from that of a tick list of experiences to a complex and significant matrix of experiences which cannot be completely controlled or determined by the significant adults in a child's life. To ignore this is to trivialise the development of meaning making.

Verónica, as we have already made clear, is not presented as a typical child. In many ways she has a privileged degree of access to traditionally high-status texts. However, we do not believe that this privileged access has been more influential overall than her experience of a much wider spectrum, nor do we have any reason on the basis of this exploration to support a view of certain texts as deleterious to the developing child. We would argue that Verónica indeed offers a telling case for future development and research. There is a need for more investigations of this kind, which explore the whole range of texts drawn on by young children and which then moves on to explore the pedagogical implications of a school curriculum which may privilege certain categories of text over others and may thus disenfranchise children whose set of assets draws more on the texts found less frequently in classrooms, at least in the UK.

Notes

1 Cri-Cri was a popular Mexican writer and performer of children's songs; Verónica has several of his CDs.
2 It is worth noting that for Verónica the immediate family includes not just parents and brother but both grandmothers and a range of aunts, uncles and cousins who are all regular visitors.
3 Morf, the character who plays the space age version of Long John Silver's parrot in *Treasure Planet*, changes shape at will, hence the balloon.

References

Barrs, M. (1988) Maps of play, in M. Meek and C. Mills (1988) *Language and Literacy in the Primary School*, Barcombe, Sussex: Falmer Press.

Barton, D. (1994) *Literacy: An Introduction to the Ecology of Written Language*, Oxford: Blackwell.

Bissex, G. (1980) *GYNS AT WRK: A Child Learns to Write and Read*, Cambridge, MA: Harvard University Press.

Bourdieu, P. (1984) *Distinction*, London: Routledge.

Buckingham, D. (2000) *After the Death of Childhood: Growing Up in the Age of Electronic Media*, Cambridge: Polity Press.

Crago, H. and Crago, M. (1976) The untrained eye? A preschool child explores Felix Hoffman's Rapunzel, *Children's Literature in Education*, 22: 135–151.

Dyson, A. H. (1997) *Writing Superheroes: Contemporary Childhood, Popular Culture, and Classroom Literacy*, New York: Teachers College Press.

Geertz, C. (1973) *The Interpretation of Cultures*, New York: Basic Books.

Hinds, P. S., Chaves, D. E. and Cypess, S. M. (1992) Context as a source of meaning and understanding, in J. Morse (ed.) *Qualitative Health Research*, London, Sage.

Lankshear, C. (2003) 'The home–school digital divide in curriculum and pedagogy, Lecture given in ESRC Research Seminar Series, 'Children's Literacy and Popular Culture', University of Sheffield, UK, July 2003. Online at: http://www.shef.ac.uk/literacy/ESRC/pdf/papers/lankshear.pdf.

Mackey, M. (2002) An asset model of new literacies: a conceptual and strategic approach to change, in R. Hammett and B. Barrell (eds) *Digital Expressions: Media Literacy and English Language Arts*, Calgary, Canada: Detselig Enterprises.

Marsh, J. (2004) The techno-literacy practices of young children, *Journal of Early Childhood Research*, 2 (1): 51–66.

McLuhan, M. (1964) *Understanding the Media: The Extensions of Man*, New York: McGraw-Hill.

Meek, M. (1982) *Learning to Read*, London: The Bodley Head.

Mitchell, J. (1984) Case studies, in R. Ellen (ed.) *Ethnographic Research: A Guide to General Conduct*, London: Academic Press.

Mitchell, C. and Reid-Walsh, J. (2002) *Researching Children's Popular Culture: The Cultural Spaces of Childhood*, London: Routledge.

Pahl, K. and Marsh, J. (2003) The space of PlayStation: performing identities and shaping textual practices, unpublished paper presented at British Educational Research Association Annual Conference, Edinburgh, September 2003.

Rheingold, H. (2002) *Smart Mobs: The Next Social Revolution?* Perseus Books.

Robinson, M. (1997) *Children Reading Print and Television*, London: Falmer.

Robinson, M. and Mackey, M. (2003) Film and television, in N. Hall, J. Larson and J. Marsh (eds) *Handbook of Early Childhood Literacy*, London, New Delhi, Thousand Oaks, CA: Sage.

Sipe, Lawrence R. (2000) 'Those two gingerbread boys could be brothers': How children use intertextual connections during storybook readalouds, *Children's Literature in Education*, 31 (2): 73–90.

Turnbull, B. (1998) Street children and their helpers; a social interface analysis, unpublished DPhil thesis, Brighton, University of Sussex.

Tyner, K. (1998) *Literacy in a Digital World: Teaching and Learning in the Age of Information*, Mahwah, NJ: Lawrence Erlbaum Associates.

Vygotsky, L. S. (1978) *Mind in Society: The Development of Higher Psychological Processes*, Cambridge, MA: Harvard University Press.

Chapter 5

Bilingual children's uses of popular culture in text-making

Charmian Kenner

Bilingual children growing up in an English-speaking country are often thought of as living in 'two worlds', one based around their home language and culture and another based around English. It is also assumed that children may experience some difficulty, or even trauma, in connecting these two worlds. In this chapter I shall challenge both assumptions. Research with children aged three to seven living in London shows first that their cultural worlds are hybridised rather than separate, and secondly that they create further hybridity through the making of texts which represent their complex cultural identities. Teachers may be unaware of children's desire to engage in this process, since schooling offers few opportunities for such text-making. The chapter aims to open a window into children's cultural worlds, so that educators can decide how best to support bilingual and bicultural development.

The examples discussed here come from two research studies concerning the literacy experiences of young children from minority ethnic communities growing up in urban Britain. The first was an action research project with three- to four-year-olds in a multilingual nursery class in South London (Kenner, 2000a). Families were asked to bring literacy materials in different languages from home into school, and parents were invited to use these materials as the basis for writing with children in the classroom. Children's responses were observed in order to discover what they understood about bilingual writing at this young age, with some of the participants being followed over three further school years. The second project focused on five- to six-year-old, by conducting case studies of children learning different writing systems: Chinese, Arabic or Spanish as well as English. The children were observed engaging in literacy activities at home, community language school and primary school (Kenner and Kress, 2003).

I shall begin by considering how the home language texts encountered by children in their bilingual communities re-contextualise traditional material in new media forms, and incorporate aspects of a globalised (mainly Anglo-American) culture. Simultaneously, children become familiar with mainstream popular culture in English via the media and peer group interaction at primary school. I shall go on to look at children's motivated engagement with this variety of textual resources, showing how they are actors in the re-making of culture. Finally, I will discuss to what extent bilingual text-making is encouraged in homes and schools.

The observations in this chapter are offered from my perspective as a researcher in the field of multilingualism, having come across data which seem to have resonance for the field of popular culture. I have provided an initial discussion of these data, in the hope that others will take the analysis forward. The multilingual aspects of popular culture provide a rich resource for further investigation.

Popular culture: a multilingual perspective

Whereas mainstream popular culture – from TV soap operas such as *Eastenders* to PlayStation games – is highly visible, children's cultural experiences in languages other than English are relatively little-known. Dyson (1996: 473) describes the enjoyment of East Asian cartoon films by Chinese American children, and Pahl (2001) shows how children weave ideas from their multi-lingual background into the construction of texts based on popular culture. In general, however, researchers have rarely considered this area. The value ascribed to English as the dominant language marginalises other linguistic communities (Bourdieu, 1991; Phillipson, 1992), with bicultural lives being either ignored or exoticised (Meinhof, 2003). The few images which make their way into the mainstream media tend to portray minority ethnic communities as trapped in a time-warp of traditionalism.

However, bilingual children's experiences are no more static and predictable than those of their monolingual peers. As shown by researchers on mainstream popular culture (Suss *et al.*, 2001), there is continual variation and change in a complex, shifting world involving global communication. Media forms such as video, cable and satellite TV and the internet are used by linguistic communities to produce new texts or to re-contextualise older ones.

This variety became obvious in the South London nursery project, as soon as we began asking bilingual families to bring into school any texts in different languages which their children enjoyed. Three-year-old Billy's favourite text in Thai turned out to be a karaoke video, in which popular love songs were acted out against the background of fishing boats on a river, with the lyrics rippling across the screen. Meera, also aged three, adored videos of 'Bollywood' films which she helped to choose from South Asian video stores in her local neighbourhood, and watched together with her family. Moham-med was learning to read in Qur'anic Arabic at the age of four, and his resources included an audiotape of children singing the alphabet as well as a more traditional alphabet chart.

By the time the second research project took place several years later, technology and its global uses had moved on considerably. Most of the families of the five- to six-year-old participants had cable and satellite TV in their own languages as well as in English. This gave access to a huge range of programmes showing varied aspects of life in their regions of ethnic origin. Using the remote control to switch between TV stations in the Arab world, for example, the viewer might see an imam responding to phone-in questions about a religious festival, a panel discussion on views about the political situation in the Middle East, or young women dancing to Arab pop music. Advances in computer technology had also been harnessed to increase the distribution of existing texts in different languages; one family owned the Qur'an on CD-ROM, and could hear the text being read out in Arabic or obtain a written English version at the click of the mouse.

Such examples show how traditional texts were available in new forms, such as the Arabic alphabet on tape or the Qur'an on computer. This re-contextualisation enabled children to make connections between past and present. A cartoon film of the classic Chinese tale *Journey to the West* signposted such links explicitly. The modern-day characters – a group of schoolchildren – took a ride into cyberspace through a computer portal to an encounter with traditionally dressed characters from the story. Three-year-old Ace, whose background was British Chinese, and her nursery classmates were gripped by this fast-moving contemporary version of the fable.

The examples also show the changing nature of cultural practices and inter-relationships depicted in the texts. Billy's Thai karaoke video used a traditional setting but the songs were given an up-to-date romantic slant in performance. Meera's Bollywood video included a motor-bike riding heroine clad in black leather, who challenged the gangster opposition. This role was far removed from the Western stereotype of the demure and passive South Asian woman. Meera also had a collection of film magazines and posters, containing interviews and photos in which the stars wore Westernised outfits of jeans, T-shirts and baseball caps and were questioned about their love lives. While such material could be seen as the colonisation of indigenous culture by Anglo-American global forces (Ritzer, 1996), the results are undeniably complex.

The dominance of Anglo culture was evident in TV programmes directly modelled on ones of Anglo origin, such as versions in other languages of the British quiz programme *Who Wants to be a Millionaire?* Other programmes were a local version of an Anglo template, such as Ming's mother's favourite programme – designated by her children as 'Chinese *Neighbours*' – where the café setting of the original Australian soap series was translated to a Hong Kong noodle bar. However, children could also see genres which had been mainly developed in non-Western countries, such as the dramatic Mexican-style soap operas watched by Brian's Colombian parents. These genres can occasionally have some effect on mainstream Anglo culture, as evidenced by recent interest in the traits of Bollywood productions and Eastern martial arts films. Again, these are complex issues which cannot be fully discussed here, but it is clear that children growing up in minority ethnic communities are being presented with multimedia texts which show considerable hybridity.

These texts offer children a multiplicity of identities, in a multilingual diasporic community (Kenner, 2004). Selina and Ming, children of Chinese origin living in London, had a window on the lives of people speaking both Cantonese and Mandarin, in Hong Kong and Taiwan. Tala enjoyed singing songs in Egyptian Arabic which she had heard on TV, as well as the songs taught to her by her mother in Palestinian Arabic. Five-year-old Recep demonstrated his strong allegiance to Turkish cultural life when pointing out, in Turkish newspapers sold in London, the singers and football teams he had watched on Turkish TV.

Many of the texts just discussed use more than one language and script and include English, arising from the multilingual realities of people's everyday lives. Meera's Bollywood film magazines were in English, a language shared among the young people from different language backgrounds living in Britain, as well as being a colonial language in India. The audiotaped soundtracks which Meera loved to dance to were usually in Hindi or Urdu, although she called them 'Gujarati' (her family language) and could understand some of the words. In many South Asian countries, children learn several different languages and in minority ethnic communities in London and elsewhere, they also experience a linguistic mix. The tape sleeves, however, were written in Roman lettering regardless of the language used, since not all children growing up in Britain would have sufficient literacy experience to read in other scripts.

Experiences of mainstream popular culture

As well as interacting with bilingual texts, children were strongly drawn to the Anglo-based cultural artefacts popular with their monolingual peers at nursery and primary school. Mainstream popular culture was already part of life in bilingual children's homes and communities. Meera's parents ran a small supermarket and Meera often brought advertising leaflets from the shop to her nursery class, incorporating them into her activities in the roleplay area. She was particularly excited about the National Lottery, which was just being set up in shops nationwide, and explained how it worked: 'You have to pick a number'. One of Mohammed's main interests was his father's car, which frequently appeared in his drawings both at home and in the nursery. He knew precisely what make and model it was (a Nissan Stanza) and wanted to write those words as part of his texts, along with the acronym 'M.O.T.' which he remembered from the roadworthiness test which he had witnessed six months earlier.

By the time Meera was seven, she was a keen football fan, supporting the North London-based team Arsenal, and her father sometimes bought her football magazines. Tala, at the age of seven, also became involved with the world of football. She and her nine-year-old brother Khalid told me excitedly that they had something to show me when I visited their house at the time of the World Cup. It turned out to be a message chalked on the pavement: 'Come on England'. For Meera and Tala, growing up in Britain, there was no apparent contradiction between supporting an English football team and enjoying Bollywood films or Arabic festivals. The famous 'cricket test' of citizenship posed by the Conservative politician Norman Tebbit ('In a cricket match between your home country and England, who would you support?') would be unlikely to pose an insuperable problem for these children. Their worlds included the option of supporting either team, or even both, just as Mohammed's cultural world ranged from the Qur'an to his dad's Nissan.

Children as actors in the making of culture

A social semiotic theory of early writing (Kress, 1997; Kenner, 2000b) highlights children's active role as producers of text. Young children use the multimodal resources available to them to create texts which represent and further their 'interest' (Kress, 1997: 11) as an individual located in a particular sociocultural context. By examining texts produced by three of the children in the research studies described above – Meera, Recep and Selina – we can explore the meanings and purposes which each child may have intended to pursue through their re-working of popular culture.

Meera: 'Football Fever'

As a seven-year-old girl of South Asian origin growing up in South London, Meera would not necessarily have been expected to be a keen supporter of a North London football team. However, football played a key part in playground culture at primary school, with children – in today's diasporic world – having a varied allegiance to teams around the country and indeed beyond. Meera seemed to have acquired her support for Arsenal from her older sister, and it was an important aspect of her peer group identity. Her knowledge of football went beyond the superficial; she vividly described details of what the referee had done wrong in a particular match, and she was following the progress of teams in the World Cup ('Argentina five–nil with Jamaica').

While boys dominated the physical space of the playground with their football games, Meera and her friend Ace carved out their own social space as girls who were knowledgeable about the topic. They did so by using a text genre beloved of children, and particularly of girls: the written list of members of an exclusive 'club'. Ace showed me a piece of paper on which was written the heading 'Football Fever Club'. Listed underneath were 'Members: Frank, Kasim, Steve' (all boys), and 'Owners: Ace and Meera'. The girls' text represented an intervention into the male-dominated world of football, making it clear that they wanted to be at the management level of the club hierarchy and putting the boys in their place as mere players – on paper, at least. This was a way of entering into negotiations about new possibilities for gender identity.

Another textual intervention made by Meera also centred on football, this time bringing together aspects of her Gujarati and English literacies, and therefore uniting her home and school worlds. Since she was very young, Meera had observed her mother doing wordsearches in Gujarati magazines. Wordsearches were also a common teaching tool in her primary school classroom. When given the opportunity at age seven to write in Gujarati at school, Meera brought a wordsearch which she and her mother had prepared at home, containing the names of different animals in Gujarati, to fit with that term's class topic. Meera's class teacher was very impressed by this and invited Meera to make a larger version, which was then displayed in the hallway for the rest of the school to see. Proud of her success, Meera announced that she wanted to make another wordsearch, this one about football because 'I support Arsenal'.

Soon afterwards, Meera arrived at school with her Arsenal wordsearch (see Figure 5.1). It was a large and complex text, consisting of a 15 × 15 grid containing nearly 225 letters. These symbols included Gujarati alphabet letters known to Meera and others which she had invented as part of her own 'Gujarati' code. Underneath the grid, Meera had written several words, each separated from the next by a comma, which turned out to be the names of footballers in the Arsenal team, transliterated from English into Meera's version of 'Gujarati'. Meera mentioned several footballers' names to search for, showing her knowledge of the team. Her writing of 'Pett' seems to have been intended to mean Petit, 'Deacs', Dixon, 'Adam', Adams, 'Patreb', Patrick Vieira, and 'Thermamp', Bergkamp, all of whom were playing for Arsenal at that time. Every one of the names can be found within the grid.

It is quite possible that this is the only recorded example of a wordsearch in Gujarati about the Arsenal football team. It is certainly most unlikely that Meera would ever have seen one. Such a text, however, flourished in her imagination and she made it into reality. What is more, she spent a considerable amount of time and effort to produce such a lovingly detailed representation of each Arsenal player in the language of her family and community. It was an important way of making visible her complex linguistic and cultural identity.

Recep: making a Turkish newspaper

London news-stands are filled with newspapers in different languages from around the world, which are read in homes around the capital. A huge variety of human experience is contained in newspapers, from politics and sport to the coverage of arts and music events, from horoscopes to the lives of pop stars and footballers. Readers of newspapers are often also viewers of

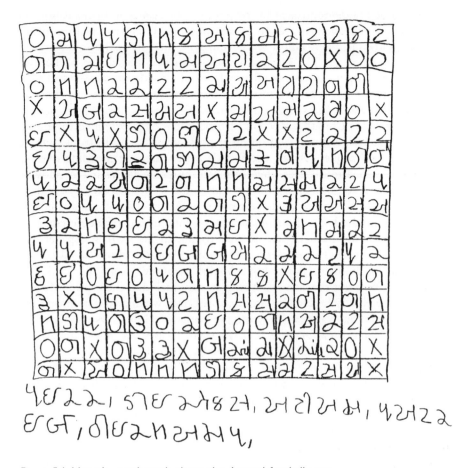

Figure 5.1 Meera's wordsearch about the Arsenal football team

multimedia such as cable and satellite TV, and through these inter-textual links they can build up a densely configured cultural world.

It might be assumed that young children have relatively little interest in newspapers, but the research project in Meera and Recep's South London school showed quite the opposite effect. One of the ways in which we created a multilingual literacy environment in the Reception class, when the children were only four- to five-years-old, was to hold a newspaper workshop once a week. Parents and relatives brought in newspapers in different languages and stayed for a while during the morning to help the children create their own texts. By choosing images and writing to cut out and paste onto large sheets of folded paper, children made their own 'newspapers' and added their own writing. This workshop was so successful in generating responses from children that it continued throughout that school year and into the next.

Recep quickly demonstrated his recognition of events and personalities in the Turkish newspaper brought in by his mother. He cut out pictures of his favourite Turkish singer, Hülya Avsar, and sang lines from the songs he had heard her perform on TV. He had a comprehensive knowledge of Turkish football teams and included a dramatic photo of a tackle on the football field in his newspaper. He spotted a picture of two famous soap stars and chose to include that as well.

We were able to see that Recep's cultural knowledge extended to politics and history as well as music and sport. In pride of place on his front page he put a photo of Jacques Chirac, the French prime minister, bending over to kiss the hand of Tansu Çiller, then prime minister of Turkey. This showed that Recep watched news programmes and would have been aware of Çiller's importance. He also recognised the picture of Atatürk, the founder of Turkey, which appeared alongside the banner headline in one of the newspapers. Recep cut out the headline and picture to put in his own newspaper and asked his aunt to help him write the name 'Atatürk' above it. We then discovered that he had a book about Atatürk at home.

When cutting out the images, Recep usually included the caption or part of the associated article. He also produced his own writing to accompany the chosen image. For example, he wrote the name of Hülya Avsar underneath the singer's picture (see Figure 5.2). In several cases, he made use of the writing from the newspaper as a basis for his own. He carefully wrote out several lines from the text about the soap opera, placing these above and below the photo of the stars, including 'Restauran' – he probably recognised the word 'Restaurant'. Similarly, he used part of a word from the caption for the football photo to make his own caption.

Recep's reaction to the newspaper workshop was all the more striking because he was not always keen to write in his primary school classroom, although he took part enthusiastically in other class activities. But from the moment when I asked him 'Does anyone in your family write in Turkish?' and he replied 'My grandmother', we seemed to find the key to his home literacy world. When I asked if he could show me how his grandmother wrote, he covered a poster-sized sheet of paper with symbols and continued to write for the rest of that classroom session. He did not even want to go outside when playtime came because, he said, 'I haven't finished'.

For Recep, Turkish newspapers represented the cultural life of his community, and were therefore strongly linked with his family. He emphasised this link by including his family in his own newspaper. Alongside the picture of the Turkish prime minister on his front page, he drew a picture of his sister and wrote her name, Gülten. He placed his mother's name, Halide, next to his writing of 'Atatürk'.

Recep's newspaper thus made use of an existing genre, and he showed his awareness of its main characteristics by including the banner headline, news, and items about sport and TV. The making of his own version enabled him

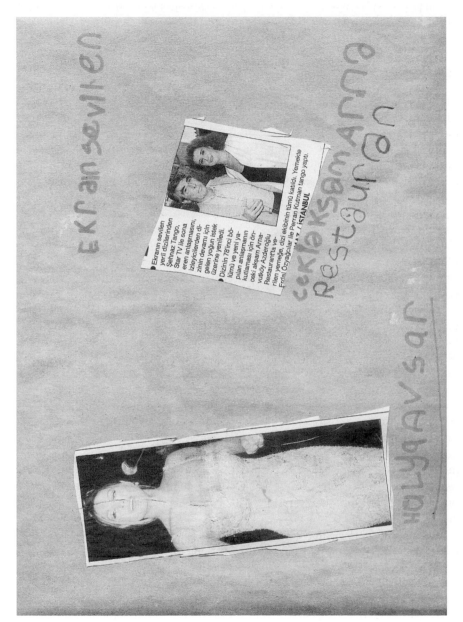

Figure 5.2 Recep's Turkish newspaper: his favourite singer and TV soap opera

to choose people and events which were particularly significant to him, and also to represent his most intimate world, that of his family. Until Recep had the opportunity to work with texts from Turkish popular culture, the extent of his knowledge from everyday life remained invisible to his primary school teachers, along with his desire to write.

Selina: Chinese 'Spice Girls'

I observed Selina learning to write at her Chinese Saturday school, producing each Chinese character with precision and practising it over and over again to ensure that the stroke pattern had been memorised. As with the other young children in her class, her attention to visual detail was striking. Selina took pride in her knowledge of Chinese writing and enjoyed showing her primary school classmates how to create the complex patterns required for different characters.

At home, Selina and her ten-year-old sister Susannah spent an hour every evening in a Chinese class around the kitchen table, taught by their mother. Susannah also helped Selina to practise the characters for next Saturday's Chinese lesson, so that she would be well prepared. There was thus a considerable emphasis on the importance of learning to read and write in Chinese within the family.

At the same time, Selina was given plenty of opportunity at home to develop her interests in Western pop culture. Her mother and sister read pop magazines with her and each chose their favourite songs. Selina was a particular fan of the band 'S Club 7' and made her own 'magazines' about them on folded sheets of paper with her sister's help (see Figure 5.3 for her characterisation of Rachel, one of the members of the group). This interest was shared with her friends at primary school.

Selina's cultural life thus included a variety of experiences constructed in English and in Chinese. She looked keenly for evidence of such connections in the wider world, and was excited when she found that her local department store was selling bracelets with Chinese motifs engraved on them. She also noticed that a member of the Spice Girls pop group had a Chinese tattoo on her arm, and was greatly interested to discover that this represented the group's slogan of 'Girl Power'.

Selina asked her mother how to write the characters for 'Girl Power' in Chinese, and also the character for 'love'. She made a text which centred around a heart icon with the English word 'Love' above it, surrounded by the Chinese characters for 'love' and 'Girl Power'. She also included the word 'Powergirl' written in English. The heart motif was a favourite one in the English-based texts Selina produced at home, along with flowers and butterflies. So this new text brought together images and words which carried particular emotional meanings for Selina: the strength of 'Girl Power', combined with the gentleness of 'Love' symbolised by the heart icon, with

Figure 5.3 From Selina's 'S Club 7' magazine

both words appearing in English and in Chinese. On the same sheet of paper she drew another heart flanked by two butterflies with the message 'I like people kind to me and if they be my firend [*sic*]'. The whole text could be interpreted as an appeal from Selina for acceptance as a child growing up with Chinese writing and English popular culture as integral parts of her cultural experience.

English and Chinese were further united in texts made by Selina about her family. She combined a drawing of her mother with the Chinese character for 'love' written above her head and the words 'I love my mother' in English below. Her sister Susannah was similarly represented in the centre of another page with the Chinese characters for 'Girl Power' above her and 'I love my sister' below (see Figure 5.4). These texts demonstrate the centrality of her mother and sister in Selina's life, and show that her emotional life was lived in more than one language. In the case of her sister, Selina brought

Figure 5.4 Selina's drawing of her sister with 'I love my sister' (changed from 'I like my sister') below, and 'Girl Power' in Chinese above

their shared experience of Western pop culture to bear on the text. Instead of Rachel from S Club 7, it was Susannah who starred as a strong female participant in a world where 'Girl Power' could also be expressed in Chinese.

Bilingual text-making in homes and in schools

Texts such as Meera's Gujarati football wordsearch, Recep's Turkish newspaper and Selina's representation of 'Girl Power' in Chinese were produced in settings where multilingual hybridity was accepted or encouraged. One such setting was children's homes. The other was their primary school classrooms, where a space for multilingual literacy had been opened up either by asking families to bring materials from home to school or by asking bilingual children to conduct peer teaching sessions with their classmates.

Bilingual homes as hybrid semiotic environments

At home, children and parents were observed to switch frequently between their different spoken languages, and literacy activities took place in both writing systems. While parents wished their children to grow up able to speak and write in their own first language, they recognised that English was the dominant representational system and that children's lives were inevitably bilingual and biliterate. In terms of cultural experience, they made efforts to maintain links with their community heritage but also accepted children's engagement with popular culture in both languages. This relatively open attitude towards popular culture links with the views of parents in other studies (Marsh and Thompson, 2001; Weinberger, 1996; Xu, 1999).

A great variety of cultural artefacts and practices were thus found to be present in children's homes. In Selina's living-room, for example, Chinese New Year banners were on the walls alongside her parents' wedding photos and posters of Selina's favourite pop groups. Selina's mother taught her how to make models of swans using the traditional Eastern craft of origami, but instead of folding coloured sheets of paper, they used hundreds of Lottery tickets. Each ticket was folded in such a way as to show the black and red design, and then tucked into the one below to gradually build up the model. The materials to hand resulted in a hybrid cultural product.

Hybridity was represented and constructed through a range of semiotic systems. As well as those of spoken and written communication, home decoration and handicrafts already described, the screen media discussed earlier offered a great variety of experience. In addition, one father highlighted the semiotic system of posture, explaining that his children preferred 'Arabic sitting' (on cushions on the floor rather than on chairs or the sofa) when watching TV. The type of food served at home was another example of hybridity; in one case, chicken nuggets and chips were placed on the table alongside Chinese dishes as part of the family's shared evening meal. It is also important to recognise that parents might sanction hybridity to different extents in different semiotic systems; in Selina's home, wall decoration was quite varied as mentioned above, while food was kept largely Chinese. However, cultural and linguistic mixing was generally possible in children's home contexts.

Multilingual expression in schools

In contrast to homes, primary schools tended to offer an environment which was far more monolingual and monocultural. Although some schools displayed posters in different languages and offered premises for community language teaching, and all celebrated festivals from children's different cultural backgrounds, almost all teaching and learning was conducted in English with English materials. England is constructed as a monolingual society despite its growing multilingual population, and schools operate as institutions within this wider frame. The resulting constraints tend to restrict children's possibilities for multilingual expression.

However, the two research projects discussed in this chapter demonstrate that nursery and primary school classrooms have the potential to open out to other linguistic and cultural experiences. If this can be done, bilingual children have the chance to build on and expand their linguistic knowledge, and also to explore their cultural identities. Multilingual popular culture is a key resource in this process.

A growing body of work on popular culture and children's literacy in English, represented in this volume and in studies such as Weinberger (1996), indicates the importance of popular cultural texts to children as part of family and community life. Studies show the ways in which children seek opportunities to refer to such texts at school. If given the opportunity to do so, they create their own texts in the classroom which they can use to re-interpret ideas and negotiate relationships with peers (Dyson, 1997; Marsh, 2000).

Bilingual children are no exception in their fondness for popular culture. The difference is that as well as knowing 'what counts' in terms of Anglo-American culture, they also have many other experiences in their home and community lives which are not visible in mainstream magazines, TV programmes or computer games. Bilingual children are also no exception in their agency and creativity. Given the opportunity, they will share their hybrid cultural knowledge with their peers at mainstream school and produce texts which take this hybridity even further. In order for this to happen, schools need to develop 'hybrid pedagogical spaces' as argued for by Hicks (2001), which in this case are also open to multilingualism.

The children described here seem to know how to make the most of their varied cultural experiences. Other researchers have also found that children accept the multiple identities arising from different aspects of their lives with relative ease, as described by Mills (2001) in her study of third-generation British children of Pakistani origin, or in Ghuman's work (1994) with second-generation British Asian adolescents who appeared to be seeking a 'hyphenated identity'. The children in my own research studies, who are growing up in London and learning more than one language and literacy at the same time, have moved beyond existing in 'two worlds' or even in 'multiple worlds', often seeming to experience their worlds as 'simultaneous' (Kenner, 2004). However, the school system has yet to catch up.

As Marsh (2003) has pointed out, if popular culture is not allowed to inform literacy teaching in early years settings and primary schools, children will be condemned to a twentieth-century rather than a twenty-first-century curriculum. In the case of bilingual children, if they are not allowed to engage with multilingual popular culture in their classrooms, they will have to live out not only a twentieth-century identity, but also a monolingual one.

References

Bourdieu, P. (1991) *Language and Symbolic Power*, Polity Press.

Dyson, A. H. (1996) Cultural constellations and childhood identities: on Greek gods, cartoon heroes, and the social lives of schoolchildren, *Harvard Educational Review*, 66 (3): 471–495.

Dyson, A. H. (1997) *Writing Superheroes: Contemporary Childhood, Popular Culture, and Classroom Literacy*, New York: Teachers College Press.

Ghuman, P. (1994) *Coping with Two Cultures: British Asian and Indo-Canadian Adolescents*, Clevedon: Multilingual Matters.

Hicks, D. (2001) Literacies and masculinities in the life of a young working-class boy, *Language Arts*, 78 (3): 217–226.

Kenner, C. (2000a) *Home Pages: Literacy Links for Bilingual Children*, Staffordshire: Trentham Books.

Kenner, C. (2000b) Symbols make text: a social semiotic analysis of writing in a multilingual nursery, *Written Language and Literacy*, 3 (2): 235–266.

Kenner, C. (2004) Living in simultaneous worlds: difference and integration in bilingual script-learning, *International Journal of Bilingual Education and Bilingualism*, 7 (1): 43–61.

Kenner, C. and Kress, G. (2003) The multisemiotic resources of biliterate children, *Journal of Early Childhood Literacy*, 3 (2): 179–202.

Kress, G. (1997) *Before Writing: Rethinking the Paths to Literacy*, London: Routledge.

Marsh, J. (2000) Teletubby tales: popular culture in the early years language and literacy curriculum, *Contemporary Issues in Early Childhood*, 1 (2): 119–136.

Marsh, J. (2003) Early childhood literacy and popular culture, in N. Hall, J. Larson and J. Marsh (eds) *Handbook of Early Childhood Literacy*, London: Sage.

Marsh, J. and Thompson, P. (2001) Parental involvement in literacy development: using media texts, *Journal of Research in Reading*, 24 (3): 266–278.

Meinhof, U. (2003) Paper given at British Association of Applied Linguistics Annual Meeting, 4–6 September, Leeds, UK.

Mills, J. (2001) Being bilingual: perspectives of third generation Asian children on language, culture and identity, *International Journal of Bilingual Education and Bilingualism*, 4 (6): 383–402.

Pahl, K. (2001) Texts as artefacts crossing sites: map making at home and school, *Reading, Literacy and Language*, 35 (3): 120–125.

Phillipson, R. (1992) *Linguistic Imperialism*, Oxford: Oxford University Press.

Ritzer, G. (1996) *The McDonaldization of Society* (Revised Edition), Thousand Oaks, California: Pine Forge Press/Sage.

Suss, D., Suoninen, A., Garitaonandia, C., Juaristi, P., Koikkalainen, R. and Oleaga, J. A. (2001) Media childhood in three European countries, in I. Hutchby and J. Moran-Ellis (eds) *Children, Technology and Culture: The Impacts of Technologies in Children's Everyday Lives*, London: RoutledgeFalmer.

Weinberger, J. (1996) *Literacy Goes to School: the Parents' Role in Young Children's Literacy Learning*, London: Paul Chapman.

Xu, S. H. (1999) Young Chinese ESL children's home literacy experiences, *Reading Horizons*, 40 (1): 47–64.

Part II

Children and Technologies

Chapter 6

Watching *Teletubbies*

Television and its very young audience

Susan Roberts and Susan Howard

There is a limited body of research on the television viewing responses of children in the first two years of their lives. Although we know that such very young children do watch television and do develop enthusiasms for particular programmes or characters (Anderson and Levin, 1976; Lemish, 1987), studies of very young viewers have focused almost exclusively on the development of their visual attention to television (Anderson and Levin, 1976; Anderson *et al.*, 1981; Anderson and Lorch, 1983; Ruff *et al.*, 1998; Ungerer *et al.*, 1998). That is, studies have focused on how soon and how often very young children start viewing with concentration. They have not attempted to provide direct insight into the diverse range of responses to television of viewers under the age of two.

This gap in the research literature may partly reflect the methodological difficulties involved in working with children who are in the early stages of language acquisition, but, we suspect, it probably has more to do with a general reluctance to see such young children as 'viewers' and a lingering concern, perhaps, about the power of television to corrupt the innocence of childhood. Being a member of an audience, however, is no longer an exceptional event; rather, it is constitutive of everyday life even for the very young.

It may be useful to expand a little here on what we know about the under-two-year-old viewer. Most studies have measured the amount of time these very young children may view television. Such studies have typically found that children spend between two to four hours a day in the same room as an operating television set (Singer and Singer 2001: 15). However, it should be noted that there is a clear distinction between the amount of television children are 'exposed' to and the amount they actually watch. In a rare longitudinal study which asked mothers to track their children's attention to television during the first two and a half years of their lives, Ungerer *et al.* (1998) found that very young children tended to ignore general programmes. If the set were switched to pre-school programming, very young children tended to watch more attentively. About a third of mothers rated their children's viewing as relatively sustained (as opposed to sporadic responding) for about half their viewing time from approximately 12 months of age, if the child were viewing preschool programming. By the time children were 30 months, their interest in and attention to television were rated significantly more intense than at 12 months of age.

This chapter outlines a study which set out to investigate directly the responses of children under the age of two to a television programme. Methodologically, the kinds of research tools that are normally available to researchers are of little value when working with children as young as this. We could not, for example, interview or survey such young respondents, but we could observe them and it was on this that we based part of our research design.

Background to the study

Fortuitously, at the time we were planning this research, the British programme *Teletubbies* was launched on Australian television. The programme and its four principal characters quickly became very popular with its target audience in Australia, as it had elsewhere (see Howard and Roberts, 1999/2000). We recognised that there were distinct methodological advantages for our research in using a text that was specifically designed to appeal to this age group rather than using programmes that were designed for older children.

The episode of *Teletubbies* that we randomly chose was typical of most episodes in terms of setting, structure and content. Each episode is set in either the Tubbydome (the bunker in which the Teletubbies live) or in the rolling landscape outside (the episode we used was set exclusively outside). Each episode also has some highly distinctive and recurring items. Probably the most unusual of these is an image of the sun which has the face of a real, chortling baby who appears to be responding with delight to the action going on below. Other regularly appearing items are a whirlygig which sends out sparkling lights and a periscope that comes up out of the ground. The former tends to signify the beginning and end of the episode's action and the latter is accompanied by a voice-over which asks questions or makes comments on the action. Each episode typically has a central live-action segment with footage of children of various ages and in different places engaged in everyday activities. This segment is shown twice at the insistence of the Teletubby characters. In the episode we chose, the live action was an adult jazz band performing a lively version of 'The Grand Old Duke of York' on a school oval while five- and six-year-old boys and girls dance and run around to the music.

Within the episode we chose, two other segments require comment. The first we have called 'Magic Drum'. Here, two of the characters, Tinky Winky and Po, find and play with a drum which has magical qualities because every time someone beats it, the sound appears to make something in the landscape change. At one point, the shape and location of clouds change, and at another, the colours of the flowers change with each drumbeat. The second segment we titled 'House'. Here, the Teletubbies gather on a little hill and the façade of a two–storey house gradually appears, feature by feature. The viewer is led to believe there is someone in the house because the sound effect of footsteps going up and down stairs precedes the turning on and off of a light behind each curtained window and the appearance of a silhouette on the curtains of the lit room. Eventually, a puppet flings back the curtains, opens a window and sings. The window then closes and the house gradually disappears. In both these segments there is a broad theme that raises issues for the young viewer about the links between sound and vision, between cue and event and between cue and reality. In other words, the puzzles here require thought about causes and their effects.

We recruited 20 children, 10 boys and 10 girls under the age of two years. Most of our participants were around 18 months; the youngest was 14 months and the oldest 24 months. All were familiar with *Teletubbies* from home viewing and two were proclaimed enthusiastic fans by their mothers. All children came from English-speaking home backgrounds. Access to the children was initially gained through local pre-school/child care centres, two were located in comfortable middle-class suburbs and the other two in predominantly working-class suburbs. Participants were invited to watch the chosen *Teletubbies* episode either in their own home, or at their pre-school or childcare centre. They could watch alone or with others, in a lap, on a couch or on the floor, and they were free to move about as they wished – in other words, we tried to recreate as normal a viewing situation as possible for each child in that context.

While the child watched the *Teletubbies* video, we used a small camcorder to video the child. With the episode of *Teletubbies* running and the camera focused on the young viewer, we were able to record each child's behaviour in front of and around the television. Each tape captures the child's facial expressions, movements, gestures, verbalisations, attention to and away from the screen and presence in front of the screen or elsewhere. What we did then was to splice the *Teletubbies* video with each of the videos of the children so that the *Teletubbies* footage and the child doing the viewing could be seen simultaneously. By carefully synchronising the start of the episode in the small-screen insert with the start of the episode the child actually watched, we were able to see quite clearly what the child was doing at any point in the video and we could see what image/action/event/sound the child may have been responding to.

The episode

Faced with this rich visual data, we then had to devise a method for analysing it. In order to do this, we first deconstructed the episode into segments. We formally deconstructed the chosen episode of the programme into its overall structure by asking – how does this episode allocate its time? Using Ellis'

(1982: 116) definition of segment as 'coherent group of sounds and images, of relatively short duration that needs to be accompanied by other similar such segments', we divided the episode into the following segments:

1   Opening segment (first appearance and introduction of *Teletubbies* characters)
2   Programme segment (first appearances of the distinctive, recurring images of whirlygig, periscope and baby sun)
3   Live action segment – jazz band performance
4   Repetition of jazz band performance
5   Teletubbies march to music
6   Magic Drum segment
7   House segment
8   Closing segment, end-credits (including final appearances of the recurring images).

The programme hangs together in a unified way partly because some distinctive images are repeated (the baby sun, the periscope) and partly because the segments are linked by common themes. In this episode, the common themes were music and sound – each segment features music, or the sound of isolated instruments, objects or the human voice.

We subdivided many of the segments into their component shots or sequences, depending on how they were structured. Some segments were edited in such a way that they invited subdivision into their separate sequences. The closing segment was one such segment because it comprised a compilation of sequences including the baby sun, whirlygig and periscope; the Magic Drum segment contained clearly self-contained sequences such as those featuring the clouds and flowers. Other segments, on the other hand, such as the jazz band performance, were constructed more smoothly and continuously using such filmic conventions as shot/reverse shot. We left these segments as whole segments.

In all, we subdivided the whole episode into 43 different sequences or segments. Consequently, some of the sequences were only a few seconds in duration, while some segments lasted several minutes. This was an inevitable outcome of deconstructing the episode as a meaningful text rather than dividing up the episode in some other, more mechanical way (see Sproull, 1973, for an analysis of time-based rather than text-based responses to a TV program.)

Interpretative criteria

We believed it was important to develop a new protocol for the analysis of the data rather than to approach it with a set of criteria drawn from research with older children. To this end we watched the tapes intensively

– together and separately – and allowed patterns in the data to emerge. These patterns involved the children's body movements, vocalisations and facial expressions.

Our final set of categories emerged after intensive viewing and vigorous debate about how to interpret particular responses. We discussed and explored our perceived biases and discrepancies, we scrutinised each other's field notes and we asked our research assistants to trial our emerging categories with some of the videotape data. At the end of this process we felt confident not only that our analytical categories constituted reasonable (albeit adult) interpretations of the children's responses to events and images in the episode, but also that we were being consistent in recognising and classifying (coding) these responses. Our final interpretative analytical categories were as follows.

The first interpretative category of 'attention level' we based on the concept of *viewing intensity* (Cupitt and Jenkinson, 1998).

A Attention level
A1 Barely watches (e.g. mostly engaged in some other activity with only occasional glances at screen).
A2 Watches a little (e.g. partially engaged in some other activity; watches some sequences from time to time).
A3 Watches half the time (e.g. distracted from time to time but watches whole sequences or for substantial periods).
A4 Watches most of the time (occasionally attention wanders elsewhere, but mostly watches the screen).
A5 Watches with great concentration (e.g. rapt – could be very active or very still; eyes on screen continuously).
A6 No response (e.g. back to the screen; engaging in activity elsewhere; sleeping).

The second category constitutes behaviour that was indicated by participants joining in with what was happening on screen. This could be physical – singing or dancing along with the characters; imitating the characters' movements clapping at the end of an action or waving hello or goodbye to characters – and it could also be verbal, involving talking to characters, answering their questions and so on.

B Parasocial response
B1 Physical (e.g. joining in with the action on the screen by singing, dancing, imitating movements; clapping at the end of something; waving goodbye).
B2 Verbal (e.g. joining in with the action on the screen by answering questions, talking to characters).

The third category reflected participants' familiarity with TV texts in general and the *Teletubbies* text in particular. Naming characters, anticipating action, spontaneously using catch phrases, linking the programme with *Teletubby* merchandise all fell into this category:

C   TV literacy response
C1 Naming characters without prompting.
C2 Understanding *Teletubbies* conventions (e.g. recognising the baby sun, the whirlygig).
C3 Using catch phrases like 'Big hug!' without prompting.
C4 Having *Teletubby* toys, reaching for them, lining them up.

The fourth category involved participants using language that they heard being used in the programme. This might involve repeating the names of objects or special phrases that the characters use (e.g. 'Big hug!'):

D   Verbal echoing
D1 Copying catch phrases.
D2 Verbal mimicry or other examples of language use.

The fifth category involves those responses that show the participants were, on the whole, actively engaged with the more complex material being presented in the episode and were actively trying to make sense of it:

E   Cognitive response
E1 Signs of puzzlement, as indicated by frowns of concentration ('What's going on here?'; 'How did that happen?').
E2 Body gestures that indicate questions ('Where did they go?', 'Where are they?').
E3 Labelling objects (e.g. drum, rabbit, hat).
E4 Showing surprise at an event (gasp!).

Responses in the sixth category of *Pleasure* were probably the easiest to identify from our rich visual data and they often occurred accompanying other responses (e.g. sharing with a companion, parasocial responses). In order to identify pleasure, we looked for the typical indicators: facial expressions, verbal expressions, and physical expressions.

F   Pleasure
F1 Facial expressions (e.g. smiling, laughing, excitement).
F2 Verbal expressions (e.g. vocalisations accompanying some other sign of pleasure).
F3 Physical expressions (e.g. leg kicking, arm waving, gross body movement that is not a response to music).

Figure 6.1 Alison touches the TV screen

The next category involved physical action focused on the TV set and screen. The participants' physical viewing space was often set up by adults (parents, child care/pre-school workers, the researchers) with a judicious distance between child and screen. This situation was frequently adjusted by the participants who moved their chairs closer to the TV set at the outset. Others ran to be nearer to or touch the set during particular sequences.

G   Action around the TV set
G1 Touching the screen (as Alison is doing in Figure 6.1).
G2 Pointing to the screen.
G3 Moving closer to the screen.

The final category involved participants' behaviour that clearly indicated they wished to share the experience with a companion. Those children watching in child care centres often had a companion sitting with them while those in family settings often watched with a parent or sibling. The following behaviours in our view constituted 'sharing'.

H   Sharing with a companion
H1 Turning to companion.
H2 Smiling at companion.
H3 Talking to companion about the action.
H4 Pointing out something to companion.
H5 Touching companion in response to action.

In order to analyse each child's patterns of response, we prepared a program proforma that divided the program into its 43 sequences and segments. We plotted each child's responses, using the analytical criteria, on separate proformas. These responses were systematically tallied, the memorable responses along with the more mundane. It was then possible to identify general patterns of response across the whole episode and across the whole cohort.

At the end of the coding process, we had two unique insights into the children's viewing behaviour. The first gave us clear profiles for each individual child, showing what sequences and segments appealed and how the child viewer responded. The other gave us a profile for the whole cohort of viewers showing patterns of response that occurred throughout the episode. While all the interpretive categories yielded interesting and useful data, we will concentrate on the four that stood out in terms of frequency of response. These are: attention, parasocial response, cognitive response and pleasure.

Attention

The conventional wisdom is that young children have very short attention spans and a limited ability to focus on any one stimulus for an extended period of time – our data here contradict this belief. There were several participants whose attention levels remained at A5 levels for most of the entire episode. From the visual data, the only way to describe these children's responses is rapt. Some were rapt and very still, gazing at the screen with a fixed, almost unblinking, intensity; others could barely contain themselves with excitement but were nevertheless totally focused on the screen.

Some individual sequences produced very high attention levels. The most interesting finding here is that sequences that featured intriguing sound effects drew significant amounts of attention. The mysterious drumbeats at the beginning of the Magic Drum segment; the light switch clicks corresponding to the lights going on and off in the House segment; and the moment when the Teletubbies (who are hiding behind a hill) all jump up and say Boo! were all sequences which attracted significantly higher than average A5 attention responses than did other sequences. In Clouds, the drumbeats are also present because they signal the change in the clouds' position; however, it is difficult to say whether it was the sound effects or the intrigue of the sound/vision puzzle that claimed the viewers' attention here. The other sequence to attract great attention was a brief close-up shot of real rabbits grazing on grass near the Tubbydome. The attraction here seemed to be recognition – many of the children responded with great excitement, pointing to the screen, chortling, turning to a companion if one were present.

The findings reported here for attention are important in so far as they challenge the myth of the poor ability of very young children to focus and concentrate on something for any length of time. Our data here show that when the program is interesting to the child, there is no problem with sustained attention (see also Ruff *et al.*, 1998). In the past, the rapt but physically still behaviour of intensely interested children may well have been misinterpreted as 'mesmerisation' – evidence of the so-called harmful deadening effects of television on young viewers' minds (see Winn, 1985). Our visual data show, however, that the rapt and still child is not comatose – the body posture, the facial expression all indicate engagement with the object of the gaze. On the other hand, the rapt but intensely excited behaviour of other children may well have been misinterpreted as 'hyperactivity' – evidence of television's so-called harmful ability to incite uncontrolled behaviour (see Winn, 1985). Again, our visual data can be interpreted differently. Rather than unfocused hyperactivity, our excited participants' gaze was firmly focused on the television screen and their facial expressions, body language and physical movements all indicated intense pleasure, anticipation and joy.

The salience of sound effects in programme content for young viewers has been known for a long time. Huston *et al.* (1981) and Huston and Wright (1983) demonstrated that funny voices and interesting or sudden sound effects in cartoons would attract the attention of three- to five-year-olds or draw them back to the screen when attention had wandered. The 10–18-month-old children in the study by Lemish (1987) were also drawn to television by musical, unusual, or noisy sounds. The sounds cue novelty, and the appeal of the novel or unusual in drawing attention is well understood. What is interesting in the present study is that not only were sound effects particularly effective in gaining our young viewers' attention, but, in the case of Magic Drum and House, they were also effective in holding attention. In other words, the children's sustained attention in these segments is due to something other than a momentary interest in the novel. We would argue that these particular sound effects are part of more complex puzzles that the viewer is being invited to solve. Thus, the children's attention here can be seen as a function of a strong need to make cognitive sense of the world.

Others working in this field have considered the link between attention and the need to make sense of television content. Lemish (1987: 40), for example, states that attention to familiar content (babies, animals, etc.) made by the children in her study is based on the fact that it makes sense to them. Further, Pingree (1986) and Anderson *et al.* (1981) both found lowered rates of attention in young viewers when programme content was rendered incomprehensible. Ruff *et al.* (1990, 1998), in studies examining individual differences in young children's sustained attention in different contexts, also found that sustained attention 'was influenced by the salience of events, suggesting the effects of motivation' (1990: 1) and varied 'with the demands of the task and [the children's] ability or interest in meeting those demands' (1998: 454).

Turning from the cognitive to the affective domain, we have described how many of our participants attended to aspects of the *Teletubbies* episode in a rapt but highly excited, intensely happy fashion. With the exception of Lemish (1987), very few studies have made any link between attention/ interest and excitement/pleasure. Indeed, traditional scientific studies (Pingree, 1986; Ruff *et al.*, 1998) ignored this aspect of attention altogether and neither measured nor observed children's affective responses while they watched videotaped 'stimulus material'. In our examination of the categories E (cognitive response) and F (pleasure) below, we examine further the links between both attention and 'making sense' and attention and 'pleasure' for the young viewers in this study.

Parasocial responses

The most important category of response here was a physical joining in with the action on the screen, most notably in the Marching and Jazz Band segments. In the first segment, the Teletubbies perform a very simple 'line dance' routine to a tune with a pronounced marching rhythm; in the second, the adult jazz band plays 'The Grand Old Duke of York' to an audience of five- to six-year-old children who dance or run around to the music. Our viewers responded in a variety of ways. Often with great visible pleasure, they bounced, danced, waved their arms and legs and/or clapped to the music in both segments. Some of them grabbed a toy to dance with, some picked up their blanket or little chair, some moved their arms and legs vigorously while staying seated, some patted or prodded their companion. What was very obvious was that this movement was not random. Even though these children were moving 'each in his or her own tempo' (Wright, 1991: 167), it was very clear that they were responding to the rhythm, the tune and the dancing action on the screen.

This highly pleasurable physical response to simple, strong rhythm is something with which we are well acquainted in three- to five-year-old children, so it should come as no surprise that we found that such sounds also produce the same delighted response among the very young. Lemish (1987) also found a similar range of responses among her young viewers, some of whom were as young as 11 months. It seems that long before we are able to coordinate our bodies to move in time with rhythm, it exerts a powerful influence over us and compels us to join in.

Two key sequences that produced parasocial responses occurred in the Opening segment and related to the introduction of the Teletubby characters. In the first, a voice-over counts as each Teletubby shoots out of a hole in the Tubbydome roof. A few minutes later the voice-over names each character by way of introduction. For both sequences, the young viewers' response was either to wave and/or say 'hello' to the characters. Some children may also have simultaneously named the characters (a television literacy response) but this was not necessary for a parasocial response. In the last sequence in the Opening segment, the word 'Teletubbies' is formed from a long balloon which is blown up until it bursts. The children's response here was either to cover their ears or say 'bang' or 'pop' at the appropriate moment. One child made blowing noises as the balloon was being blown up. In these two latter categories, the children are showing both early learning of conventional social responses (e.g. greeting behaviours) and knowledge of social events (e.g. knowing how balloons are blown up, knowing what happens when they burst).

Cognitive responses

The responses in this category clustered most evidently around the Magic Drum segment. Here, to recap, Tinky Winky and Po find a magic drum which, when beaten, makes a sound that appears to change, among other things, the location of clouds in the sky and the colour and placement of flowers in the grass. Examples of children's responses here included:

- pointing upwards or to the outside sky during the Clouds sequence, as Belinda (in Figure 6.2) is doing;

Figure 6.2 Belinda points to clouds

- saying 'clouds' (labelling);
- exhibiting shoulder shrugging in a gesture of puzzlement at the beginning of the sequence when the narrator says of the mysterious drumbeats, 'And nobody knew what it was';
- responding with what appeared to be puzzled pleasure (smiling frowns) at the connection between the drumbeat and the transformation of the image (cloud position, flower colour);
- gasping in surprise and turning to a companion (if one is available) when the drumbeat seems to change the visual image.

In the Magic Drum segment, both the voice-over and the characters exhibit surprise at the effect the drum is having; thus, the viewer is being directed to the central sound/image, cause/effect puzzle and the question, 'What's going on here?' Interestingly, there were very few observable cognitive responses during the House segment. Even though many children were clearly attending to this segment very closely, they provided very few of the physical or verbal responses that had been evident in other segments. The inference-making required of the child viewer here is quite sophisticated. Without voice-over guidance or character demonstration, the inference that someone was going up and down stairs inside the house turning the light on and off in each room had to be drawn solely from sound effects (footsteps, light switch clicks) and visuals (a light going on behind the curtains in different windows and the subsequent silhouette of a character on the curtains). In this segment, the inferential connection between a number of different clues is considerably more complex and subtle than it is in the Magic Drum segment. While the children's attention was clearly *engaged* during this segment, they gave none of the observable responses that indicated they were *understanding* the cognitive puzzle that was being presented.

The Opening and the Closing segments, both of which contain numerous small sequences, also produced a number of cognitive responses. In the Opening segment, a close-up shot of rabbits produced a number of labelling responses ('rabbits', 'bunny') and so did the first appearance of the baby sun ('baby'). When the Teletubbies run and hide behind a little hill, the voice-over asks, 'Where have all the Teletubbies gone?' and several viewers responded here with shrugs or verbal responses ('all gone'). When the balloon bursts some children responded with playful gasps, suggesting they anticipated this outcome. In the Closing segment, there is a regular feature, a 'going to bed' ritual, acted out among the Teletubbies. Most of the cognitive responses in this segment centred on this action, with children showing they understood the 'rules' of this playful ritual and adding in bits of their own 'going to bed' scripts (also a parasocial response). In this, there is a link with the way young children learn to deal with print. The participants here are engaging in what Cochran-Smith (1984: 174) calls, in a print-literacy context, life-to-text interactions: 'readers/listeners will take knowledge that they have gained from direct or secondary experiences outside of texts and use this knowledge to make sense within texts' (see also Martinez, Roser and Dooley, 2003).

We would suggest that the children's responses in this category show that they were, on the whole, actively engaged with the more complex material being presented in the episode. The Magic Drum segment shows them making inferences and predictions as they try to make sense of the sound/image, cause/effect, fantasy/reality puzzle (and our hunch is that this was happening in the conceptually more difficult House segment too). Even though the Tubbydome and its environs are somewhat futuristic, action and detail throughout the episode provide opportunities for recognition and naming of familiar objects (babies, rabbits), situations (dancing to music) and rituals (e.g. Peep Bo!, Boo!, bedtime rituals, hide and seek). In our view, these under-two-year-olds are engaging in the intellectual task of making sense of the way the world works, which, in this particular episode, involves them being quite skilfully challenged and scaffolded in the cognitive tasks of recognition, prediction, inference–making and fantasy and reality comparisons.

Pleasure

The beginning of the Magic Drum segment, where the mysterious drumbeats are heard, attracted the greatest pleasure response – a clear link, in our view, between attention/interest and excitement/pleasure. The sequence begins with the voice-over saying, 'One day in Teletubby land, there was a strange noise' and this is accompanied by a single drumbeat. As the drumbeats continue, each of the Teletubbies is shown listening, and finally the voice-over says, 'But no one knew what it was'. Po and Tinky Winky subsequently find the drum and discover its magical powers. This drumbeats sequence, in the best storytelling traditions, creates suspense, anticipation and a kind of delicious excitement about a mystery that is about to unfold. The children certainly seemed to be responding to this dramatic tension by behaving in all the ways that we had identified as pleasure – they squirmed with glee, they bounced up and down, they beat their hands on the floor, they stood closer to the set and jigged – all the while, their gaze was firmly on the television image. Even those who turned to smile at a companion here quickly turned back to the television.

The same response of excited anticipation accompanied sequences in the Opening segment – a segment that is regularly repeated each episode and is accompanied by the programme's theme music. The opening sequence where the baby sun rises to gaze down on the Teletubby landscape and that point in the segment where each Teletubby first appears by shooting through a hole in the Tubbydome roof produced in some viewers what can only be described as barely controlled ecstasy. Bodies, faces, voices all express intense excitement and a sense of 'I know what's going to come and I can hardly wait'. One 18-month-old girl (identified by her mother as a committed fan) was so excited she had great difficulty coordinating her physical excitement with her need to keep her eyes on the action and the necessity of bringing her special chair closer to the screen.

As all of the children were more or less familiar with the *Teletubbies* programme, repeated viewings would have acquainted them with the opening scenes and sounds. The action in the Opening segment is not intrinsically thrilling – even, we assume for under-two-year-olds and especially if one has seen it several times – so the stimulus for the hugely excited response can therefore probably be attributed to anticipation. What is interesting here is that not only have our young viewers recognised familiar patterns in a television text, they have also learnt that these patterns have a kind of symbolic significance – they are cues that experiences, which in the past they have found very pleasurable, are about to occur again. In this way, the opening scenes in the *Teletubbies* episodes are performing much the same function as the words 'Once upon a time' at the beginning of stories. Whereas it used to be believed that children under two were only supposed to be able to think about what they could immediately see and/or do (viz. the sensori-motor period, Piaget, 1952), we suggest that our young viewers' responses are contributing to the evidence that very young children can think rather more flexibly and usefully than this.

The pleasure in the Jazz Band segments, the Marching segment and another sequence that we have called the Game was, to different degrees, produced by a combination of music and action. Those children who danced to the Jazz Band and the Marching segments showed great pleasure while they were doing so. In the Game, the pleasure derives from something more than this simple activity. A voice comes through the periscope singing 'The Grand Old Duke of York' and the Teletubbies march up and down the hill as directed by the words of the song. With the final line, 'And when they were only half way up they were neither up nor down', the Teletubbies get quite muddled and fall in a heap on the ground giggling. Here we have the irresistible combination of simple actions linked to music plus a situation where familiar characters get themselves in a pickle while trying to do something tricky. The pattern of response in our viewers was for mild pleasure to be exhibited for the bulk of the sequence (possibly a sign of enjoyment of the music/action combination), but the greatest pleasure response occurred at the end of the sequence as a result of the Teletubbies all falling down in a giggling heap (we suggest a response to the humour of the situation).

Laughter and other responses indicating pleasure occurred when the balloon bursts and when the Teletubbies leap out from their hiding places to surprise the viewer in a variation of the age-old peep bo! game. In these sequences we find two basic elements of humour – surprise and playing a trick on others. In the Game, we find rudimentary slapstick. We would suggest that what we are seeing here is evidence of a developing sense of humour in children under the age of two. Whether these responses to humorous situations have been learnt from experience or whether they are manifestations of some other emotional response is hard to determine.

Conclusion

Children in the period of early childhood (from birth to two years of age) generally do not figure much in media-related research and yet we know that very young children do watch television and express enthusiasm for some pro-grammes more than others. Reasons why this age group has been neglected in research terms are probably twofold. First, one must consider the meth-odological difficulties of working with such very young children. Second is the pervasive and powerful ideological belief that early childhood is a period of innocence and sanctity – as Sefton-Green (1999: 1) puts it, some kind of 'walled garden' quarantined from the concerns of the adult world. The intro-duction of *Teletubbies*, the first television program deliberately designed for under-twos, certainly mobilised moral panic discourses that lent support to this latter view (see Howard and Roberts, 1999; 2000).

Undeterred by these methodological and ideological difficulties, the present study has demonstrated the efficacy of observation as a methodological tool, and we further show how one can gather, simply and reliably, very rich data about very young children's television viewing using quite simple equipment and techniques. On the basis of the data we gathered, we were able to begin the task of theorising the interactivity of our young respondents with media texts. In our analysis of the children's responses we found a pervasive match-ing of reality and television image in, for example, their recognition of familiar objects, situations and routines. In addition, the children engaged with cognitive puzzles that required them to exercise developing theories of cause and effect, prediction and inference. A strong feature of the data was the young viewers' discovery of pleasure in seeing familiar characters; in responding to music and rhythm; in recognising tricks and rudimentary slap-stick. Indeed, while other traditional studies have ignored young children's affective responses to television, this one has highlighted our participants' pleasure and excitement as they watched a particular program.

In relation to the question of attention, we have been able to show that our participants exercised powers of concentration and attention for periods of time that were previously thought unlikely for such young children. Further, we argue that our participants demonstrate that attention to televi-sion is not only affected by the cognitive meaningfulness of the material, it is also affected by the level of enjoyment or pleasure that is afforded by it. Indeed, if our analysis of the Magic Drum sequence is correct (highest scores for cognitive responses, attention and pleasure), the usefulness of the tradi-tional cognitive/affective binary is called into question. Our young partici-pants' responses show that what is intellectually intriguing can be simultaneously pleasurable and thus clear boundaries between the cognitive and affective domains are blurred. Recent research in the area of the brain and reading is challenging the whole notion of what has seemed like an impermeable membrane between cognition and emotion. Coles (2003) in reviewing some of this research, concludes that 'there is no question that research on brain activity and reading that fails to account for the fugue of cognition and emotion is severely insufficient research' (Coles, 2003: 174).

We suggest that in relation to the media, very young children are neither the romantic constructions to which Sefton-Green (1999) draws our attention, nor are they stuck with the extreme limitations of 'sensori-motor' thinking, as was once posited. We have shown our young participants using a television text both for pleasure and for making sense of their worlds and in this they are no different from older children. Indeed, we would suggest that programs like *Teletubbies* enable very young viewers to exercise and develop those skills and dispositions that make their older brothers and sisters savvy operators in a pervasive media environment (see Buckingham, 1990).

References

Anderson, D. R. and Levin, S. R. (1976) Young children's attention to Sesame Street, *Child Development*, 47: 806–811.

Anderson, D. R. and Lorch, E. P. (1983) Looking at television: action or reaction? In J. Bryant and D. R. Anderson (eds) *Children's Understanding of Television: Research on Attention and Comprehension*, pp. 1–33, New York: Academic Press.

Anderson, D. R., Lorch, E. P., Field, D. E. and Sanders, J. (1981) The effects of TV program comprehensibility on preschool children's visual attention to television, *Child Development*, 52: 151–157.

Buckingham, D. (ed.) (1990) *Watching Media Learning: Making Sense of Media Education*, London: Falmer Press.

Cochran-Smith, M. (1984) *The Making of a Reader*, Norwood, NJ: Ablex.

Coles, G. (2003) Brain activity, genetics and learning to read, in N. Hall, J. Larson and J. Marsh (eds) *Handbook of Early Childhood Literacy*, London, New Dehli, Thousand Oaks, CA: Sage.

Cupitt, M. and Jenkinson, D. (1998) *Infants and Television*, Sydney: ABA.

Ellis, J. (1982) *Visible Fictions: Cinema, Television, Video*, London, Routledge.

Howard, S. and Roberts, S. (1999/2000) Teletubbies downunder: the Australian experience, *Televizion* (Journal of Internationales Zentralinstitut für das Jungend- und Bildungsfernsehen), 12 (2): 19–25.

Huston, A. C. and Wright, J. C. (1983) Children's processing of television: the informative function of formal features, in J. Bryant and D. R. Anderson (eds) *Children's Understanding of Television: research on attention and comprehension*, pp. 35–68, New York: Academic Press.

Huston, A. C., Wright, J. C., Wartella, E., Rice, M. L., Watkins, B., Campbell, T. and Potts, R. (1981) Communicating more than content: formal features of children's television programs, *Journal of Communication*, Summer, pp. 53–66.

Lemish, D. (1987) Viewers in diapers: the early development of television viewing, in T. Lindlof (ed.) *Natural Audiences: Qualitative Research of Media Uses and Effects*, Norwood: Ablex.

Martinez, M., Roser, N. and Dooley, C. (2003) Young children's literary meaning making, in N. Hall, J. Larson and J. Marsh (eds) *Handbook of Early Childhood Literacy*, London, New Dehli, Thousand Oaks, CA: Sage.

Piaget, J. (1952) *The Origins of Intelligence in Children*, New York, International Press.

Pingree, S. (1986) Children's activity and television comprehensibility, *Communication Research*, 13: 239–256.

Ruff, H., Capozzoli, M. and Weissberg, R. (1998) Age, individuality and context as factors in sustained visual attention during the preschool years, *Developmental Psychology*, 34: 454–464.

Ruff, H., Capozzoli, M., Dubiner, K. and Parrinello, R. (1990) A measure of vigilance in infancy, *Infant Behavior and Development*, 13: 1–20.

Sefton-Green, J. (1999) (ed.) *Digital Diversions: Youth Culture in the Age of Multi Media*, London: UCL Press.

Singer, D. G. and Singer, J. L. (2001) *Handbook of Children and the Media*, Thousand Oaks, CA: Sage.

Sproull, N. (1973) Visual attention, modelling behaviours and other verbal and non verbal meta-communication of pre-kindergarten children viewing *Sesame Street*, *American Educational Research Journal*, 10: 101–114.

Ungerer, J., Cupitt, M. and Waters, B. (1998) *Infants and Television*, Sydney: Australian Broadcasting Authority.

Winn, M. (1985) *The Plug-In Drug: Television, Children and the Family*, New York: Penguin.

Wright, S. (ed.) (1991) *The Arts in Early Childhood*, Englewood Cliffs: Prentice Hall.

Chapter 7

The CD-ROM game

A toddler engaged in computer-based dramatic play

Cynthia R. Smith

James led me by the hand to a mirror where we could both see ourselves easily and smiled up at me through his reflection. 'Look Mama!' he squealed in delight, 'Click here if you want me to read you the story and click here if you want to play in the story.' His voice was robot-like in tone as he pointed in turn to the lower left side and lower right side of the mirror as he offered the choices. For James, the rectangular shape of the mirror represented the computer screen, as he acted out the start-up instructions at the beginning of his make-believe CD-ROM storybook. This scenario marked James's discovery of a new object to transform for use with computer-based dramatic play. One of the defining characteristics of dramatic play (also called socio-dramatic play) is a child's transformations of objects and use of role-play to act out stories they invent (Christie, 1991). James transformed the mirror into a computer screen, and he became the CD-ROM storybook operating from within the computer by altering his voice and using the language typical of the software.

The purpose of this chapter is to describe a perspective involving the existence of computer-based dramatic play and the role it plays in both literacy development and children's learning processes. This perspective will be largely based on the work of Vygotsky (1978) and Rosenblatt (1978) while using Rowe's (1998) conception of book-related dramatic play as both a framework and comparison. In working toward that purpose, I defined computer-based dramatic play as dramatic play that reflects symbol use related to computer technology stemming from computer-based experiences. The example of James and me in front of the mirror is an example of computer-based dramatic play. James called it 'The CD-ROM Game'.

James's experience with CD-ROM storybooks

I documented James's exploration of CD-ROM storybooks from age two-and-a-half to three-and-a-half as part of a larger study comparing three types of storybook media (Smith, 2001). The use of single case descriptions to explain literacy development has emerged as an acceptable practice among literacy researchers. Studies by Bissex (1980), Crago and Crago (1976), Harkness and Miller (1982), Snow (1983), and Yaden, Smolkin, and Conlon (1989) set precedence for further single case studies. Researchers who study their own children and single case examples conduct studies that derive their strength from context, presenting the natural environment of literacy development and learning. It is within James's natural environment that I observed his interaction with CD-ROM storybooks and his subsequent play behaviors.

The purpose of the original study was to describe James's interaction with various storybook media and to analyze the similarities and connections within and across three types of storybooks: traditional paper storybooks, child-created texts (language experience books), and CD-ROM storybooks. The proportion of engagement in episodes across and within storybook sharing experiences was unique for each medium under investigation, suggesting that each storybook medium contributed uniquely to James's overall storybook knowledge and literacy development.

The year-long study documented James's learning path of CD-ROM story-book use. The study began with James's first experience with CD-ROM storybooks and concluded with his ability to complete a CD-ROM story-book as an independent playroom activity. James's father and I were both graduate students during the course of the study and thus spent a good deal of time plucking away at the keys of our computer. James found this intriguing, and he often asked to sit in our laps as we worked. He asked about things he noticed on the screen and wanted to type on the keys. The first time James experienced a CD-ROM storybook, he watched his father interact with the text and hypertext. He quickly understood the concept of clicking to engage the hypertext and began to instruct his father where to point and click. He wanted to see the same hypertext objects repeated and instructed his father to 'Do again, Daddy!'

Initially, I introduced James to ten CD-ROM storybooks at a rate of two per week for a period of five weeks, so he could become familiar with each text and with the new technology. James used a mouse especially designed for young children by Microsoft called an EasyBall. It resembled a large yellow softball cradled in a white holder with a rectangular blue button on the front. James manipulated the mouse by moving the yellow ball in the cradle and selected items on the screen by pushing the large blue button. The EasyBall was designed for his two-and-a-half-year-old motor skills, which made the interaction with the artefacts of the technology more appropriate for his developmental abilities.

James and I read a wide range of CD-ROM titles such as *Stellaluna* (Cannon, 1996), *The Polar Express* (Van Allsburg, 1996), *Shiela Rae, the Brave* (Henkes, 1996), *Green Eggs and Ham* (Seuss, 1996), *Little Monster at School* (Mayer, 1994), and *The Adventures of Peter Rabbit and Benjamin Bunny* (Potter, 1995–6). After the initial introduction, the CD-ROM storybooks became a playroom activity that was chosen by James and not planned by me.

However, I occasionally purchased a new CD-ROM storybook and invited James to read it with me.

The discussion in this chapter will focus on the data collected in the original study of James. A second analytical pass was made through the data with the lens focused on play behaviors in response to technology interactions. Data sources such as video tapes, transcripts, parent diaries, reflective summaries, and coding sheets were searched and episodes of interaction were compared. Episodes emerged from the data sets that contained play behaviors related to CD-ROM storybook interaction and were coded as vignettes that were used as defining moments for analysis.

Dramatic play

In order to define computer-based dramatic play, it is important to begin with a general description of play. In very broad terms, play is generally defined by researchers as a set of characteristics, such as those described by Bruner (1983):

1   Play implies a reduction in the seriousness of the consequences of errors and of setbacks.
2   Play is characterized by a very loose linkage between means and ends.
3   Play is very rarely random; it follows a scenario.
4   Play is a projection of interior life onto the world in opposition to learning through which we interiorize the exterior world and make it part of ourselves.
5   Play gives pleasure.

(Bruner, 1983: 60–61)

These characteristics include all types of play, for example, the play you see toddlers engage in when they pick up a block and pretend it is a telephone to call grandma and the play you see adolescents engage in with their skateboards on a ramp after school. To further examine play behavior, researchers (Bergen, 1988; Christie, 1991) subcategorize play so that the adolescents are engaged in a form of play called *practice play* to refine their skateboarding skills and the toddler is engaged in *dramatic play* to transform real-world objects into make-believe ones for role play. Two additional subcategories of play are *constructive play* and *exploratory play*. Constructive play is when a child creates something to solve a problem. Exploratory play involves children experimenting with the reactions of others through acting on objects or people.

Dramatic play can be considered as uniquely different from the other types of play in the sense that it does not include creating objects to solve problems, practising a skill, or experimenting with the reactions of others. More specifically, dramatic play occurs when children transform real-world objects into make-believe ones and act out stories and scripts they invent (Christie, 1991). For example, when the toddler uses the block to call grandma on the telephone, she is transforming the real-world object, the block, into a telephone. Also, the toddler creates a script of the telephone conversation that occurs between her grandma and herself. She is engaged in dramatic play rather than exploratory play, because she is not experimenting with the reactions of others. She is not practising telephoning skills, thus she is not engaged in practice play. She is also not creating an object to solve a problem; therefore, she is not engaged in constructive play.

Computers and dramatic play

Play is the foundation of a young child's experience, so it is logical that the effects of exposing young children, like James, to computers would be revealed through their play. However, little is currently known about dramatic play as a response to computer use. Computer-based dramatic play is a unique area of investigation.

Researchers have examined play *at* the computer or the use of computers *for* play (Escobedo, 1992; Labbo, McKenna, and Kuhn, 1996; Liang and Johnson, 1999). Studies in this area of research focus on categorizing the types of play during computer use to verify its developmental appropriateness and its ability to facilitate the construction of new concepts. Escobedo, for example, found that children moved through a progression of play behaviors similar to the path they would follow for any other new play materials. She also suggested providing child-oriented activities and sufficient play time at the computer in order to reach the optimum level of symbolic play that leads to opportunities for literacy learning. Liang and Johnson suggested that computers can be used to enhance literacy development through play and recommended Talking Books (CD-ROM storybooks) and multimedia centers as environments for play. Labbo, McKenna, and Kuhn examined children in their preschool setting when a computer was used as a prop in a play center. They found that using the computer as a prop at play centers resulted in expanded symbol use, keyboarding skills, understanding of computer processes, and increased vocabulary for the children in the study.

Studies like these are building foundational connections between computers, play, and literacy learning. This type of play is contextual play and is perhaps practice play. The children are learning a skill and practising it with the actual object. During the study, James did engage with this type of play. There were times when he clicked hypertext items over and over just to watch them respond. There were also times when he moved the mouse across the screen, just to watch it move. He was playing on the computer screen and within the hypertext. However, when he began to transform a mirror into the computer and create his own scripts during dramatic play, the experience changed. Now the research lens must also change. Instead of connecting computers, play and literacy; the focus needs to shift to connect computers, *dramatic* play, and literacy.

Computer-based dramatic play: the CD-ROM Game

James's CD-ROM Game is an example of computer-based dramatic play. The mirror James transformed into the computer screen served as a window that opened a new world of computer-based dramatic play for him. His dramatic play grew more elaborate over the course of the study as his experience with the technology increased. For more than a week (during February, 1998), James played the CD-ROM Game nearly every day for the majority of his play time. Afterward, he played spontaneously throughout the day and less frequently. He generally played independently, but would sometimes invite his father and me to serve as his audience or scripted characters. The mirror he found was part of a dressing table where he could easily see himself. It was shaped like the rectangular computer screen, but was slightly larger. He used the mirror as a symbol and began the game each time in front of the mirror by saying, 'Click here if you want me to read you the story and click here if you want to play in the story.' He held up both hands to show where to click in the mirror. This scenario is a part of the actual CD-ROM storybook experience and occurs prior to beginning each CD-ROM storybook.

When readers choose to play in the story, the story is still narrated (read); however, after the narration for the page is complete, the story does not automatically turn to the next page. This allows the readers to flexibly explore the hypertext on the page and progress to the next page at their own pace by clicking the *next page* icon. When the CD-ROM progresses to the next page, the narration begins first and the readers cannot engage hypertext until the narration is complete. When readers choose to have the story read to them, the pages automatically turn and readers are unable to engage the hypertext on each page. There were times when James chose to have CD-ROM stories read to him, but most often he chose the option of playing in the story.

During the CD-ROM Game, James acted out parts of storybooks, switching between the part of the narrator and hypertext characters that were being clicked. He even moved from room to room in the house, each time he pretended to click and turn the page. Each room of the house was a new page, complete with narrated text and new hypertext objects to click. Sometimes items in the room were hypertext objects that he would make come to life when clicked.

Flying Berts and Giraffes

James chose to use his stuffed Bert (from *Sesame Street*'s Bert and Ernie) as a hypertext object. Each time Bert was clicked he flew in a circle around James's room and landed back on his pillow and said 'Night, night.' During another episode, James kept saying, 'Click,' and throwing a stuffed giraffe up into the air. He clicked it several times in a row, throwing it up in the air, and then replacing it on his bed each time after it was clicked.

Other times, James became the hypertext object to be clicked. For example, on several occasions he sat on the ottoman in the living room with his legs crossed and pointed to the top of his head and said, 'Click.' Then he jumped up using movement or gesture in some way to show a hypertext response, sometimes adding dialogue or silly songs that he created. When finished, he returned to his original sitting position. Then, he typically clicked to the next page by yelling 'Click!' and running to the virtual next page, which was in his bedroom. There, he became the narrator by standing still and tall and reciting a page of text for the story he invented.

James's CD-ROM Game contains the characteristics of dramatic play as identified by researchers (Christie, 1991; Rowe, 1998; Rubin, Fein, and Vandenberg, 1983). The CD-ROM Game included the make-believe transformation of objects when he transformed his home into the CD-ROM storybook using each room as a separate page of the story. He also transformed the mirror into the computer screen, the stuffed animals into hypertext objects, and himself into hypertext objects, book characters, and the narrator. The CD-ROM Game also included a role-playing component as James acted out the stories and scripts he created in his make-believe CD-ROM storybooks that encompassed and became his home.

Theoretical strands

Two theorists distinguish my thinking about computer-based dramatic play: Vygotsky and Rosenblatt. Using their theories as a foundation, I present four strands that describe the mental processes James revealed during computer-based dramatic play: (a) abstract transformation of objects and roles, (b) internalization of technical tools, (c) efferent stance involving computer-based dramatic play, and (d) aesthetic stance involving computer-based dramatic play.

Abstract transformation of objects and roles

James's ability to transfer what he learned about the CD-ROM storybooks from one context to another – from the actual context of the computer experience to the context of the entire house symbolizing the computer – is not unlike the process that children must develop when they learn symbol use to become literate. They must develop the notion that the squiggles they see on paper symbolize or *stand for* the words they speak. Vygotsky (1978) describes experiences like James's use of the mirror and his role in the CD-ROM Game as abstract transformation of objects and roles in play and attributes this behavior to having a direct relationship to symbol use in reading and writing. Using Vygotsky's notion of abstract transformation of objects and roles in play, James's behavior can be viewed as facilitating literacy development as he transforms the real-world objects around him into make-believe objects to create his own CD-ROM storybooks complete with narration of invented text. Roskos (2000) supported this theory by stating, 'It is becoming clearer that in play and literacy, certain foundational mental processes may be shared.' According to Roskos the process of letting something stand for something else is similar to the way that words in print stand for language. The ability to use and understand symbolic representations in one context can then be transferred to another context. James discovered how to use and transform the abstract symbols necessary to develop literacy when he engaged in dramatic play through his creation of the CD-ROM Game.

Internalization of technical tools

James and I shared CD-ROM storybooks together in a social setting which involved much talk and interaction, and then James later acted out the CD-ROM storybooks by transforming signs and tools to internalize what he learned during the social interaction. Vygotsky (1981) proposed that children learn the effective use of symbols and tools and then internalize that discovery as part of their cultural development. Vygotsky stated, 'all higher mental functions are internalized social relationships' (p. 164). For example, in the same way that an infant learns that the word 'bottle' stands for bottle through socialization with adults, James learned new sign systems in a *social plane* while sharing CD-ROM storybooks with me, and then transferred that knowledge to a *psychological plane* through his independent dramatic play. James's use of technology and his subsequent transformation of the tools and concepts of the technology were part of his cultural development and were internalized as he grew in his understanding of the technological concepts. According to Vygotsky, 'It goes without saying that internalization transforms the process itself and changes its structure and functions' (p. 163). In James's case, the internalization of the effective use of symbols and tools regarding CD-ROM

Table 7.1 Proportion of engagement in episodes for specific storybook experiences, Summer 1997 (Smith, 2001)

Episodes of interaction	Traditional	CD-ROM
Artefacts	0%	20%
Story text	47%	15%
Illustrations/hypertext	27%	31%

storybooks is revealed in his dramatic play. His experiences and resulting play behaviors illustrate that he internalized the technological concepts and was then able to recreate the events by transforming real-world objects and creating stories and scripts, removed from the original context of the CD-ROM storybook-sharing event.

The specific tools of the technology, whether a paper book or an electronic book, also play a role in the mental functioning that occurred and should be considered in understanding James's play behaviors. One of the main themes that emerges from Vygotsky's work, according to Wertsch (1989), is the belief that technical tools mediate human activity. In my original study (Smith, 2001), James's proportion of engagement was unique for traditional paper books and CD-ROM storybooks for the seven episodes of interaction. The use of various technical tools is a plausible explanation for that difference. For example, Table 7.1 illustrates that in the summer of 1997 during the second data comparison point, James focused on the artefacts, story text, and illustrations/hypertext at different rates for each type of storybook.

The use of tools of the technology (i.e. paper book or electronic book) mediates James's interaction with the different storybooks and thereby influences his mental functioning. During this specific time frame (see Table 7.1), his exploration with CD-ROM storybooks involved some time spent talking about how to click and where to click (the artefacts), while no time was spent talking about page turning or book holding during traditional storybook reading. He is talking much less (15% versus 47%) during CD-ROM storybooks than traditional storybook reading about meaning-making of story text. And, he is talking about the pictures and hypertext at a similar rate, yet he did focus more on the hypertext (31% and 27%). The various technological tools shaped the social interaction that occurred during the storybook reading and the mental functioning that occurred; the technical tools mediated the activity.

The technical tools also mediated James's activity during dramatic play. If he had not experienced the technical tools, he could not later pretend to be a hypertext object. Without his experience with CD-ROM storybooks as tools, he would be missing an entire repertoire of play in his dramatic play.

This dramatic play in turn affected his mental functioning as it reflected his internalization of cultural practice. Thus, returning to the concept of how children learn new symbol use and practice that as part of their cultural development, James developed his CD-ROM Game as a way to internalize his effective tool use. In effect, the process of internalizing the tools led to his ability to transform the objects in abstract ways and the types of tools used mediated his thinking and actions during the dramatic play.

Efferent stance involving computer-based dramatic play

Rosenblatt (1978) suggested that reading generally involves two stances, an aesthetic stance and an efferent stance. During James's computer-based dramatic play he adopted both stances in response to his reading of CD-ROM storybooks. The stance defined by Rosenblatt as efferent involves learning information from the reading. This *learning* stance, as defined by Rosenblatt, also describes James's behavior as he learned to use the tools of his culture as described by Vygotsky (1981). Following the CD-ROM storybooks experience, James took an efferent stance while engaged in computer-based dramatic play as he internalized the tools and symbols of his culture; thus, his efferent stance and his new understanding of cultural tools were revealed. Rosenblatt's theory of adapting an efferent stance supports Vygotsky's theoretical position that James's thoughts and activities were mediated with respect to tool and symbol use, and then internalized as part of his cultural development. For example, James learned how to read and respond to CD-ROM storybooks and grew in his understandings by internalizing them during his play through the CD-ROM Game. This transformation of understanding to abstract objects and other contexts involved taking an efferent learning stance during computer-based dramatic play.

Aesthetic stance involving computer-based dramatic play

James also adopted an aesthetic stance (Rosenblatt, 1978) as evidenced by the joy he shared with me in the opening scenario of this chapter. James could barely contain his enthusiasm as he invited me to see his new discoveries and to be an audience to the new game he invented. He was having a wonderful experience reliving and reconstructing the CD-ROM storybooks in the new sign system he created. He was playing and the play was pleasurable.

This aspect of the computer-based dramatic play is important both from a theoretical perspective and from a practical standpoint. Theoretically, if the pleasure had not been part of the experience, then it would not be considered dramatic play. The characteristics of dramatic play and play in general must include a reduction in seriousness and must be pleasurable (Bruner, 1983). From a practical viewpoint, if James did not find it entertaining on his own, then he would not be motivated to continue playing the CD-ROM

Game. The joy that was evident in James's computer-based dramatic play demonstrated he was adopting an aesthetic stance and it defined the experience as dramatic play.

Computer-based dramatic play and literacy

James's symbolic computer play behaviors are similar to the types of play that typically result from sharing storybooks with children. His play revealed an understanding of the technology as well as the story. He demonstrated an understanding of hypertext by pretending to be hypertext objects and transforming real-world objects into hypertext objects. He further demonstrated his understanding of the CD-ROM storybooks by retelling and dramatically interpreting stories while playing the CD-ROM Game. He not only acted out the story, but also used his technological understandings by utilizing the entire house as the storybook and creating a page of the story in each room. His play behaviors were similar to those found by Rowe (1998) and Wolf and Heath (1992) in their studies of book-related dramatic play.

This section of the chapter will compare my study of James's experience with CD-ROM storybook events to Rowe's (1998) work in which she studied her son, Christopher's, experience with traditional storybook events. Specific parallels can be drawn between book-related dramatic play as defined by Rowe and James's computer-based dramatic play. James and Christopher were both approximately two-and-a-half years old during the studies and were both sons of literacy researchers. Both boys were only children at the beginning of the study and were subjects of a home-based case study for the length of one year. Both were the sons of professional parents. Interestingly, both boys were intense theme-based learners. For example, when James became interested in space, he wanted to read space books, draw spaceships, create a solar system, and build space models of clay and blocks. He pursued this interest for a long period before moving on to his next topic of interest: dinosaurs. Rowe describes Christopher in the same manner. James and Christopher seem to be highly similar subjects for comparison.

Rowe (1998) defines book-related dramatic play as 'dramatic play that reflects either explicitly or implicitly the meanings signed in books' texts or illustrations, or in the book-reading events in which children encounter books' (p. 10). I defined James's computer-based dramatic play in a broader fashion to encompass not only the CD-ROM storybook experience, but the experience of using the tools and artefacts of the technology. Thus, when James pretended to be part of the computer screen *and* when he pretended to be a CD-ROM storybook character, both were examples of computer-based dramatic play.

Rowe (1998) suggested that there were seven characteristics of play that provided both motivation and opportunity for literacy learning during the course of her study: (a) connection, (b) ownership, (c) flexibility, (d) openness, (e) multiple sign systems, (f) transmediation, and (g) community. The following section will present each of the seven characteristic followed by vignettes used as defining moments as evidenced in my study of James as I observed and analyzed his computer-based dramatic play.

Rowe (1998) argued that the *connections* during book-related dramatic play were bidirectional, meaning that the themes from the book reading events were incorporated into play and then brought back into the book reading events. For Rowe's son, Christopher, the play provided an important link between books and his world of play. Similar experiences were also notable in James's CD-ROM storybook explorations and subsequent dramatic play experiences.

I'm a Cool Cat

During engagement with the CD-ROM storybook, *Sheila Rae, the Brave* (Henkes, 1996), James clicked on a cat sitting on top of a fence. The cat sang a song called, 'I'm a Cool Cat'. Later during computer-based dramatic play, James pretended to be the cat and replicated the cat sitting on top of the fence by reenacting the hypertext movement and song. He created some new lyrics, but kept the chorus and melody. Later, when he chose to re-read *Sheila Rae, the Brave*, he pointed to the cat and said, 'I'm that cool cat, Daddy-O!'

James connected to the CD-ROM storybook in a new way due to his computer-based dramatic play. In effect, his play created new opportunities for meaning–making during the book reading event. Conversely, the CD-ROM storybook reading event created the opportunity for new dramatic play opportunities. It was a bidirectional connection.

Rowe (1998) suggested that *ownership* provided her son Christopher with an opportunity to explore literacy through book–related dramatic play. During Rowe's study, Christopher was able to initiate play as a response to book reading events and tailor it to his interpretations of the world around him; he had ownership in the dramatic play events. This was also true for James. He was free to choose not only whether to engage in storybook sharing events after the initial introduction of the CD-ROM storybooks, but to decide what to play during his time in the playroom. James created the CD-ROM Game on his own and used it to further explore and extend his understanding of the CD-ROM storybook events. He freely transformed the real-world objects into the parts of the computer to create his own version of the CD-ROM experience in his make-believe land which encompassed his entire home. He owned the experience and orchestrated it from beginning to end, sometimes inviting an audience and sometimes playing independently of others.

Flexibility is the third characteristic that Rowe (1998) suggests created a supportive medium for literacy learning in her study of book-related dramatic play. Rowe observed a range of play behaviors as Christopher responded to his learning about books. James's play was also flexible and often changed quickly from one aspect of the CD-ROM storybook to another as he used dramatic play to explore sign systems, meaning-making regarding the story text, technological aspects of the software, and hypertext understandings.

I'm Yally

After reading the CD-ROM storybook, *Little Monster at School* (Mayer, 1994), James played a version of his CD-ROM Game and pretended to be a character in the story named Yally. He said, 'I'm Yally. I eat too much candy and I get sick. Blaaagh.' In the story, Yally eats only candy for lunch, and James inquired about it during the CD-ROM storybook reading. He did not understand why Yally would eat so much candy. He told me that he thought Yally would probably get sick. Even though that is not what happened during the story, James changed the outcome during his dramatic play reenactment. It simply made more sense to James according to his sense of how things work in the real world to make this change in his script. A moment later, James was pretending to be a hypertext object in the classroom that Yally was holding on one of the pages. It was a plant that Yally was trying to grow, but it would not grow. James clicked on himself as the plant and said, 'You have to water me Yally.' Then he pointed in the air and clicked to the next page, ran to another room in the house, and acted out a new page of the storybook.

In this short example, James pretended to be a book character and was working out a difficulty he had with the events of the story, a hypertext object that he felt needed a voice in the story, and the actual technology of the software as he became the icon to click to the next page. His play was flexible and held multiple purposes during the computer-based dramatic play.

Openness is the fourth characteristic that Rowe (1998) assigns to book-related dramatic play as a supportive medium for literacy learning. By openness, Rowe suggests that the play she observed in her study was free from outside rules and interference from adults. Christopher was free to act out specific aspects of books as he saw fit and create new text or sometimes use close approximations of the actual language from the texts. This was also true during my observations of computer-based dramatic play. For example, in James's dramatic interpretation of Yally, he decided to act out the scene where Yally was eating lunch at school, rather than start from the beginning of the text. Yally was not the main character, but rather a supportive character in the story. And the lunch scene was a small part of the overall plot of the story. James also changed the text and outcome to be more in line with his expectations of the social world. James often used the dramatic play as an outlet for making sense of the world and for working out social meanings.

Click here for a nice story

James seemed to be working out the difference between a nice story and a mean story and nice characters and mean characters. This work lead to an adaptation of the opening scenario of his CD-ROM Game. He began his game by saying, 'Click here if you want a nice story and click here if you want a mean story.' He even found toys to represent each choice. He held up a Dalmatian for the nice story choice and Cruella Deville for the mean story choice. The openness of the dramatic play allowed James to flexibly explore this new learning in his own way.

Multiple sign systems were the fifth characteristic that Rowe (1998) described as contributing to literacy learning through book-related dramatic play. The use of multiple sign systems in James's case involved the use of props (the mirror turned computer screen), language (the robot-like computer voice and his Yally voice), settings (turning the house into a computer), and drama (movements and gestures, such as clicking and flying Bert). The use of these multiple sign systems provided greater access to meaning and the opportunity for James to explore CD-ROM storybooks in new ways.

Transmediation is the sixth characteristic that Rowe (1998) described as contributing to literacy learning through book-related dramatic play. Initially, James constructed meaning in the CD-ROM storybook sign system. Next, he reconstructed that meaning in another sign system using the entire house and various props within the house, such as the mirror, stuffed animals, furniture, and himself as symbols that were within the computer during his original construction of meaning. The act of reconstruction of meaning in this new context using new sign systems has been called transmediation by researchers (Eco, 1976; Rowe, 1998). Rowe argues that the interplay between book reading, transmediation, and dramatic play creates new potentials for literacy learning. According to Rowe, book-related dramatic play influences book reading, which in turn influences dramatic play and vice versa.

In her opinion, the children (her son and his classmates) in her study were different readers because they were engaged in book-related dramatic play and they played differently because they were engaged in storybook reading.

Like they did it on the computer

In October 1997, James reenacted the storybook *Harry and the Haunted House* (Schlichting, 1994) with his father as an invited scripted character. He said, 'I want to play like they did on the computer. Come on Daddy!' James remembered the actual dialogue and the scenes and even the hypertext responses on each page. Throughout the dramatic play, James and his father tiptoed around our home acting as if it were the haunted house. At the end of the dramatic play, James picked up the traditional paper version of the book and pointed out the illustrations to his father. He told his father what the hypertext items did in each picture. 'That girl sings.' 'The fire has eyes and makes a face.' 'When I click on this . . .' As soon as James finished telling about the hypertext, he asked if his father would read him the story again. These connections from text to dramatic play and back to text support Rowe's notion of transmediation.

Community is the final characteristic that Rowe (1998) described as contributing to literacy learning through book-related dramatic play. Rowe's study included both home and school environments for book-related dramatic play. In James's specific situation, community plays a lesser role, because only his home environment was utilized for computer-based dramatic play. However, James did engage his father and me in his dramatic play on occasion. He most often engaged us as audience members or as scripted book characters. For example, we could participate, but he fed us our lines of script by leading us with 'Now you be Stellaluna's Mommy, and you say. . . .' The dramatic play remained in his control. Even though I was sometimes an actor in the role play, it was his creative dramatic play. In Rowe's work, the other children in the community sometimes shaped the dramatic play, but in James's case I was an observational community member. I observed the dramatic play unfold rather than interfered with its development. I was an audience member when invited and a script speaker when asked, but my participation did little to reshape the dramatic play that James created.

The parallels drawn between Rowe's (1998) findings and James's experiences are based strongly on the foundational response to literature present in both studies. While Christopher responded to traditional storybooks and James responded to CD-ROM storybooks, both were engaged in dramatic play as a response to story following a storybook sharing event. It is not surprising, then, that so many of James's experiences were similar to those of Christopher's. The added dimension of the technology and how James used it during the dramatic play made his experience unique, but the seven characteristics of book-related dramatic play were evident throughout James's computer-based dramatic play.

It is difficult, given these types of naturalistic inquiry, to compare findings and make generalizations across the two studies. It is clear, however, that Christopher and James both engaged in dramatic play behaviors that contribute to literacy learning. It is also clear that the types of dramatic play behaviors that the children exhibited were similar. For each of Rowe's (1998) seven categories, defining moments emerged from the data analysis of James's experience that supported the existence of computer-based dramatic play experiences.

Conclusions

The purpose of this chapter was to describe computer-based dramatic play and the role it plays in both literacy development and children's learning processes. In order to do so, I used the work of Vygotsky (1978) and Rosenblatt (1978) and compared James's defining moments of computer-based dramatic play to Rowe's (1998) conception of book-related dramatic play. The following are major themes that emerged throughout the chapter to both reveal the existence of computer-based dramatic play and establish its connection to literacy development and children's learning processes as well as implications for teachers and researchers who work with young children.

Computer-based dramatic play is defined as dramatic play that reflects symbol use related to computer technology stemming from computer-based experiences. James's CD-ROM Game is an example of computer-based dramatic play. The computer-based dramatic play includes the defining characteristics of dramatic play, such as the transformation of real-world objects into make-believe ones and the acting out of stories and invented scripts (Christie, 1991). The CD-ROM Game included a make-believe transformation of objects when James transformed his home into the actual CD-ROM storybook using each room as a separate page of his story. He transformed the rectangular mirror into the computer screen, the stuffed animals into hypertext objects, and himself into an array of computer-based items. The CD-ROM Game also included a role-playing component as James acted out the stories and scripts he created in his make-believe CD-ROM storybooks that encompassed our home. Defining computer-based dramatic play in this way allows early childhood educators and researchers a new arena in which to talk about how children engage with technology. Up to this point, most of the research and teaching for this population has focused on what children are doing with computers, not what happens as a result of engaging with computer technology.

Computer-based dramatic play has a theoretical foundation to support its role in literacy development. The abstract transformation of objects and roles evident in James's CD-ROM Game has a direct relationship to his literacy development according to Vygotsky's (1978) theoretical position. In the same way that children must learn that letters stand for words, abstract symbols are used in dramatic play to stand for something else. In addition, the process of internalizing the tools that led to his ability to transform the objects in abstract ways is also linked to his learning processes. According to Vygotsky (1981), the type of tools used mediates James's thinking and activity. Thus, the computer-based dramatic play is a result of the new technology used and James's internalization of the technical tools of his culture. Finally, James adopted both an efferent and an aesthetic stance during computer-based dramatic play. The efferent stance supports his attempt to internalize his new technological understandings through dramatic play and his aesthetic stance supports his motivation and expression of joy during the dramatic play. The theoretical foundation established between computer-based dramatic play and literacy development suggests that young children can benefit from exposure to CD-ROM storybooks and time to dramatize them during play. However, more long-term studies are needed with larger numbers of participants to make generalizations about such correlations.

Comparisons were revealed between computer-based dramatic play and book-related dramatic play to support its role in literacy development. Rowe's (1998) work describes the ways in which her son, Christopher's, dramatic play was linked to his literacy development and she suggests as evidence seven characteristics of dramatic play that provide motivation and support for literacy learning. I provided examples from James's computer-based dramatic play for each of the seven categories. It is difficult to know the extent to which the two studies are comparable, given the naturalistic nature of the studies. The children were relatively the same age and seemed to come from similar home experiences, even having mothers with similar education and interests. It seems reasonable to make connections between the boys' experiences, given the descriptions shared by Rowe and the examples provided here about James. It also seems reasonable to conclude that both boys' dramatic play experiences, book-related dramatic play and computer-based dramatic play, provide opportunities for literacy learning.

The combination of both traditional and CD-ROM storybooks in early childhood classrooms may provide a powerful basis for dramatic play. Book-related dramatic play and computer-based dramatic play can support literacy development for young children. These experiences separately, book-related dramatic play and computer-based dramatic play, were linked to the foundations of literacy development. The experiences combined could lead to multiple literacy awareness that would be powerful during dramatic play experiences. During my original study of James (Smith, 2001), three types of storybook experiences were explored and revealed a development of multiple storybook literacy as each type of storybook contributed uniquely to his overall literacy development and understanding of story. I believe the same types of phenomena could occur with dramatic play, although it needs further invest-igation and this chapter contained only a simple comparison. Perhaps, if groups of children were exposed to different types of media during dramatic play that included technology, then their play would reflect the different types of thinking for each medium and the multiple literacies would be revealed during dramatic play as well. It is a question I still have after writing this chapter and one I pose to future researchers and practitioners.

References

Bergen, D. (1988) Stages of play development. In D. Bergen (ed.), *Play as a Medium for Learning and Development* (pp. 49–66). Portsmouth, NH: Heinemann.

Bissex, G. (1980) *GYNS AT WRK: A Child Learns to Write and Read*. Cambridge, MA: Harvard University Press.

Bruner, J. (1983) Play, thought, and language. *Peabody Journal of Education*, 60, 60–69.

Cannon, J. (1996) *Stellaluna*. Navato, CA: Broderbund's Living Books.

Christie, J. F. (1991) Psychological research on play: Connections with early develop-ment. In J. Christie (ed.). *Play and Early Literacy Development* (pp. 27–43). Albany, NY: State University of New York Press.

Crago, H. and Crago, M. (1976) The untrained eye? A preschool child explores Felix Hoffman's Rapunzel. *Children's Literature in Education*, 22, 135–151.

Eco, U. (1976) *A theory of semiotics*. Bloomington, IN: Indiana University Press.

Escobedo, T. H. (1992) Play in a new medium: Children's talk and graphics at computers. *Play and Culture*, 5, 120–140.

Harkness, F. and Miller, L. (1982, October) A description of the interaction among mother, child, and books in a bedtime reading situation. Paper presented at the annual Boston University Conference on Language Development, Boston, MA.

Henkes, K. (1996) *Sheila Rae, the Brave*. Novato, CA: Broderbund's Living Books.

Labbo, L. D., McKenna, M. C. and Kuhn, M. R. (1996) *Computer Real and Make-believe: Providing Opportunities for Literacy Development in an Early Childhood Sociodramatic Play Center*. (ERIC Document Instructional Resource No. 26 ED396254.)

Liang, P. and Johnson, J. (1999) Using technology to enhance early literacy through play. *Computing in the Schools*, 15, 55–64.

Mayer, M. (1994) *Little Monster at School*. Novato, CA: Broderbund's Living Books.

Potter, B. (1995–6) *The Adventures of Peter Rabbit and Benjamin Bunny*. Novato, CA: Broderbund's Living Books.

Rosenblatt, L. (1978) *The Reader, The Text, The Poem: The Transactional Theory of the Literary Work*. Carbondale, IL: Southern Illinois University Press.

Roskos, K. (2000) Creating connection, building construction: Language, literacy, and play in early childhood. *Reading Online* [On-line], Available: http://www.readingonline.org/articles/roskos/index.html.

Rowe, D. W. (1998) The literate potentials of book-related dramatic play. *Reading Research Quarterly*, 33, 10–35.

Rubin, K., Fein, G. and Vandenberg, B. (1983) Play. In E. Hetherington (ed.) and P. H. Mussen (Series Ed.). *Handbook of Child Psychology: Vol. 4. Socialization, personality, and social development* (pp. 698–774). New York: Wiley.

Schlichting, M. (1994) *Harry and the Haunted House*. Navato, CA: Broderbund's Living Books.

Smith, C. R. (2001) Click and turn the page: An exploration of multiple storybook literacy. *Reading Research Quarterly*, *36*, 152–183.

Snow, C. E. (1983) Literacy and language: Relationships during the preschool years. *Harvard Educational Review*, *53*, 165–189.

Suess, Dr. (1996) *Green Eggs and Ham*. Novato, CA: Broderbund's Living Books.

Van Allsburg, C. (1996) *The Polar Express*. Somerville, MA: Houghton Mifflin Interactive.

Vygotsky, L. S. (1978) *Mind in Society: The Development of Higher Psychological Processes*. (M. Cole, V. John-Steiner, S. Scribner and E. Souberman, eds. and Trans.). Cambridge, MA: Harvard University Press.

Vygotsky, L. S. (1981) The genesis of higher mental functions. In J. V. Wertsch (ed.). *The Concept of Activity in Soviet Psychology*. (pp. 144–188). Armonk, NY: M.E. Sharpe.

Wertsch, J. V. (1989) *A Sociocultural Approach to Mind: Child Development Today and Tomorrow*. San Francisco: Jossey-Bass.

Wolfe, S. and Heath, S. B. (1992) *The Braid of Literature. Children's Worlds of Reading*. Cambridge, MA: Harvard University Press.

Yaden, D., Smolkin, L. and Conlon, A. (1989) Preschoolers' questions about pictures, print conventions, and story text during reading aloud time at home. *Reading Research Quarterly*, *24*, 188–214.

Chapter 8

Narrative spaces and multiple identities

Children's textual explorations of console games in home settings

Kate Pahl

Introduction

In this chapter I argue that console games provide a space in which children can discover new textual practices, and explore narratives of space and identity. I consider how such games offer recursive narrative spaces, enabling children to enter discursively realised 'figured worlds' and to create narratives that are structured through iterative and patterned sequences. Console games also provide a space for children to explore their multiple identities. In order to explore how they realise children's identities, I pay particular attention to children's *texts* made in response to console games. In developing ideas around children's construction of identity and narratives in response to console games, I draw upon Holland *et al.*'s concept of identity in practice (Holland *et al.*, 2001) together with Bourdieu's concept of *habitus* (Bourdieu, 1977, 1990; and Bourdieu and Wacquant, 1992). Drawing on Bartlett and Holland's (2002) argument that Bourdieu's notion of habitus needs to be explored in relation to the making of texts, I argue that by textually exploring these games, children are modifying the habitus of the home. I also draw on literature from the ethnography of communication on narrative and performance (Michaels, 1986; Hymes, 1996), as well as work on communicative practices in the context of changing global and cultural contexts (Lankshear and Knobel, 2003; Gee, 2003). Putting these ideas together, alongside the literature on children's popular culture and literacy (Marsh and Millard, 2000; Buckingham and Scanlon, 2002; Burn, 2003; Dyson, 2003) I develop the argument that console games offer children a rich narrative space within which multiple identities can be explored in a number of textual forms.

The study

The data explored in this chapter were derived from a three-year ethnographic study of communicative practices in homes. The particular ethnographic method drawn upon was linguistic ethnography. Here, linguistic ethnography is defined as ethnographically grounded detailed analysis of communicative practices (Maybin, 2003). Three homes were visited on a regular basis for two years. The focus was on texts, visual and linguistic, and on practices surrounding the texts. The homes were selected on the basis of there being a boy of about six years of age within each home, with a mix of working-class, and middle-class homes. Access was organised through my working as a teacher in a family literacy class in a school in North London. One mother attended the family literacy class, another mother attended, and helped run, a class at a neighbouring school, and one was a teacher, living locally, recommended by one of the teachers working on the family literacy project. The families' backgrounds included Turkish and Indian heritages. The families agreed to take part in the project, and I gradually gained the trust of the families and became involved with their lives on a continuing basis.

The children in the study drawn on here were:

- Sam, seven, son of Parmjit, Indian heritage, teacher;
- Fatih, six, son of Elif, Turkish heritage, student of English;
- Edward, six, son of Mary, born in India, Irish origin, Learning Support Assistant.

The initial research interest was on boys and meaning–making. Each field visit involved the writing of field notes and recording of conversations. Texts were collected from the boys if they were available, photocopied and re-turned to the home. After about a year of fieldwork in each home, a tape recorder was used and conversations were recorded. Included in the dataset were videos made by the mothers of the boys, as described below. Each home had access to console games, but the ethnographic study did not focus initially on them. Texts about the games arose in the context of the children's 'interest' (Kress, 1997). The data presented in this chapter were drawn from both the first and second years of the study and represented specific instances, selected as 'telling cases', that is, cases which can be theoretically generative, of children's texts in response to console games (Mitchell, 1984).

The term 'console games' is used in this chapter to describe games whereby a hand-held console is used alongside a television screen. This console is provided with buttons that control the activity on the screen, allowing the player to manipulate characters and take them through moves. Common types of these consoles include the PlayStation 2 manufactured by Sony and Nintendo's games console, now developed into a Game Cube. In this chap-ter, three games are referred to. The first is *Super Mario*, manufactured by Nintendo, which concerns a character called Super Mario and is a level-based game. The second is *Spyro the Dragon*, which is a game involving an ima-ginary dragon in a fantasy world, in which the player has to undergo a series of difficult tasks, and can be played on a PlayStation console. The third is *World Wrestling Federation (WWF)*, which is a game that can be played on a Play-Station 2 console, involving two wrestlers in a ring, and the game involves making special moves until you have your opponent on the floor. In a recent study, working-class families were more likely to have a TV-linked console games machine than the middle classes, 72 per cent compared with 61 per cent (Livingstone, 2002).

The 'space' of console games

The argument developed in this chapter is that console games can offer a space for children that can harness and develop text making. Games offer 'figured worlds', which invite alternative ways of being and enacting (Holland *et al.*, 2001: 41). These ways of being are play spaces, offering rich textual possibilities. I draw on Holland's concept of identity, centred around the concept of practice together with cultural forms. Holland *et al.* argue that 'Identity is a concept that figuratively combines the intimate or personal world with the collective space of cultural forms and social relations' (Holland *et al.*, 2001: 5). I connect Holland's practice-infused concept of identity with Bourdieu's practice theory, particularly his theory of habitus as a set of 'dispositions' which structure identities in practice, and may be improvised upon (Bourdieu, 1977, 1990). This 'taken for granted' identity in practice offers a space, I argue, for children to engage with in an 'as-if' universe, which Holland *et al.* described as a 'figured world' (Holland *et al.*, 2001).

Holland *et al.* locate their practice-infused view of identity within their concept of 'figured worlds', which are collectively realised 'as-if' realms. They describe how 'Figured worlds take shape within and grant shape to the coproduction of activities, discourses, performances and artefacts' (Holland *et al.*, 2001: 51). Here, I suggest that the 'figured worlds' of console games such as *Spyro* and *Super Mario* offer an opportunity for children to 'play' with different identities, and to re-fashion identities in relation to those worlds. In all three case study examples described below, the children's identities were culturally, discursively and textually realised in relation to the 'figured worlds' of console games. These 'figured worlds' relied upon artefacts which upheld and discursively represented them. Artefacts included 'avatars', imaginary characters created in order to play the game which children could identify with, and images and narratives which entered children's text making. Children's texts retained traces of the social practice of playing console games imbued with stories and characters such as Super Mario (Rowsell, 2000).

Console games are ideally suited to the concept of the 'figured world'. They are games which are culturally fashioned and offer the opportunity to engage with other identities. Here is Sam, describing his play from a tape recording made in his bedroom, at home:

Sam: Whoops he's he got me
       When the stars go round my head that means that I get hurt.

The 'me' is not the 'real' Sam, who later describes how his tooth came out (see below) but the Sam who is the avatar, in combat. This move into embodiment, and the ability of the player to project into an alternative reality, has also been noted by Gee: 'people learn to situate meanings through embodied experiences in a complex semiotic domain and mediate in the process' (Gee, 2003: 26). This concept of embodied identity is also one which can be linked to Bourdieu's concept of 'habitus' as a set of 'durable, transposable dispositions' (Bourdieu, 1977: 72). Console games offer an opportunity to improvise upon the habitus, as a place for embodied action. They invite children into a practice-infused space where identities can be modified. Here, I analyse children's textual forms in relation to the shifts in identity the texts produce, and I consider how games such as *Super Mario* offer these children a space in which to shift and improvise upon identity. In doing so, I construct console games as being spaces of improvisation and play.

Console games have begun to be studied in recent years in the context of work on children's digitised literacy practices in the home (Buckingham and Scanlon, 2002; Burn, 2003; Marsh, 2003). This chapter draws on recent work by Gee, which argues for console games to be seen as a learning tool (Gee, 2003). However, few studies have looked specifically at text making. In this study, the concept of 'texts' included a multiplicity of communicative practices. One way of seeing 'texts' is as being 'articulations of discourses', and this is the definition used in this chapter (Kress and van Leeuwen, 2001: 24). In the study, texts included drawings, performance captured on video, talk while playing the games and talk about them. These different communicative practices all related to the games, but here the focus is on what these textual responses offer children's identity formation in the home. In addition, the role of narrative is explored, and the way in which console games offer children alternative narrative structures that may not be congruent with 'schooled' settings (Street and Street, 1991).

Console games offer the player a different structural form of telling and embodying stories. Instead of a rounded, closed, form in which the story begins, and then ends, in many games, such as *Super Mario*, or *Spyro*, discussed below, the player has to master certain objectives, or tasks, and then move on to the next 'level'. The narrative therefore has a recursive quality, as the player finds himself or herself in a similar, but slightly altered space, on the next level of the game. This way of thinking about narrative has been previously explored by Berger (2000) and in a more theoretical way by de Certeau (1984). Console games offer alternative narrative structures from which children can create their own meanings. These new narratives can be structured in relation to the form of the game.

Hymes (1996) and others previously observed how alternative narrative structures were disadvantaged within classrooms. Michaels (1986) observed African-American first graders telling stories, and noticed that these children did not progress in 'Sharing time' because their narrative structures were different. Out of these observations developed Michaels' argument that these children engaged with and used narrative in a different way from that of the other children (Michaels, 1986). This insight can be related to the narratives that children produced drawing on the structures embedded in console games, which focused on action differentiated through levels (see Fatih's talk below). The concept of narrative was developed by Hymes in the context of his work on the ethnography of communication (Hymes, 1996). Hymes' insight that narrative was formed through a recursive, iterative use, and was linked to both performance and text, was useful for understanding narrative as an iterative form, honed through iterative practices within homes. More recently, Lankshear and Knobel (2003) have argued that new textual practices need to be understood as such, in order for work on the new literacies to adequately assess new competencies. The narrative structures of console games thus offer a challenge to 'schooled' notions of literacy (Street and Street, 1991).

Identity in console games

When playing console games, the children in this study became involved in the characters, the 'avatars', and existed 'out of time' while they played the game. Gee describes the gaming identity as being a 'projective identity', that is:

> Playing on two senses of the word 'project', meaning both to 'project one's values and desires onto the virtual character' . . . and 'seeing the virtual character as one's own project in the making, a creature whom I imbue with a certain trajectory through time defined by my aspirations for what I want that character to be and become . . .'
>
> (Gee, 2003: 55)

Gee's account describes the process of active involvement with a character, a process that is different from an identity outside of the game. For example, Fatih, below, focused on the theme of 'levels' as a way to structure his story about *Super Mario*. The 'I' sits in a different way in the game's space. The children in the study allowed for a transformation of identity, when playing console games, re-enacting the games, and in relation to the 'characters' they were playing. Here is Sam, talking, as he is playing *Spyro*, a game which offers an avatar and a series of combats in different settings:

Sam: He's gotta get me one more time, or two more times
       Oh man ate my supper!
       Poha . . . coming near me

Sam's intonation totally changes from playground argot to 'mum' speak:

Sam (to me):	Hey look
	Look
	I lost my teeth the other day
	I was worried that I swallowed it but/
Kate:	/What you are going to do with it?
Sam:	Put it under the pillow

(See list of transcription conventions on p. 144.) Here the 'switch' from the identity of the playing child, and the identity of the child who has lost his tooth is evident, both in intonation and content. Sam's 'projective identity' in Gee's terms, is at variance with his identity as a child who shows me his teeth.

Another aspect of console games is that the game offers a different timescale from that of 'real life', when teeth are lost and dinner is ready. The different timescales involved in playing games and 'real-life' timescales, as realised in homes, were evident, and contested. Parents often regulated games' playing time, and had set times when playing was allowed. However, children responded to the different timescales console games offered them. They became interested in the difference between their gaming identity and their real identity, or, conversely, the links between the 'playing' self and the 'real' self. Here is Fatih, talking of his 'gaming' self:

> When I was five years old I didn't know how to do these. I come to the castle and I come to the boss and he was on a boat and I went into . . .
> (Fieldnotes, 4 December 2000)

Fatih draws on the 'I' who couldn't play the game when he was five, and then switches almost immediately to the 'I' which was in the game, and came to the castle. Fatih has linked the longer-term process of his growing up with the shorter-term event of mastering levels. The object mediating these time processes is the game *Super Mario*. Console games such as *Super Mario* offer a record of the player's iterative mastery of particular levels, thus offering a way of viewing time in a particular sequential way.

Lemke (2000) described different kinds of timescales, which linked long- and short-term processes through a material object, which functioned both symbolically and materially. He described how a Samurai sword held meaning across generations. In feudal Japan, a storied and sacred family sword passed down across the generations can be used for beheading a commoner. If the Samurai chooses a common and ordinary battle sword, this artefact has a different meaning, as it has a different relation to family tradition. While this is a rather remote example, it shows how different material objects carry with them different semiotic affordances and are attached to different timescales. Lemke's description of the way in which particular artefacts hold within them particular traditions and embody a process of cumulating meaning can be applied to games such as *Super Mario*, in that through the iterative levels children can enter alternative timescales where different embodied identities can be realised.

In a different tradition, that of ethnography, Bourdieu's concept of habitus also can be applied to the way in which the playing of games, and the response to them through text making, constitutes improvisation upon the habitus (Bourdieu, 1977; 1990). Bourdieu's concept of habitus, the 'regulated improvisations' that structure the dispositions of the household, can be applied here to the way in which children improvised upon the habitus of the game, and used it to develop different identities in practice (Bourdieu, 1977: 78). For example, the *WWF* play fighting game described later has this quality. Habitus, as a set of dispositions, can be applied equally to the way the home is structured, the 'idea' (Douglas, 1991) of the home, and to the movements and dispositions of the people who inhabit that space (Bourdieu, 1990). It occupies the 'taken for granted' space of everyday life (Bourdieu and Waquant, 1992).

Habitus builds the everyday, and is improvised upon in the process. Gee describes the process of how content is built upon by developing identities:

> Content, the internal part of a semiotic domain, gets made in history by real people and their social interactions. They build that content − in part, not wholly − in certain ways because of the people they are (so-cially, historically, culturally). That content comes to define one of their important identities in the world. As those identities develop through further social interactions, they come to affect the ongoing development and transformation of the content of the semiotic domain in yet new ways. In turn, that new content helps further develop and transform those identities. The relationship between the internal and external is reciprocal.
>
> (Gee, 2003: 29)

Gee describes how identities can be shaped through the interaction and forming of new semiotic domains when playing video games. Likewise, in this study, it was found that console games such as *WWF*, *Spyro* and *Super Mario* allowed the development of new identities in practice, the evidence for which is a multiplicity of texts including home videos, drawing and talk, all recorded within the homes of the children.

Recontextualisation

The process of playing console games and responding to the game by text making involves a process that can be described as *recontextualisation*. The term comes from Bernstein (1996). Bernstein described what happened to pedagogic discourses when they moved into different fields. He described the process of recontextualisation of discourses as:

> selective appropriation of a discourse or part of a discourse from the field of production, and a principle of *re-location* of that discourse as a discourse within the recontexualising field.
>
> (Bernstein, 1996, 2000 edition: 113, his italics)

Bernstein's description of the process of recontextualisation, from de-location to re-location of a discourse, was suggestive in relation to texts crossing sites. Bernstein had a focus on pedagogic discourse. Dyson's use of the concept of recontextualisation, or 'remix' when applied to children's texts and practices crossing sites was grounded in detailed observations of children's text making in out-of-school contexts (Dyson, 2003). For example, one child in her study, Noah:

> originally experienced Space Jam with his real family as a multimodal story, complete with pictures, music score and dialogue. Then [. . .] Noah recontextualized and transformed that original experience into childhood practices of group singing and dramatic play.
>
> (Dyson, 2003: 346)

While Bernstein's concept of recontextualisation seems to apply to the pedagogic principle and to discourses only in relation to a particular, specific process, Dyson applied recontextualisation to both practices and texts grounded in cultural material and socio-cultural contexts. This is how I applied the concept to console games as I watched children take characters from the games, and move them into different fields, or take narratives which they then used and improvised upon, in different settings.

In the following three examples, different aspects of the space of console games are explored. In the first example, the game offered an opportunity for two children to be videoed by their mother re-enacting the fight they had previously engaged in when playing the game on the console. In doing so, they improvised upon the characters of the game, and recontextualised the content. In this example, they play with identity and create performative identities in practice, enacted through discourse and gestures. In the second example, the *Super Mario* texts, the child, Fatih, described the *Super Mario* game to me both in oral discourse, and in drawings. The drawings show how he has put together a hybrid, syncretic text that responds to the game and develops his identity in relation to the game (Duranti and Ochs, 1996). The third example is of a child talking while playing the *Spyro* game, in which the child's identity shifts are tracked through his oral discourses around the game. All three examples, a performance on video, a set of drawings and talk, and talk while playing, are seen as textual responses to gaming.

Where performance and text live: the *WWF* video

This example comes from the home of Mary, who was a Learning Support Assistant, and her son Edward, who was seven when the video was made. When the data were collected, I had been visiting the home every two weeks for about a year and a half. *WWF* was a console games version of a television programme of staged wrestlers, in which a number of differently named characters compete within a ring. The focus is on the moves and the aggression between the partners. It went through 'cult' status for a while, and was both a satellite television programme and a console game, whereby characters can be chosen and a fight can be enacted using two players, on a console.

About a year into the field work, I had observed Edward playing on his *WWF* game, and had taken field notes about it:

> We spent some time watching Edward play the *WWF* wrestling game on the console, and Mary described how they did it at play centre, and how the boys got involved. She said that initially they had been very excited and aggressive, less so now.
>
> (Fieldnotes, February 2001)

More than six months later I returned and was sitting in Mary's front room, when she asked me if I would like to see a home video of Edward and his friend 'playing' at *WWF*. Mary said I would like to see the video because it was very funny.

> The setting was the living room floor. This was thick pile carpet with two glass cabinets either side of the wide screen television and a floor to ceiling glass window leading out onto a small balcony. The boys were mimicking the *WWF* fight but were play acting it using special high pitched voices. P lived next door, and was a good friend.
>
> (Fieldnotes, 31 November 2001)

Transcription

The following video clip was chosen from a much longer clip that Mary had taken one evening of the boys.

Edward: And then I . . . /
Both: Oh!
          (P is on floor)
Edward: (in an undertone) And then I come – oh! (raises P's legs)
Both: Nah! Oh!
Edward: We don't know who's going to win!
          (P pursues Edward onto the settee and begins to pretend box him)

P: Hardcore hardcore hardcore hardcore (on settee)

           Oh my god oh my god what's this get off oh! Oh! Oh!

           (gets off settee)

Both: Oh! Oh! Oh!

           (unintelligible)

Edward: He can't get off schooly! Oh! Stick brace!

P: No! Don't do it! AHH! (Edward sits on him, with a wiggle, on settee)

Edward: Eeeh!

Both: (laughter)

Edward: (in an undertone) You run I'm going to jump you oh (lies down)

P: He's going to get the old school now! Old school!

           Get up! Get up you, you liddle person ah!

This text, created using a home video camera by Mary in response to her 'interest' in Edward's construction of his gestural 'text', is an example of recontextualisation. The children have responded to one cultural form, *WWF* fighting, and have recontextualised it into another form, that of the 'pretend fighting' in the front room. They have 'recontextualised' the violent fighting of *WWF* and have translated it into the performance above. This had gentle qualities, while being enacted using the violent language of the fighters, who speak in high-pitched voices.

The children have used the 'figured world' of *WWF* as a 'cultural resource' but then transformed the cultural resource into something else (Holland *et al.*, 2001). The response is made through the medium of gesture. It is a multimodal text as artefact, which operates as an artefact in that it 'opens up' the figured world of *WWF* (Holland *et al.*, 2001). This was then used as archive for family narratives. The video became, as a repeated, iterative family artefact, a way of seeing the past in the present, and a means of enjoying the performances the boys gave. The family returned to the video to watch it as they considered it to be funny, and it was referred to in subsequent field visits.

In the *WWF* clip, the boys used a variety of identities in practice including:

- the pretend 'identity' of the fighter with the high-pitched voice, 'old school!';
- the 'behind the scenes' orchestrator giving instructions, as when Edward says, 'Pretend' or announces a move, as in 'and then I come';
- the attacked fighter as in, 'No, don't do it!';
- the excited crowd as in 'hardcore, hardcore, hardcore!';
- The tough American fighting guy, 'you liddle person'.

In this way, they demonstrate an awareness of performance and narrativised identities within that performance. Habitus became something to be altered

Figure 8.1 A still from the home video of the WWF game

through the use of gesture, and in doing so, the 'dispositions' of the children were improvised upon (Bourdieu, 1990). The example shows how the gestural 'artefacts of the moment' are taken up as the boys' identities in practice are constructed on the video 'text' (Holland *et al.*, 2001). The 'figured world' of *WWF* is transformed through the gestural artefacts captured on video. In this example, the *WWF* game has been transformed into a home video, with the boys acting out the role of contestants and transforming those roles in the process. This becomes a space where:

> performance and text live, the inner substance to which performance is the cambium, as it were, and the crystallized text the bark. It is the grounding of performance and text in a narrative view of life . . .
>
> (Hymes, 1996: 118)

Hymes' words describe the way in which performance can work with text to form a narrative, which is returned to again and again. This video was returned to as an iterative family narrative. It could also be seen as a staged performance. The performative aspect of the process of playing this game was captured on video. Figure 8.1 shows a still from the video, in which the boys 'introduce' themselves as fighters through a small screen, which acts as the 'television' or 'frame' through which the game is enacted.

The still captures the way in which the performative identities of the boys were constructed in relation to the viewer, and the 'props' of the *WWF* arena, as seen at the top of the screen, are used to evoke the 'figured world' of *WWF*. From this moment, the boys went into action.

That's Super Mario and that's the bird

In homes, the researcher would often be given a set of texts which the child had drawn on a particular topic. Often these texts would be unsolicited, and on a particular theme. As an example, one set of texts collected over time was Fatih's *Super Mario* texts. These were drawings and narratives that were noted down when visiting Fatih's home.

Fatih's mother, Elif, was from a village in central Turkey, and came to the UK when she was a teenager for an arranged marriage. Fatih was five when the research began. Fatih was obsessed with playing *Super Mario*, and often became so keen to play, his mother regulated the game so that he did not play for too long. Super Mario involves a character, *Super Mario*, who has to go into a castle and perform a series of complicated actions, including driving away enemies and finding stars, in order to pursue this key goal. Among the 'baddies' there is a 'bomb' and a 'sonic'. The game became recontextualised into drawings which were responses to playing the game. In the first episode I came in to hear Fatih's excited discussion about his game.

> Fatih immediately began telling me about the *Super Mario* game he was playing, about the stages, the castle, the bricks, what he does. He was very excited.
>
> (From fieldnotes, 4 December 2000)

Fatih produced some drawings, which he proceeded to describe to me. Figure 8.2 shows a man pursued by a round two-legged thing, with a bird beneath it. Fatih described the drawing to me:

> That's Mario and that's the bird. That's sonic and that's the bomb the bomb's chasing him he hasn't got no head.

Fatih has constructed his text using the *Super Mario* characters, Mario, the sonic and the bomb. However, *Super Mario* does not have a bird in it, and I was interested in the appearance of the bird.

Fieldwork data and collection of texts from Fatih's home and classroom reveal a layered accretion of meaning around the concept of 'bird'. From interviews with Fatih, birds were salient, because they appeared to represent

Figure 8.2 'That's Mario and that's the bird.'

himself. 'Kus', bird, in Turkish, was used by Fatih's mother as a pet name for her children, and the family's real name was the name of a bird. The text betrays its origins in relation to both Super Mario, and the interest in 'bird'. In the drawing, Fatih's identification with Super Mario is layered alongside his identification with the 'bird'.

Fatih also produced a drawing of the castle Super Mario goes into when he attempts the game. Figure 8.3 shows the Super Mario 'castle' along with the levels, as indicated at the bottom of the drawing. Super Mario is at the top of the castle. Fatih has drawn heavily on the game's topographical layout, and his texts explore the different scenarios he is presented with. They act as an iterative form, narratives which enact the experience of playing *Super Mario*. These narratives are returned to through Fatih's own oral stories and drawings. Fatih places himself within this process, when he says that when he was young he could not do what he can do now. This is an example of a recursive narrative text that echoes the game's structure in relation to Fatih's identity in practice.

The narratives in *Super Mario* offer one particular timescale, that of the game. However, Fatih is also representing different timescales, the timescale of his identity, and the bird, a culturally infused sign which is presented

Figure 8.3 Super Mario's castle

alongside the *Super Mario* drawing. The timescale of the child growing up in a set of cultural spaces is presented alongside the game's timescale. Lemke has described how different timescales, for example home timescales, intersect with, for example, classroom timescales, and these different timescales can then be analysed (Lemke, 2000). Fatih returned to the *Super Mario* text a year later, when he described the process of playing.

This is the second place. You pass the first castle and then you go like this and play the game and you have to play the fish game when you play the fish game you go like this. When it plays the fish game it comes to the ghost house here. You play this game you play execute. The ones the first, first go like that and that. If you open the yellow piece you have to play this game. This is a team.

(From Fieldnotes, 9 December 2001)

The game becomes a series of stages on a journey. Fatih's conceptualisation of his gaming on paper both looks back to the game, and draws on the structuring and shape from the graphics in the game, but is also a re-working of the game. Fatih articulates his agency within the game's structures, with his structured sequential talk, 'if you open the yellow piece you have to play this game'. The talk was accompanied by a series of sequenced drawings. Fatih's *Super Mario* texts were moments when he articulated his own relation to the game, his understanding of the game, and they therefore both use and reflect upon cultural processes. Identity is re-fashioned in response to the process of playing the games.

Oh, I'm dead

There have been several studies of children's experience of playing games in the bedroom (Buckingham and Scanlon, 2002; Livingstone, 2002). Here, the focus is on the child's oral talk while playing. Sam, six, was from a middle-class home in North London. His mother, Parmjit, was a teacher. The example below was recorded as part of a period of the fieldwork when the tape recorder was being used, within the context of the ethnographic study. The tape reveals the way in which the relationship between the researcher and Sam was mediated through an interest in the game. The tape is of Sam playing a game called *Spyro*, in which a fantasy dragon has to go into a landscape and overcome particular challenges, or die. Part of the decision-making involved in the game was to choose a scenario. In the first example, Sam is introducing me to the game, and is also introducing the 'story' of the game.

Kate: Sam is now telling us about his PlayStation game/
Sam: /yeah that was just a story but I am playing the game.
Sam: Well this is some of the forest and there's this thing that goes around Spyro and it's a little kind of um some sort of bug, light bug or something
When you like burn a frog . . . or a sheep or something
A butterfly comes and then it eats it
And if I go, into which one shall I go into
Autumn plains or Winter tundra?

Here, Sam reifies the 'story' ('that was just a story'), turning it into an object within the game, but dismisses it to say, focusing instead on his agency, 'but

I am playing the game'. He then describes the setting which can be chosen (Autumn plains or Winter tundra), before taking action and going into his identity as player. Very quickly, the 'I' switches to become the projective identity (Gee, 2003), the 'I' of the player:

Sam: Look, look watch this . . .
Trying to squash me watch what . . .
Try and think what I have to do OK?
Kate: I think . . .
Sam: Try and have a clue and think what I have to do
(Sounds of the game being played.)
Kate: What are you actually trying to do?
Sam: Actually trying to hit him like that
Did you see that one of his life's went one of those went
Sam: Oh no I hate it when he does that
Sam: It's very . . . good this game.
Its my favourite game . . .
but I'm very good at this.
You're not going to be this good.
Cos he's the second boss. He's very . . .
He's so <u>hard.</u>
Whoops he got me
When the stars go round my head that means that I get hurt.
Wow . . .

Here, Sam's projective identity moves from commentary on his prowess, 'I'm very good at this', followed by his sudden shift to 'Whoops he got me' and his identification with his character with the stars going round in his head. Sam's demise as a character is swift and sudden:

Sam: Wow! Watch it! Whoopsi daisy
Sam: Oh I'm dead.
(long silence)
Kate: Oh dear
Sam: Four lives
Squashed.
I'm not completely dead I just lost a life.

Sam's identity shifts are complex; he moves between commentary on the game (I'm very good at this), to his nervous concern about his character (Watch it) to his entire transformation and demise (Oh, I'm dead). These meta-commentaries, like the inserted stage directions Edward and his friend placed into their re-enactment of *WWF* (and then I come) are reminiscent of the frequently observed 'play orchestration' of children engaged in socio-dramatic play (Garvey, 1984).

Finally, Sam becomes another identity, when playing as his character:

Sam: I'm gonna hit
          Oh I got me and him
          He got me and I got him
          Ooo gotta get him two more times and then he's dead meat

This 'tough guy' talk, much like the talk enacted as part of the 'play fighting', moves swiftly into Sam's demonstration of his lost teeth to me:

Sam: Hey look
          Look
          I lost my teeth the other day

The switch in identities is made possible by the way in which console games offer an embodied identity, an avatar, which is the 'I' of the player, and not the 'I' of the child. Burn described this:

> if you're playing an avatar-based game, you are likely to see the character in third person terms, as a character presented to you by the audiovisual technologies of the game; but also as a projection of yourself, your representative in the game ('avatar' is a Sanskrit word meaning the descent of a god to earth). We might expect, then, some oscillation between third person and first person references.
>
> (Burn, 2003)

The concept of an oscillation in identity is helpful in analysing the shifts in identity afforded by games. Sam oscillates between a number of different identities including:

- the 'fighting man' as in 'I'm gonna hit';
- the skilful player, as in 'I'm very good at this';
- the victim, as in 'Whoops he got me';
- the narrator, as in 'This is some of the forest';
- the child, in real life, who has lost a tooth, 'I lost my tooth'.

These identities are mediated according to where Sam is in the game, his level, and his past experience of the game. Saving the game is part of the playing process, as previous moves are saved in order to go to the next level. Playing this game allows the past to be rolled up within the present; it offers a recursive, narrative self, that is forever journeying up a series of levels, through a hazard-strewn landscape.

Conclusion

This study was a small-scale ethnographic study of three London homes. However, it offered some indications that children's use of console games extends to narrative, performance, text making, and complex identity work. Given this potential, and given the way in which these cultural resources were present in many homes, it would be possible to transfer these forms of knowledge into classroom settings. The principle of recontextualisation has possibilities for classroom practice. This crossing over has enormous peda-gogic potential, and is, I would argue, currently under-used within class-rooms. The question remains, what kind of cultural resources are drawn on in classroom settings? In this study, as with recent work by Dyson (2003), children recontextualised material they had experienced as gamers and drew upon this material when making texts. A focus on the narrative affordances of console games when constructing classroom writing tasks could prove pedagogically useful, and could lead to different forms of writing, which acknowledge level, setting and space. This kind of work with children using visual writing frames in classrooms is currently an area of interest in curriculum development (Millard, 2003).

The theoretical implications of this work are also fruitful. By linking the concept of Holland's 'figured worlds' together with Gee's concept of em-bodied identities, it was possible to understand how the children in the *WWF* video both drew on a figured world, and improvised upon it physically and discursively (Holland *et al.*, 2001; Gee, 2003). The concept of modified habitus in texts is also worth exploring, through the practices of the everyday, and then how they come to be transformed, or improvised upon, in text making (Bartlett and Holland, 2002). Gee's concept of projective identity, together with Burn's observation of identity switches in games offer fruitful analytic tools with which to explore how children draw upon the avatars presented to them when playing console games (Burn, 2003; Gee, 2003). Another theoretical grouping could be the analysis of semiotic objects to-gether with their timescales that Lemke offers, alongside Bourdieu's concept of a set of dispositions, or 'habitus' which guides the use of objects and semiotic affordances within the home (Bourdieu, 1977, 1990; Lemke, 2000).

Finally, the switches in identity observed within Fatih, Sam and Edward's text making could be tracked over time, to explore how these identity shifts could be traced across domains and sites of communicative practice. Console games offer a space in which identity can be linked to agency, and embodied action is possible in 'as if' figured worlds. Some of the children in this study lacked material resources, and yet these games offered a 'figured world', which led to textual possibilities (Holland *et al.*, 2001). Rather than see homes that offer such affordances as 'deficit', the richness and diversity of these textual possibilities could be explored and recognised.

Transcription conventions

/ indicates an overlap.
Underlined indicates emphasis
. . . Indicates a pause.
[. . .] indicates pseudonym substituted in text.

References

Bartlett, L. and Holland, D. (2002) 'Theorizing the space of literacy practices', *Ways of Knowing*, 2 (1): 10–22.
Berger, A. A. (2000) 'Arthur's computer (narrative) adventure', *TelevIZIon*, 13 (1): 40.
Bernstein, B. (1996, reprinted 2000) *Pedagogy, Symbolic Control, Identity: Theory, Research, Critique*. Oxford: Rowman and Littlefield, Publishers.
Bourdieu, P. (1977) *Outline of a Theory of Practice*. Trans. R. Nice. Cambridge: Cambridge University Press.
Bourdieu, P. (1990) *The Logic of Practice*. Trans. R. Nice. Cambridge: Polity Press.
Bourdieu, P. and Wacquant, L. (1992) *An Invitation to Reflexive Sociology*. Oxford: Polity Press.
Buckingham, D. and Scanlon, M. (2002) *Education, Entertainment and Learning in the Home*. Milton Keynes: Open University Press.
Burn, A. (2003) 'Skaters, avatars and poets: performance, identity and new media in English', *English Teaching, Practice and Critique*, 2 (2).
De Certeau, M. (1984) *The Practice of Everyday Life*. (Trans. Steven Rendell.) Berkeley: University of California Press.
Douglas, M. (1991) 'The idea of a home: a kind of space', *Social Research*, 58 (1): 287–307.
Duranti, A. and Ochs, E. (1996) 'Syncretic literacy: multiculturalism in Samoan American families', National Center for Research on Cultural Diversity and Second Language Learning. *Research Report No. 16*. University of California, Santa Cruz, USA.
Dyson, A. H. (2003) '"Welcome to the Jam": popular culture, school literacy, and the making of childhoods', *Harvard Educational Review*, 73 (3): 328–361.
Garvey, C. (1984) *Children's Talk*. London: Fontana Press.
Gee, J. P. (2003) *What Video Games Have to Teach us About Learning and Literacy*. New York: Palgrave Macmillan.
Holland, D., Lachicotte, W., Skinner, D. and Cain, C. (2001, second printing) *Identity and Agency in Cultural Worlds*. Harvard: Harvard University Press.
Hymes, D. (ed.) (1996) *Ethnography, Linguistics Narrative Inequality: Towards an Understanding of Voice*. London: Routledge.
Kress. G. (1997) *Before Writing: Rethinking the Paths to Literacy*. London: Routledge.
Kress, G. and van Leeuwen, T. (2001) *Multimodal Discourse: The Modes and Media of Contemporary Communication*. London: Cassell.
Lankshear, C. and Knobel, M. (2003) *New Literacies: Changing Knowledge and Classroom Learning*. Buckingham: Open University Press.
Lemke, J. L. (2000) 'Across the scales of time: artifacts, activities and meanings in ecosocial systems', *Mind, Culture and Activity*, 7 (4): 273–290.

Livingstone, S. (2002) *Young People and New Media: Childhood and the Changing Media Environment*. London: Sage.

Marsh, J. (2003) 'One-way traffic? Connections between literacy practices at home and in the nursery', *British Educational Research Journal*, 29 (3): 369–382.

Marsh, J. and Millard, E. (eds) (2000) *Literacy and Popular Culture: Using Children's Culture in the Classroom*. London: Paul Chapman/Sage.

Maybin, J. (2003) 'Introduction' to the Colloquium on Linguistic Ethnography at the Interface with Education, British Association of Applied Linguistics Annual Meeting, Leeds 2003.

Michaels, S. (1986) 'Narrative presentations: an oral preparation for literacy with first graders', in J. Cook-Gumperz, *The Social Construction of Literacy*. Cambridge: Cambridge University Press, pp. 94–116.

Millard, E. (2003) 'Towards a literacy of fusion: new times, new teaching and learning?', *Reading Literacy and Language*, 37 (1): 3–8.

Mitchell, J. C. (1984) 'Typicality and the case study', in R. F. Ellen (ed.) *Ethnographic Research: A Guide to General Conduct*. London: Academic Press, pp. 238–241.

Rowsell, J. (2000) 'Textbooks as traces of actors, systems, and contexts'. Unpublished PhD thesis, King's College London.

Street, B. V. and Street, J. (1991) 'The schooling of literacy', in D. Barton and R. Ivanic, *Writing in the Community*. London: Sage, pp. 143–166.

Chapter 9

'Pronto, chi parla? (Hello, who is it?)'

Telephones as artefacts and communication media in children's discourses

Julia Gillen, Beatrice Accorti Gamannossi and Catherine Ann Cameron

Cultural prevalence, academic neglect: historical, geographical and ideological imperatives on research of children and telephones

Telephones are one of the most significant, and yet one of the most academically neglected, items of popular culture in the child's world. If you take almost any study of the impact of popular culture upon children's literacy, or story-telling, or formation of gendered identity, a whole host of cultural media and artefacts are mentioned – from TV to toys, computer games to magazines – but not telephones. Marsh (2004) is a rare example of a study where mobile phones are integrated into a study of young children and popular culture.

For many years parents, carers and indeed educators have been aware of the fascination that telephones hold for children. In Italy, for example, mobile phones are pervasive in primary schools and kindergartens (for three- to five-year-olds), both within and outside the formal curriculum. For a time many primary school children were bringing their own telephones into school, as the national preoccupation with emergency calls filtered down the age groups; however, many head teachers have now prohibited this. In kindergartens, teachers have created structured activities with toy telephones to encourage explicit use of language and to cement links between the ways children learn informally at home and in the school environment. Structured pretence play settings such as 'homes' and 'offices' make copious use of toy telephones. Adults have a coordinating role in other, more closely directed play, designed to promote oracy skills through telephone-related channels, such as beakers connected with taut string. In Italy, the game known in Canada as 'cocktail party', in which a message is passed through a long chain of speakers, is called 'telefono senza fili', i.e. 'telephone without wires'.

However, despite rich practice found in many countries where the telephone is a highly salient cultural tool in the child's everyday experience, this is not necessarily manifest in academic attention. Occasionally telephones have surfaced in curricula documents; we will take another country highly penetrated by telephone use for many years, as an example. In 1996, 98.7 per cent of Canadian households had telephones (a higher prevalence than TVs at the time), and 14.1 per cent had cellular telephones (Dickinson and Sciadas, 1997). References to the telephone in curricula documents are occasional and scattered, and it is difficult to ascertain an underlying rationale for their inclusion. Mentions can appear in clusters, then disappear, even for many years. To mention two examples: in the mid 1990s, Boards of Education in Ontario specified (toy) telephone activities such as practising telephone answering routines for kindergarten through Grade Three (North York Board of Education, n.d.). In an earlier period Canadian policies relating to older children also sometimes recommended the use of telephones: a summary of a teachers' resource guide for Italian language learning prominently suggests studying cultural practices in Italy around the use of public telephones (Etobicoke Board of Education, 1985).

Turning to the research arena, there has been a historic lack of attention to the telephone in relation to children. This contrasts hugely with the situation in regard to adults: in the 1970s especially and the early 1980s there were hundreds of studies on adults by social psychologists interested in terms of the telephone's particular challenges and demands as a communicative tool or channel (see, for example, Rutter, 1987 for a bibliography). Even over the period of the past twenty years, research on telephones and children, whether conceptualised as specifically linked to oracy or otherwise, has been minor in scale. Part of the aim of this chapter is to adumbrate the very limited progress that has been made and to suggest, if in places only by implication, how and why it might be useful to extend such research.

The mid 1980s saw the beginning of a period when a small number of researchers became interested in telephones in the context of children's language and learning (that is, with the use of the telephone as a focus rather than an aid to research, e.g. for the conduct of interviews). Most of this research was located in experimental settings where adult researchers have set the agenda for study of adult–child telephone conversations (e.g. Bordeaux and Wilbrand, 1987; Holmes, 1981; Warren and Tate, 1992). In these studies the possibility of an inhibiting effect of artificiality of research design and adults' dominating linguistic behaviour is overlooked: see for example Bordeaux and Wilbrand's (1987: 264) conclusion that 'children from two to five years do not use telephone discourse imitating behaviors or discourse rules'. Holmes (1981) set up highly artificial situations for child–adult telephone conversations, and although she characterised the children's performances as generally adequate, she found that they rarely took the initiative. The approach of Warren and Tate (1992) is dominated by the assumption that children are less than competent and that their deficiencies are measurable. In contrast, the Italian semiotician Mininni (1985) made a useful small study incorporating longitudinal observations of his own child, in which he noted early capacities for spontaneous, imaginative pretence telephone talk and investigated how these capabilities were carried over into actual telephone dialogue.

This chapter is written by three researchers working both together and separately on projects on various aspects of children's telephone use in three different countries: the UK, Italy and Canada. Although from the outset we held the Vygotskyan perspective that one must consider cultural and historical factors in the deployment of mediational means, it has been surprising for us to realise the degree to which children's experiences of the mobile phone is considerably influenced according to the *country* in which they find themselves.

Our earlier studies (e.g. Cameron, Hunt and Linton, 1988; Cameron and Wang, 1999; Gillen, 2000a, 2002) have also focused positively on children's use of the telephone as an ecologically valid site for investigating recontextualised language. However, before we turn to this work in any detail, let us quickly jump to a recent observation conducted for this chapter by the relatively simple expedient of entering a preschool centre in the English Midlands, to observe whether and how telephones feature in the lives of these under-fours. Soon after one of us entered the 'under-two's room' we saw toy telephones – actually discarded, very contemporary in appearance, working mobiles – being gleefully appropriated from amongst a box of varied toys. Lewis and Braydon put the smallest such objects in their back pockets and walked away again. Shortly afterwards Megan, just one year old, picked out a phone and handed it to her friend just nine months older. He put it to his ear and began vocalising. The nearby educarer told me that he often pretends to call either his mother or Bob the Builder – a popular TV animation character who wears a mobile telephone on his belt. On the other side of the globe, an ecological study we are conducting in five diverse cultures video-captured a mountain-dwelling Peruvian toddler entertaining herself using a small candy box found in her mother's shop as a mobile phone.

Even this short glimpse tells us much about the 'new communications landscape' (Kress, 1998) in so far as our children are engaging with phones. The extent to which we are 'connected' with one another – in contact virtually wherever we are – was increased enormously over the last decade or so. Text-messaging has brought a new literacy practice into the everyday environment. Children's interest in telephones is now overwhelmingly connected with mobile telephones as opposed to old-fashioned fixed landlines; of course the latter have become commonly portable, therefore clouding the former fixed distinction, at least as perceived by children. Many of the telephones that feature in our investigation are 'toys' – that is either replicas of telephones manufactured as toys, or, even more prevalent now, discarded or even loaned 'working' phones temporarily in the child's possession and being used as toys. Even the youngest children appear to share the adult cultural evaluation that smaller size equals greater desirability.

Despite the barrage of media attention given to them, mobile phones have attracted extremely slight research attention in relation to children, although there are some understandable reasons why this is so. For example in the UK, governmental policy has generally discouraged the use of mobile phones by children aged under 16, owing to continuing worries concerning their safety (IEGMP, 2000; Department of Health *et al.*, 2000/2002). This has led to a wariness relating to including references to them in curricula documents and an official stance that although they may be useful in emergencies, caregivers might be wise to discourage this use by children under 16. One cannot be sure whether a negative stance towards telephones is wholly founded on concerns about health, or whether it might be connected to other instances of prejudice towards new technologies where adults fear loss of control (Luke and Luke, 2001; Marsh, 2004). Very recently, there have been signs of 'softening' in this, presumably in part owing to recognition of the prevalence of mobile phones. Recently, ownership among British school children stood at 17 per cent for primary and 58 per cent for secondary level (National Statistics, 2002) and given that use must be broader than ownership, it becomes less tenable to ignore them. In 2003, the government appeared to move in ways that tried to capitalise on the positive aspects of this phenomenon, while preserving their earlier cautions. For example, a Department of Education and Science website directed at parents, to support their children's learning at Key Stage 1 (age five to seven), deals with telephones as a topic in Information and Communications Technologies in the following way:

> *'I'm on the train . . .'*
> Love them or hate them, it's hard to avoid mobile phones these days. But it can be interesting to compare the ways people use mobiles with the way they use normal phones. What does your child think: do people speak differently on mobiles? Do they say different sorts of things? Do people talk longer on mobiles or on the phones in the house? Do they often talk loudly on one type of phone and more quietly on the other? Ask your child if they can think of reasons for the differences. See if your child can tell you some of the advantages and disadvantages of both types of phone. *Some researchers think that mobile phones may be unsafe, especially for children under the age of 16. As a precaution, the government has advised schools that it is best for children only to use mobile phones in an emergency.*
> (Department for Education and Science, 2003)

In this chapter, our intention is not to oppose health fears and, for example, recommend the use of mobile phones for children, but rather to recognise some of the reasons why telephones might be attractive, to explore facets of 'toy' as well as authentic phone use and also to offer some thoughts and ideas as to how paying attention to children's fascination with telephones (in safe ways) could be worthwhile for students, caregivers, educational practitioners and indeed all those involved with children's learning, considered in its broadest as well as relatively teleological senses. We aim to offer some frames for thinking about this surely unique artefact.

In her paper relating to technological affordances offered to young children (see below for discussion), Margaret Carr reminded us of Wertsch's perspective on such issues:

> Wertsch (1995, p. 56) has suggested that 'the goal of sociocultural re-search is to understand the relationship between human mental function-ing, on the one hand, and cultural, historical, and institutional setting, on the other.' He describes this relationship as being located in mediated action, where the 'mediational means' include social and discursive prac-tices as well as the materials and tools available.
>
> (Carr, 2000: p. 61)

This provides us with some useful notions with which to explore the tele-phone. Obviously, owing to the speed of technological change at times, we cannot assume as we write that the situation is now the same as when the reader considers it; however, along with Scandinavian countries, the Philip-pines, and Japan, two of our primary research locations, the UK and Italy, are societies where the mobile phone is both highly prevalent in relation to many other countries, yet also where each country is characterised by its unique telecommunications culture. If one compares these to Canada and the USA, for example, as late as the mid 1990s the mobile phone was relatively little used and therefore less likely to figure in children's worlds in North America. For although North America was at the forefront of developments in cellular technologies, its disjointed infrastructure resulted in charges to recipients as well as callers and a consequent relative reluctance to give out numbers; even business use was slow to rise in comparison with the UK (Agar, 2003). In comparison with the USA's 45 per cent figure of rate of mobile phone ownership in 2002, the UK stood at 77 per cent and Italy at an explosive 84 per cent – an extraordinary more than ten-fold leap in the latter country in six years (ITU, 2003). Canada is closer to the US than to the UK and Italy in mobile adoption with 48 per cent household ownership in 2001, a three-fold increase in five years (Statistics Canada, 2003), presumably for the infrastructural reasons mentioned earlier. Further, long-standing very high landline availabil-ity has possibly mitigated against a perceived need for mobile phone access. In complete contrast, children growing up in the Philippines will almost certainly have virtually no experience of fixed-line phones: in 2003 there were just 4 telephone lines per 100 head of population (United Nations, 2003). Yet in the latter, the use of texting on pay–as–you–go mobiles is per-haps more predominant than in any other country, being used interpersonally to keep members of Catholic extended families working away from one another in contact, and politically to organise so powerfully as to threaten governments (Agar, 2003).

Although our endeavours in this chapter certainly do not include the aim of writing definitive comparisons between the telecommunications cultures in specific countries in so far as they affect children, it is important that we remain aware how historical, geographical, economic, and ideological differences may be traced in children's activities and how these are, and may be, researched; this will remain a theme throughout our chapter.

Our approaches to research: affordances and language

As the dual concerns of our title suggest, in our research projects we investigate children's interactions with telephones in two aspects, the affordances of the telephone as a material object and a specific examination of particular issues around language elicited by this channel of communication. These two approaches are indeed entwined as will become apparent; however, this chapter focuses more on our work in the first, broader aspect.

Our first broad approach, as mentioned earlier, has benefited from consideration of Carr's (2000) concept of *affordances*. Drawing on the work of Norman (1988, 1993) and Roth, Woszcyna and Smith (1996), Carr proposes that the notion of affordances

> refers to the perceived and actual properties of an object or artifact, those properties that determine just how it could possibly be used (Norman, 1988, p. 9) and how the technology facilitates or hinders learning of various kinds . . .
>
> (Carr, 2000: 63)

Carr constructs three categories of affordance: transparency, challenge and accessibility, which we find helpful yet also inseparable; our investigations will demonstrate their links or application at various times of engagement. We shall elucidate Carr's concepts by working through them in turn in respect to our area of study: children and telephones.

Transparency

Transparency – by which we mean the sense in which a tool's function might readily be grasped – is indeed the first challenge for a young child. One of us discovered while holding a newborn niece in her family living room, that whereas she jumped in a startled way in response to certain sudden noises, she showed no such reaction to the (louder) telephone ring (Gillen, 1998). Of course hearing is developed in the womb, and she was born familiar to the sound, and therefore presumably in some degree to that one-sided witnessing of telephone calls she came quickly to experience. Carr's second affordance, challenge, is surely experienced, as the infant has to work out the relation between the object, the telephone, and the behaviour it induces. Overheard telephone talkers speak with an apparently different rhythm from that of face-to-face conversationalists: they alternate utterances with pauses not necessarily accompanied with a single clearly identifiable focus of attention. It is evident that part of their attention has been removed from their physically located environment.

To demonstrate this, the following are extracts from a researcher's observation journal of the telephone-related activities over a period of six months of her daughter, K. Just as in sociocultural studies of children's encounters with other types of media (e.g. Dyson, 2001), one can see processes of appropriation, recontextualisation and, indeed, ways in which interactions can assist children in their meaning-making processes.

Entry 1   Age 0′ 6″ (0 years 6 months)
K on floor while I was speaking on phone not paying her any attention. Suddenly I saw her smiling at me, silently, striving to make eye contact, looking a bit worried (as though I was talking to her – nobody else was there) as if my communication was perturbed.

Entry 3   Age 0′ 6″
K is sitting crying quietly when phone rings. She stops and only resumes when call is finished.

Entry 7   Age 0′ 7″
K knocked phone off table during dinner. 20 minutes later returned to it while crawling on floor, picked up receiver and played with it vocalising 2 syllable vowel [aya] unlike usual babble. She brought receiver part nearer face than rest. Shortly after repeated [aya]. Phone was taken away from her. Shortly afterwards I heard her saying [aya] while engaged in a completely different activity.

Entry 10   Age 0′ 8″
K vocalising sounds similar to 'hiya' and [aya] while I talk on the phone.

Entry 11   Age 0′ 8″
I talk on phone near K. I hand phone to Conor (brother aged 2′ 10″) who talks. She 'joins in' with great excitement, repeatedly vocalising a sound similar to 'hiya' with brief pauses.

Entry 13   Age 0′ 9″
I held K while talking on phone to G (adult friend). I said 'blow kisses' and she began to. G spoke to K – I held phone to K's ear. He said 'Hello

Kathleen,' and she chuckled in delight. Then sat still looking fascinated at phone.

Entry 14   Age 0′ 11″
I phoned Nana (K's great-grandmother). I was saying, 'yeah . . . yes . . . yeah' and suddenly noticed that K began saying (in a phase when I was silent) 'yeah . . . yes . . . yeh' – with shorter intervals between the sounds than mine.

Entry 16   Age 0′ 11″
K picks up phone holds it to ear but with outer part of the receiver to her ear and says, 'yeah (3 second pause approx.) yeh (3) uh (3) yeah (3).'
(Gillen, 2003: 483–484)

Of course it would be foolish to suggest that in her first year this child has grasped how the telephone works, as implied by the notion of transparency. However, to mention the earliest such vignette we have found in child language research, Bates, Camaioni and Volterra (1979: 12) describe watching twelve-month-old Carlotta and her mother playing with a telephone:

C. is sitting on her mother's lap, while M. shows her the telephone and pretends to talk. M. tries to press the receiver against C.'s ear and have her 'speak', but C. pushes the receiver back and presses it against her mother's ear. This is repeated several times. When M. refuses to speak into the receiver, C. bats her hand against M.'s knee, waits a moment longer, watches M.'s face, and then, uttering a sharp aspirated sound *ha.* touches her mother's mouth.

Even before she is a competent speaker herself, Carlotta knows enough about the telephone to enjoy her mother's performances and to undertake the facilitator's role, thus refusing being positioned as the junior agent in the interaction. One might fairly make a comparison with the notion of emergent literacy (Cameron, Hunt and Linton, 1996; Hall, 1987; Teale and Sulzby, 1986), and perceive a developing understanding, a partial grasp of certain aspects of a complex phenomenon that is actively pursued by the learner. We now have a good deal of evidence that in contexts where telephones are ubiquitous, many children by three years of age accurately interpret the point of communicating by telephone and demonstrate avid interest in doing so (the aspect of transparency most strongly emphasised by Carr). Pretence phones are one way in which children gain experience in using the medium, and parental prompting to communicate with supportive family members and friends at a distance aid in their apprenticeship as telephone users. Joining the community of telephone users involves recognising that in such a distanced communication context, more explicit language that effectively recontextualizes information for an interlocutor makes for more satisfying exchanges.

Challenge

K's experience with the telephone has already illustrated some aspects of challenge posed by the phone. However, 'challenge' is perhaps most usefully thought about not as an intrinsic property of the object – we have shown that to a considerable extent this can be comprehended by the second year of life – but rather as related to the cultural dispositions of the human agent. Drawing on Papert (1980), Carr (2000: 64) points out that 'familiarity and passionate interest . . . alter the perception of challenge'. Telephones are a superb example of this. Mininni (1985) contrasted his daughter's loquacity (especially, in the very early years, on a toy phone) with the bewilderment of his elderly father, 'who was only able to repeat "yes" – or, sometimes, "no" –, at nearly regular intervals when he first had to use the phone to call me . . .'. This led Mininni to propose the term 'specific dialogic subcompetence' for the learned ability to know how to manage a telephone conversation (Mininni, 1985, 1986).

A generation later, we suggest the situation is not so different with mobile phones. To generalise from statistics and our experiences in the three countries where our studies are conducted, we can contrast the attitudes towards the telephone as broadly age-related. However, it does seem clear that the telephone has become a centrally integrated part of the dispositions and activities that we might, following Bourdieu (1977), term the 'habitus' of young people. In Italy more than 94 per cent of people aged 14–24 own a mobile phone (GSMBox, 2003). Many middle-aged people make much use of mobile phones, but are more likely to struggle in circumstances such as changing products from one manufacturer to another, or not to 'bother' with functions they are less inclined to find easy to learn, such as downloading ringtones or using SMS messaging. Some older people still manage to do without them, partly, we think, because they class them in the category of 'luxury' items rather than believe them to be as essential an item in one's life as a television (cf. research into the salience of the concept of 'digital choice' as distinctive from the 'digital divide'; Oxford Internet Institute, 2003). Nonetheless, one must resist a simplistic correlation of age and positive attitudes towards the mobile. In their investigation of mobile phone ownership and attitudes among 10- and 11-year-olds in the UK, Charlton, Panting and Hannan (2002) found that a small minority had concerns over receiving threats and rude messages, but also expressed concern that non-ownership may lead to social exclusion.

Carr (2000: 64) proposes that another aspect of challenge afforded by an artefact relates to its degree of flexibility: if an (implicit) task presented to a child is too open-ended they might be overly daunted, and if too constrained it rapidly becomes boring. Here we provide an example of a Canadian primary school child choosing to grasp the opportunity, while on the telephone with her working mother, to ensure that her music home work be completed successfully:

Sophie: Um, do you know when you have . . . a staff line? . . . What . . . on top of the fifth line . . . , is that G?
Mother: Mmm, let me try to picture it in my head. E, G, B, D, . . . F, I think. I think it's F . . . .
Sophie: No, it's not on the line, it's on top of the line.
Mother: Oh above the line. Oh well that would be G for sure . . . .
Sophie: Sorry about that.
Mother: Well you probably explained it right, I just wasn't . . . keeping it straight. Yes, that's . . . definitely G . . . .
Sophie: Heh heh he he.

Sophie initiates a complex exchange with her mother (and even takes responsibility for her mother's telephone comprehension failure), supporting our assertion that the context of a telephone exchange engenders 'passionate interest' in joint meaning-making between the child and her communicative partner.

Telephones present a range of different kinds of affordances. One might press buttons to elicit various sounds (a principle behind many toy phones, however narrow or broad the range of semiotic responses). One might engage in the games; as with PC and video games, children can rapidly come to understandings of the rules and winning strategies. One might engage with multiple fascias – a phenomenon itself traceable to creative thinking on the part of a major brand, the Finnish company Nokia – to find a juncture between a substance in oversupply – woodpulp – and connections to 'fashion' within popular culture, thus expanding demand (Agar, 2003). Fascias in their bright colours reference currently popular themes such as console games, or brands with longevity, for instance from Disney. The 'flexibility' of a tool as experienced by a child, is necessarily subject to sociohistorical factors. A quick examination of the 2003 Canadian Sears' seasonal 'Wish Book' catalogue shows the prevalence of commercial theme telephones as gifts for both adults and children, touted as fun ways to keep connected.

Toy mobiles also demonstrate the importance of the mobile phone within the inter-connectedness of children's popular culture. These toys are often related to a particular theme, e.g. Barbie mobile phones. Apparently new phones are now coming online which double up as bracelets and necklaces. A popular culture researcher recently remarked to one of us that the mobile phone has replaced the ladies' powder compact of a bygone age, with which it bears a striking resemblance; such accessories are replicated too as children's toys, with even colourful infant soft-toy mobile replicas available for the infant who 'has everything'.

Accessibility

We move on to Carr's third element of affordance – accessibility. This is not an entirely discrete separation from the issues discussed in the last section, but rather lays emphasis, in Carr's terms, on 'the form of participation enabled, or afforded, by its use'. The key for telephone use is the responsibility taken by participants for engaging in effective communication. We agree with Carr in this context about the usefulness of Lave and Wenger's (1991) notion of engagement in communities of practice.

To return to the English preschool recently visited, it seems to us that even within this apparently 'enclosed' setting, where telephone contact with the outside world is definitely not part of the normal experiences of children during the school day, there were various ways in which the staff were facilitating learning characterised as peripheral participation, that is authentic use of the telephone as a means of communication. To take one such example, a child who realised they were a plate short at mealtime, was permitted to speak on the internal phone to the kitchen. The children frequently, in their pretence play, demonstrated internalised understanding of diverse emotional and practical functions for telephone communications. One child, who was in some distress when her mother left, probably was unaware of quite what was happening when later the mother phoned and simply spent a few seconds with the phone 'held out' by an educarer so that she could hear the atmosphere of contented, quiet play in the room that included her child. However, on another occasion when a child was distressed, she did speak to her mother by phone. Far more frequent, though, were pretence calls to caregivers, some of which were modelled or participated in by the educarers. Emotional comfort, particularly at painful transitional times, can be gained through actual or pretence telephone calls to a loved one (Spero, 1993; Gillen, 2000b). Similarly, in the early days of the use of voice mail, Canadian parents of kindergarten children were grateful even to connect asynchronously with teachers for reassurance regarding their child's transition to school (Cameron and Lee, 1997). However, as the plate episode indicates, the telephone is also of course employed as a timesaving shortcut: one child had recently phoned 'the Chinese' (i.e. takeaway) and ordered 'sausages and rice'.

In these ways, pretence play can be an element of accessing the behaviour of a specific 'discourse community' (Swales, 1990). Children in play access the registers of placing telephone orders (Gillen and Hall, 2001); in real life they become participants in text-messaging practices (Marsh, 2004). From this sense of utilising the telephone in becoming at least an emergent member of a specific 'discourse community' (Swales, 1990) that uses the telephone for a certain range of functions, we can further explore children's use of language on the telephone.

Our previously quoted Canadian child Sophie has a powerful 'specific dialogic sub-competence', to return to Mininni's (1985) phrase mentioned above, to detect quickly and withstand her mother's subtle attempt at pre-closing, 'So it sounds like you guys had a good day?', demonstrating her capacity to control the extent as well as the content of her participation in the conversation:

Sophie: Anyway . . .
Mother: So it sounds like you guys had a good day?
Sophie: Oh I am not done
Mother: Oh well, well you know what honey you have got to finish pretty soon because I've got to get home for supper
Sophie: And then Dad said . . .
Mother: And then we can talk in person
Sophie: And then Dad came, he said 'Look' and he said, 'it's time to go' and then it was like 'Lunch break' . . . and we had that thirty minutes to eat our lunch and go to the library cause we're all Hermione juniors. He he
Mother: Oh I see of course because Hermione would go to the library
Sophie: And then our next class was going to be care of magical creatures, no our next class is going to be brooms it's going to be with um Professor Hooch

This adroit diversionary narrative tactic, by returning to invoke a game she called 'Witchies and Wizards' that involved 'Harry Potter' characters she and her friends had enacted earlier in the day, extended the dialogue another forty-four discursive turns until she finally relented and accepted her mother's bid for phone-call closure.

Mother: I'll call you from the video store, okay?
Sophie: Okay
Mother: Okay we'll see you soon
Sophie: Bye
Mother: Bye pumpkin

Sophie, by age seven, is well launched towards becoming a full member of a community of telephone-talking practitioners.

Conclusion

Telephones, as elements of popular culture, are of course referenced in other media and thus affect children in a multitude of different directions. Apart from direct experience of telephone, children learn about telephone use in a number of other spheres including that of fictional narrative. We have already referred to Bob the Builder's frequent use of the telephone; a highly prominent precursor in UK children's popular culture was Fireman Sam.

This character, prominent in books, toys, TV cartoons and other manifestations, featured the use of the telephone in countless storylines. Two child protagonists in the UK preschool were often shown making 'emergency' calls to him, whether about minor fires or a cat getting stuck in a tree; the firefighting colleagues took such calls from landlines and telephone boxes and were occasionally shown making written records.

In Italy, the telephone also has a prominent place in children's literature and related media. For many years the most popular book for children has been a very old one called *Tales on the Phone* (*Favole al telefono,* Rodari, 1962). The background story is that a father, Signor Bianchi, had to travel a lot around Italy because of his job and every night he called home to tell his little daughter a different goodnight story, so this book is the collection of Signor Bianchi's tales. The author apologises because some of them are very short, but Signor Bianchi had to pay for his telephone calls, so some of his stories had to be short to spare money. The book is very famous and it is often used by parents to tell goodnight stories to their children, but the interesting thing is that through story-telling they give their children the sense of distanced and recontextualised communication, one of the most important characteristics of telephone conversation.

We have suggested that in order to study the affordances of the telephone one needs to consider the object an instantiation of material culture, thus only comprehensible if one considers social as well as physical properties. D'Andrade (1986, cited by Cole, 1997: 249) explains: 'Material culture – tables and chairs, buildings and cities – is the reification of human ideas in a solid medium.' The attention lavished on the external physical and gaming features of the telephone are of course related to its communicative function, itself in a period of rapid technological changes. It is likely that most readers of this chapter are very well aware of the tremendous quantity and quality of 'human ideas' organised as considerable economic resources into the development of new functions of the mobile phone, whether focused on extending its breadth of semiotic channels, e.g. with pictures and videos, its inter-relationship with use of other technologies such as satellites, the internet, and so on, or convergence with others such as personal digital assistants (PDAs). What is going on here is not a pure 'march' of technology riding on the back of scientific progress, but a complex interplay of economic, cultural and political factors coming together in commercial form (Winston, 1998). New 'inventions' are rarely as new as they are painted to be, rather they are taken up when the right constellation of factors coalesces (ibid.). One example of a communicative practice was the picture postcard; the technology had been around for some time but it was in 1902 that their accessibility and affordability in the UK suddenly tipped them into popular use, reaching almost a billion per year (Staff, 1979). Phillips (2000: 12), reaching for a simile to convey its place in popular culture, declares the postcard 'the phone call of the early part of the century'. On the other hand, phones communicating images tilted on the cusp of mass introduction for decades: public videophone boxes were installed in Berlin and Leipzig in 1936 (Burns, 1998; Fisher, 2003) – though Jews were forbidden to use them. One can look now at the website of the International Telecommunication Union (ITU, 2004) if one is in any doubt as to the influence of political bodies such as the UN on the emergence of 'technological standards' (we are not implying this is deleterious).

The practice of telephoning (whether in pretence or in actual dialogic mode) as experienced by a child in a particular time and place can best be interpreted with the aid of an appreciation of the dynamic sociohistorical interplay of forces around her as much as the technology. A child re/creates her own ways of interacting with the telephone; bringing her own personal experiences and 'passionate interest' to bear. Finnegan's (2002) perspective on communication stresses multimodality in embracing both attention to the body's movement and technological tools:

> This [is] brought home to me by my 3-year-old granddaughter's mimicking of her mother's busy striding up and down as she talks on the phone (actual telephone talking, not just pretend), made possible by the (increasingly common?) cordless phone they have in their house.
>
> (Finnegan, personal communication)

Children's interactions with the telephone are a fertile arena of study, reflecting the many semiotic potentials of this rich item of popular culture.

References

Agar, J. (2003) *Constant Touch: A Global History of The Mobile Phone.* Duxford: Icon Books.

Bates, E., Camaioni, L. and Volterra, V. (1979) A functionalist approach to the acquisition of grammar. In E. Ochs and B. Schieffelin (eds) *Developmental Pragmatics.* New York: Academic Press.

Bordeaux, M. A. and Willbrand, M. L. (1987) Pragmatic development in children's telephone discourse. *Discourse Processes*, 10 (3): 253–266.

Bourdieu, P. (1977) *Outline of a Theory of Practice*, trans. R. Nice. Cambridge: Cambridge University Press.

Burns, R. W. (1998) *Television: An International History of the Formative Years.* London: IEE.

Cameron, C. A. and Lee, K. (1997) Bridging the gap between home and school with voice-mail technology. *Journal of Educational Research*, 90: 1–9.

Cameron, C. A. and Wang, M. (1999) *Frog, where are you?* Children's narrative expression over the telephone. *Discourse Processes*, 28: 217–236.

Cameron, C. A., Hunt, A. K. and Linton, M. J. (1996) Written expression as re-contextualization: Children write in social time. *Educational Psychology Review*, 8: 125–150.

Cameron, C. A., Hunt, A. K. and Linton, M. J. (1988) Medium effects on children's story rewriting and story retelling. *First Language*, 8: 3–18.

Carr, M. (2000) Technological affordance, social practice and learning narratives in an early childhood setting. *International Journal of Technology and Design Education*, 10: 61–79.

Charlton, T., Panting, C. and Hannan, A. (2002) Mobile telephone ownership and usage among 10- and 11-year-olds: participation and exclusion. *Emotional and Behavioural Difficulties*, 7 (3): 152–163.

Cole, M. (1997) Cultural mechanisms of cognitive development In E. Amsel and K. A. Renninger (eds) *Change and Development: Issues of Theory, Method and Application*. London: Erlbaum.

Department for Education and Science (2003) Learning Journey (website for parents): key stage 1 ICT topic 'I'm on the train', accessed at: http://www.parentcentre. gov.uk/learnjourn/index_ks1.cfm?ver=graph&subject=in&subpage=teach&tip=1, created 9 February 2003 (accessed 2 September 2003).

Department of Health, Scottish Executive, The Northern Ireland Executive, The National Assembly For Wales (2000, updated 2002) *Mobile Phones and Health: Information and Advice*. Public leaflet also available at: http://www.doh.gov.uk/ mobilephones/mobilephones.htm (accessed 2 September 2003).

Dickinson, P. and Sciadas, G. (1997) Access to the information highway: The sequel. *Science and Technology Redesign Project*. Ottawa: Statistics Canada.

Dyson, A. H. (2001) 'Donkey Kong in Little Bear Country': A first grader's composing development in the media spotlight. *Elementary School Journal*, 101 (4): 417–434.

Etobicoke Board of Education (1985) *Year Two Italian: Teacher's Resource Guide*. Abstract. 00101661 Canadian Education Index (accessed 1996).

Finnegan, R. (2002) *Communicating: The Multiple Modes of Human Interconnection*. London: Routledge.

Fisher, D. (2003) Terramedia: Chronomedia website. Accessed at: http://www. terramedia.co.uk/Chronomedia/years/1936.htm#Videophone (accessed 17 September 2003).

Gillen, J. (1998) An investigation into young children's telephone discourse. Unpublished PhD thesis, Manchester Metropolitan University.

Gillen, J. (2000a) Recontextualization: the shaping of telephone discourse in play by three- and four-year-olds. *Language and Education*, 14 (4): 250–265.

Gillen, J. (2000b) Listening to young children talking on the telephone: a reassessment of Vygotsky's notion of 'egocentric speech'. *Contemporary Issues in Early Childhood*, 1 (2): 171–184.

Gillen, J. (2002) Moves in the territory of literacy? – the telephone discourse of three- and four-year-olds. *Journal of Early Childhood Literacy*, 2 (1): 21–43.

Gillen, J. (2003) 'Engaged from birth: children under two talking on telephones' in A. Schorr, B. Campbell and M. Schenk (eds) *Communication Research and Media Science in Europe*, Berlin: DeGruyter.

Gillen, J. and Hall, N. (2001) 'Hiya, Mum!' An analysis of pretence telephone play in a nursery setting. *Early Years*, 21 (1): 15–24.

GSMBox (2003) Mobile News, 19 March. Accessed at: http://it.gsmbox.com/news/ mobile_news/all/95604.gsmbox (accessed 19 September 2003).

Hall, N. (1987) *The Emergence of Literacy*. Sevenoaks: Hodder and Stoughton.

Holmes, J. (1981) Hello–goodbye: an analysis of children's telephone conversations. *Semiotica*, 37 (1–2): 91–107.

IEGMP (Independent Expert Group on Mobile Phones) (2000) Mobile Phones and Health, Report of the Group (the Stewart Report). Oxon: Secretariat IEGMP.

ITU (International Telecommunication Union) (2003) Cellular Subscribers – World. 24 April. http://www.itu.int/ITU-D/ict/statistics/at_glance/cellular01.pdf (accessed 19 September 2003).

ITU (International Telecommunication Union) (2004) website http://www.itu.int/home/ (accessed 10 May 2004).

Kress, G. (1998) Visual and verbal modes of representation in electronically mediated communication: the potentials of new forms of texts. In I. Snyder (ed.) *Page to Screen: Taking Literacy into the Electronic Era*. London: Routledge.

Lave, J. and Wenger, E. (1991) *Situated learning: Legitimate Peripheral Participation*. Cambridge: Cambridge University Press.

Luke, A. and Luke, C. (2001) Adolescence lost/childhood regained: on early intervention and the emergence of the techno-subject. *Journal of Early Childhood Literacy*, 1 (1): 91–120.

Marsh, J. (2004) The techno-literacy practices of young children. *Journal of Early Childhood Research*, 2 (1): 51–66.

Mininni, G. (1985) The ontogenesis of telephone interaction. *Rassegna Italiana di Linguistica Applicata*, 17 (2–3): 187–197.

Mininni, G. (1986) 'Pronto chi parla?' Note sullo sviluppo di una sottocompetenza dialogica. ('Hello who is it?' Notes on the development of a dialogic subcompetence). *Eta, Evolutiva*, (23) (February): 44–55.

National Statistics (2002) *Social Focus in Brief: Children in 2002*. London: National Statistics. Accessed at: http://www.statistics.gov.uk/downloads/theme_social/social_focus_in_brief/children/Social_Focus_in_Brief_Children_2002.pdf (accessed 2 September 2003).

Norman, D. (1988) *The Psychology of Everyday Things*. New York: Basic Books.

Norman, D. (1993) *Things That Make us Smart: Defending Human Attributes in the Age of the Machine*. Reading, MA: Addison-Wesley.

North York Board of Education (n.d.) Guidelines for a sequential program Kindergarten–Grade 13, *Canadian Education Index Language and Linguistics* 00105871, North York Board of Education, Ontario (accessed 1996).

Oxford Internet Institute (2003) http:// www.oii.ox.ac.uk (accessed 17 September 2003).

Papert, S. (1980) *Mindstorms*. Brighton: Harvester.

Phillips, T. (2000) *The Postcard Century*. London: Thames and Hudson.

Rodari, G. (1962) *Favole al telefono*. Torino: Einaudi.

Roth, W.-M., Woszczyna, C. and Smith, G. (1996) Affordances and constraints of computers in science education. *Journal of Research in Science Teaching*, 33 (9): 995–1017.

Rutter, D. (1987) *Communicating by Telephone*. Oxford: Pergamon Press.

Spero, M. (1993) Use of the telephone in play therapy. In C. E. Sachaefer and D. M. Cangelosi (eds) *Play Therapy Techniques*. Northvale, NJ: Jason Aronson (pp. 101–108).

Staff, F. (1979) *The picture postcard and its origins*. Cambridge: Lutterworth Press.

Statistics Canada (2003) *Canadian Statistics – Families, households and housing. Housing – selected dwelling characteristics and household equipment*. Accessed at: http://www.statcan.ca/english/Pgdb/famil09b.htm (accessed 5 December 2003).

Swales, J. (1990) *Genre analysis: English in academic and research settings.* Cambridge: Cambridge University Press.

Teale, W. H. and Sulzby, E. (eds) (1986) *Emergent literacy: Writing and reading.* Norwood, NJ: Ablex.

United Nations (2003) *Cyberschoolbus: Global teaching and learning project.* Accessed at: http://cyberschoolbus.un.org/index.asp (accessed 2 September 2003).

Warren, A. and Tate, C. (1992) Egocentrism in children's telephone conversations. In R. Diaz and L. Berk (eds) *Private Speech: From Social Interaction to Self-Regulation.* Hillsdale, NJ: LEA (pp. 245–264).

Winston, B. (1998) *Media Technology and Society – A History: From the Telegraph to the Internet.* London: Routledge.

Part III

Transformative Pedagogies

Chapter 10

Popular culture
Views of parents and educators

Leonie Arthur

There is increasing recognition that families and communities play a key role in children's literacy learning (Luke, 1993; Barton and Hamilton, 2001). Cairney (2000: 355) has pointed to the family as a 'rich source of language, knowledge and ongoing support of children's learning'. Families have a range of diverse social and cultural practices. It is the responsibility of educators to find out about children's family literacies and to provide a curriculum that validates and builds on each child's literacy competencies. The importance of home–school congruence has been highlighted in literacy research studies for some time (Breen *et al.*, 1994; Hill *et al.*, 1998). Cairney (2000) has long argued for the development of effective partnerships between homes and educational settings that enable parents and educators to engage in dialogue and to develop shared understandings. Yet many educators are not well informed about children's family contexts and many hold deficit views regarding families' social and cultural practices (Makin *et al.*, 1999).

One area where educators and parents hold differing perspectives is in the area of children's popular culture interests. While many parents view popular media culture positively, it is often banned from early childhood settings (Boyd, 1997; McNaught *et al.*, 2000). This chapter aims to compare and contrast parents' and educators' perspectives on the role of popular culture in children's literacy learning in order to encourage ongoing discussion and the development of shared understandings.

The chapter draws on a large collaborative research project conducted in 1998 and a smaller project conducted by the author in 2001. The 1998 research is from Stage 1 of the Early Literacy and Social Justice Project, conducted in New South Wales, Australia. Stage 1 of this project involved the mapping of existing literacy practices in 79 early childhood settings (long day care centres and preschools) situated in low socio-economic areas and is reported in full in Makin *et al.* (1999). The data collection methods consisted of observations of the literacy learning environments in each early childhood setting, structured interviews with two educators from each setting and a total of nine focus group discussions with parents. The educators interviewed included staff with a range of qualifications and experiences. The parent focus groups included one Aboriginal group and one bilingual group where the parents' home language was used. Bilingual parents were also present in the other groups.

The 2001 research focused on the role of popular culture in children's literacy learning. Data were collected in three early childhood settings (two long day care centres and one preschool) in areas of socio-economic diversity. These were settings where educators were interested in literacy and open to the inclusion of children's interests in the curriculum. One of the settings catered predominantly for Aboriginal children and families, the other settings included children from a range of cultural and language backgrounds. Data collection methods included semi-structured interviews with parents of children aged from birth to five years and with educators working with children in this age group. Across the three settings, 12 parents and 12 educators were interviewed. Participants reflected the diverse demographics of the settings and included two bilingual parents, four Aboriginal parents, two bilingual educators and two Aboriginal educators. The 24 participants also included two male educators and two fathers.

Parents' perceptions of the role of popular media culture in their children's lives

Analysis of data from parents interviewed in 1998 and 2001 pointed to the significant role of popular media culture in children's lives. Technologies were specifically highlighted by 71 per cent of parents in the 1998 study when asked about their children's literacy learning. All of the parents involved in the 2001 study commented that viewing television and videos were a notable part of their children's daily experiences.

Parents in the 2001 study all stated that children had television programmes and movies that they were passionate about and that these popular media interests extended to a range of texts and toys. In some families children played computer games and visited internet sites connected to licensed characters. In other families children had hand-held computer games or books and magazines related to their favourite movies and television programmes. Many children also had toys connected to their favourite characters or used existing toys and props to reenact familiar narratives, as was the case in the studies reported in Marsh's chapter in this book. Some parents also noted that children's drawings were influenced by their popular culture interests.

Many of the parents interviewed in 2001 stated that children were aware of and sometimes watched some adult programmes – sometimes with parents or older family members and sometimes independently. These included television programmes such as wrestling, football, music video clips, adult movies and reality shows. In some families the television or a video was on for a substantial part of the day and children moved in and out of playing and viewing. Children's media consumption often took place alongside other

experiences. A number of parents commented that children were simultaneously watching the television or a video and drawing, writing or reading
so that viewing was in addition to, rather than instead of, other literacy
activities. One parent commented of her two children:

> Sometimes they are watching TV and writing at the same time. Some-
> times they are watching TV and reading books. But then I come in and
> the TV is turned off – although they protest and say they want it on. Its
> like background noise or music.
>
> (Parent, 2001)

Several parents commented that children were aware of popular children's
television programmes even when they did not watch them at home. One
parent stated of her children:

> But they know it all even if we don't watch it – like the Power Puff
> girls. I can't follow it much – it's just the good girls get the bad guys.
> They like it because of their peer group. They are very influenced by
> that.
>
> (Parent, 2001)

Another parent interviewed in 2001 stated that her child 'looks at some
programmes like *Digimon* because other kids talk about it'. As Luke (1999)
has argued, children's popular media culture is part of children's social repertoire and generates cultural capital that is valued within children's peer groups.
Popular media culture creates a shared frame of reference that children draw
on in their play.

In a globalised and corporate world, there is increasing intertextuality.
Products marketed to children include toys, games, magazines, books, computer and video games related to popular television programmes and movies,
as well as clothing, food, bags, and lunchboxes emblazoned with licensed
characters. As a result, popular culture icons penetrate every aspect of children's
lives (Buckingham and Scanlon, 2001). Thus, even when children do not
have access to the latest electronic and digital media and the associated toys,
popular culture characters and narratives are part of their social worlds and
'funds of knowledge' (Moll *et al.*, 1992).

A number of parents interviewed in 2001 also reported that their children
had experiences with digital technologies such as hand-held computer games,
games consoles and computers. Some children accessed websites at home
connected to their favourite media programs and characters such as *Rugrats*,
or *Bananas in Pyjamas*, or toys such as Lego and Matchbox. Other children
played with computer software that included popular media characters such
as Madeline and Winnie the Pooh. Where children did not have access to
computers at home, parents often reported on their children's experiences

with hand-held computer games and games consoles. In addition, parents noted that children accessed screen technologies at friends' homes, at the library and at shopping centres where there were frequently games consoles.

The data collected in 1998 and 2001 demonstrated that parents have a wealth of knowledge about their children's experiences and interests. Yet interviews with educators in 1998 indicated that the majority of educators were not aware of the learning that was occurring in children's homes and communities, with 30 per cent of educators stating that they were not aware of what goes on at home (Makin *et al.*, 1999). In addition, 20 per cent of educators held deficit views of family literacy practices that were dismissive of diverse experiences. Both the 1998 and the 2001 studies indicated that when educators held broad definitions of literacy and were aware of and valued children's family and community experiences, there was a substantial degree of congruence between homes and early childhood educational settings. In these settings, children were provided with experiences that validated their home and community literacies.

Parents' perceptions of the links between popular media culture and literacy learning

Most parents involved in both the 1998 and 2001 studies believed that experiences with screen technologies and popular media culture assisted their children's language and literacy learning. Parents in both these studies held broad views of literacy that reflected understandings of literacy as social practice and recognised the range of texts that children interacted with as part of everyday life.

Parent focus group data from Stage 1 of the Early Literacy and Social Justice Project highlighted the significant role of technology – including television, videos and computer games – in children's literacy learning (Makin *et al.*, 1999). Children were said to be very aware of and interested in popular culture texts and images. Parents from bilingual backgrounds particularly noted the role of technology for children learning English as a second language. One parent commented that:

> 'I get K. to play on some of the computer games . . . from there he learned how to pronounce it (English) right.'
>
> (Makin *et al.*, 1999: 80)

Kenner's chapter in this book also highlights the role of popular culture and technologies in bilingual children's social and cultural practices.

Several parents interviewed in 2001 also commented on their children's interest in computers. These parents saw computers as a valuable literacy learning tool. One parent made the following comment about her four-year-old son's computer use:

It's good. He explores and says 'I found this new game!' The system is so interactive. It provides him with an incentive to learn.

(Parent, 2001)

The same parent stated that one of the internet sites her son visited was Lego (www.lego.com). She observed that:

He can't read but he makes up words for the Lego characters and . . . he uses the Lego site to make the same thing another day with bricks.

This parent's comments highlight the way that the interactive and multimodal nature of online texts enables children to easily access and gain meaning. They also demonstrate the literacy learning potential of the integration of play and technology. Bilingual parents in the 2001 study also noted that technology assisted the maintenance and development of the home language. One child from a Spanish-English bilingual family engaged with Spanish internet sites and CD-ROMs as well as sites in English. His mother noted that these experiences provided her child with incentives to use Spanish.

The proliferation of consumer texts connected to popular media culture and the increasing intertextuality assist children to make meaning with a range of everyday texts. A total of 76 per cent of parents in the 1998 study identified the community as a site of their children's literacy learning. In particular, they observed that their children were able to read signs such as 'McDonalds' and knew how to find specific items in the supermarket (Makin et al., 1999). All of the parents interviewed in 2001 observed that their children were able to read print and logos connected to their favourite popular media culture. In some cases this was on signs in shopping centres, in other cases on clothing, in catalogues, books or magazines or on screens. The familiarity of these texts assists children with meaning making. As one parent noted:

We buy her the *ABC Playtime* magazine/comic, which she 'reads' herself from cover to cover, over and over again.

(Parent, 2001)

Parents involved in the 2001 study also observed that their children were able to join in the dialogue and sing the songs from their favourite videos. Children were also reported to be able to retell and reenact familiar videos, demonstrating understandings of narrative structure and dialogue. The parent of a two-year-old boy, for example, commented:

He plays out the videos (such as *Dinosaur*). He role-plays with (plastic) dinosaurs using lines from the videos. He knows them off by heart.

(Parent, 2001)

Parents' comments indicated that many children are highly engaged in and knowledgeable about the characters, narratives and dialogues associated with their popular media culture interests and often utilise and innovate on them in their play. In some cases, this involved snippets of dialogue drawn from repeated viewings of a video, in other cases it was the theme song of a favourite program or an advertising jingle. Children were observed by parents to demonstrate authorial agency by reinventing narratives and characters and innovating on known songs and rhymes. One parent, for example, noted that her four-year-old son composed his own songs, using the tune and rhyming structure of a familiar song from a television program or advertisement and creating his own words.

Parents were generally very supportive of children's popular culture interests and associated experiences. As one parent wrote in an email communication:

> We feel that Pop culture is an important and inevitable part of life as a child (and adult), therefore should not be made out to be the baddy in the eyes of our child(ren). It gives L. an easy escape and fantasy world away from daily life, which is the role of pop culture (?).
>
> (Parent, 2001)

Discussions with parents involved in the 2001 study indicated that although children's interest in popular culture was generally viewed in a positive light, it nevertheless presented a number of tensions and challenges, which are explored further in the following section.

Parents' concerns regarding children's engagement with popular media culture

Parents interviewed in 2001 expressed a number of concerns regarding the impact of popular media culture on their children's identities and worldviews. Concerns predominantly focused on consumerism and, to a lesser extent, on issues of ideologies.

Most of the parents stated that they often felt under pressure to purchase the latest toy, to take their child to fast food restaurants in order to get the latest promotional offer, and to buy their children clothing emblazoned with licensed characters and logos. One parent expressed her concerns about children's popular media culture as:

> It's the cost. Like Barbie − all the clothes for Barbie, the accessories, the other stuff like the pencil cases. I feel like a sucker if I buy into all that . . . I hate the whole marketing of it.
>
> (Parent, 2001)

Another parent commented that her child always wanted what he saw on television, including special brands or food promoted through connections with popular media characters. Popular media culture positions children as consumers. Seiter (1993) argued that consumer culture has created a separate peer culture and market so that children are 'sold separately'. There is a blurring of the boundaries between information, entertainment and advertisement (Buckingham, 2000) and, as noted by Kenway and Bullen (2001), the resulting 'consumer-media-culture' is particularly prevalent in children's television and on internet sites aimed at children. Resources connected to popular media culture are 'sold' not only to children, but also to parents who want to provide the 'best' for their children.

There is increasing recognition of the importance of the early years and the learning that occurs at home. Parents are encouraged by governments and educators to provide their children with educational experiences at home. Buckingham and Scanlon (2001) have outlined the emergence of 'edutainment' as publishers of digital and paper-based texts exploit parents' anxieties about their children's learning by promoting resources to parents that are said to be both educational and entertaining. One example of these resources is children's magazines such as *ABC Playtime* and *Bananas in Pyjamas* that are connected to children's television (see Carrington's Chapter 2 in this book for an analysis of these magazines). Buckingham and Scanlon (2001: 282–283) argued that these magazines:

> Address parents as pedagogues, who should be responsible for ensuring that their children acquire the 'skills' they will need for educational success; and yet they also address parents and children as consumers, as active participants in a global multi-media market.

A number of parents, particularly those with children from diverse racial backgrounds, were particularly critical of the limited cultural representations in the media. One parent stated:

> I don't get videos about princesses – I hate those. I don't like the stereotypes. And especially because she (daughter) is dark I don't like all the blonde-haired, blue-eyed princesses.
>
> (Parent, 2001)

The work of Giroux (1997) and more recently Tobin (2000) highlights the negative portrayal of indigenous peoples and the stereotyping of non-standard dialects in popular media culture. In the Disney movie *Aladdin*, for example, the 'baddies' are given urban, black, Latino accents and the goodies upper-class British accents and standard dialects (Giroux, 1997). Tobin's interviews with 6–12-year-olds point to the dangers of these stereotypes, particularly 'when the minority-group child, identifying with the aggressor, is seduced by the racial semiotics of a film as seeing people who look like her as ugly or evil' (Tobin, 2000: 55). Other issues that were raised by some parents related

to the ways that popular media present limited roles for women and reproduce discourses of violence as the preferred means of problem-solving. There
were differences in parents' responses to these issues based on gender and
class.

Mothers from middle-class, tertiary-educated backgrounds carefully monitored and regulated their children's popular media consumption and discussed
ideological as well as commercial aspects of the media with their children
on a regular basis. All of the middle-class tertiary-educated mothers raised
the gendered roles presented in the media and the objectification of women
as a concern whereas this was not raised as an issue by other parents. These
mothers made comments such as:

> There's still lots of stereotypes in it (*Little Mermaid*) – she lost her voice,
> got the man.

> I've started to watch the commercials with the kids. Like the 'Give your
> kids Chicken Tonight and be a good mum'. But how do you know she's
> a good mum. What makes a good mum?
>
> (Parents, 2001)

Popular icons such as Barbie and Superman do impact on children's subjectivities and worldviews, as well as on the way they express themselves and relate
to each other. Analysis of popular media culture (see, for example, Giroux,
1997) indicates that in most cases, males have agency and power while female
characters present narrowly defined gender roles that 'privilege romantic
relations over collegial ones between women and men' (Dyson, 1997: 178).

Gendered roles in popular media are also an issue for boys. The reality is
that male characters are more numerous than female characters in children's
television programs as well as computer and video games. For instance, 30
per cent of video games analysed by Dietz in 1998 (as reported in Anderson
and Cavallaro, 2002) did not include female characters at all and only 15 per
cent showed females as action characters or heroes. Male characters show
more bravery, ingenuity, competence and power and are more independent
and assertive than female characters (Anderson and Cavallaro, 2002). Many
boys – particularly boys from working-class backgrounds and from diverse
cultural backgrounds – are attracted to these characters and draw on them in
their play and interactions (Dyson, 1997; Marsh, 2000; Urquhart, 1996). They
engage in role play as their favourite characters; exchange and evaluate television programs, videos and computer games; and collect, swap and play with
trading cards and related toys (Urquhart, 1996). Urquart also suggests that
boys read and use popular culture to find out about the world and to pursue
competency and agency.

The middle-class mothers were particularly critical of cartoons and action
heroes and did not allow their children to watch these genres, as they believed

they promoted violence. However, working-class parents, and fathers, did not express concerns about these issues. The middle-class mothers made comments such as:

> Sometimes we watch the video (music) hits but I have to censor them.

> The TV is monitored. I don't let them watch anything with guns. If I don't like it. I can't bear it. And you have to think about how age appropriate it is.

> I don't let her (daughter) watch anything on commercial stations – there are too many stereotypes.
>
> (Parents, 2001)

Dyson (1997), Seiter (1999) and Buckingham (2000) have all suggested that there are many class-related assumptions, beliefs and values associated with the media, with middle-class families being much more likely to perceive children's programs as 'too violent' than working-class families. Seiter's research (1999: 3) has particularly highlighted the tendency for mothers and female educators of boys to 'often battle to keep little boys away from violent cartoons, such as *Mighty Morphin Power Rangers*, and forbidden video games, such as *Street Fighter*'.

While middle-class mothers carefully monitored their children's media exposure and engaged them in critiques of dominant ideologies and consumerism, they expressed concerns that the child's father was much more permissive and more consumer-oriented than they were. Comments included:

> My husband lets the kids (three-year-old girl and one-year-old boy) watch video hits. He doesn't see anything wrong with them.

> My husband spends lots of time playing computer games. And the Game Boy is his. So he isn't worried when G. (son) spends a lot of time with electronic games.

> He (my husband) loves that – all the sports gear, the labels . . . Even when it is pointed out about the exploitation, my husband still wants it. It's important when mixing in his social circle. (He says) 'I have to have it.'
>
> (Parents, 2001)

One reason for these differences may be that the advice generally given to mothers in parenting magazines, in the popular media and in educational settings, focuses on the negative aspects of popular media culture and encourages mothers to monitor and control children's media consumption (Seiter, 1999). There is much discussion in the news media and popular discourse focused on the negative effects of popular media on children. These theories, what Seiter (1999) calls 'lay theories', focus particularly on the ways that popular media are believed to cause violent behaviour and are situated within a developmentalist view of children as morally pure individuals easily corrupted by the media. Arguments about the negative impact of the media on children present simplified, linear perspectives on media effects, view learners in isolation from their social context, and perceive children to be innocent and passive beings manipulated by the media and unable to engage in resistant readings of texts (Tobin, 2000).

The influence of postmodernism and the movement reconceptualising early childhood (see, for example, Dahlberg, Moss and Pence, 1999) have challenged traditional images of children as innocent and naïve beings who passively receive and reproduce knowledge. Instead, children are perceived as competent social beings actively engaged in the co-construction of meanings, cultures and identities (Malaguzzi, 1993; James, Jenks and Prout, 1998). This view of children challenges educators to find out about and work with children's competencies and passions. Many children's passions and literacy expertise are associated with popular media culture, yet many educators are not aware of or are dismissive of these aspects of children's social worlds (Makin et al., 1999; McNaught et al., 2000).

Educators' perceptions of the role of popular media culture in children's lives

Many educators interviewed in 1998 for the Early Literacy and Social Justice Project were highly critical of the role of technologies in children's lives and did not acknowledge the positive role of popular media and digital culture in children's literacy learning (Makin et al., 1999). While parents viewed technology as a positive learning tool, many staff expressed concerns about the negative impact of television, video and computers on children's learning.

Observations in early childhood educational settings and data from interviews conducted with educators in 1998 indicated that technology and popular culture were conspicuously absent in most early childhood settings. While many settings had televisions and videos, these were generally not utilised as literacy learning tools. Many staff expressed concerns about the extent of time children spent in front of the television at home, and the quality of language input from screen technologies (Makin et al., 1999). In one early childhood setting, where the majority of the children were from bilingual backgrounds, staff privileged book-based experiences in English and held deficit views about children's home and community experiences. Staff comments included:

> But a lot of them they watch TV and that's only where they get their words from and like they're reading from commercials and McDonald's, they all know the McDonald's sign.
>
> (Makin et al., 1999: 102)

Maybe a handful out of all the kids in my class . . . might be read to every night or not at all. And usually what they get here is all that they get.

(Makin *et al.*, 1999: 98)

The parents at this setting, on the other hand, viewed technologies as an important source of learning, particularly for English as a second language. One parent commented:

And when she (the daughter) reached one year, she used to like to watch television, *Playschool*. She used to sing, she was only one. She used to know all the words, and then by two she knew the ABC just by watching *Sesame Street* and *Playschool*.

(Makin *et al.*, 1999: 101–102)

Educators interviewed for the Early Literacy and Social Justice Project generally held deficit views of children's experiences with popular media culture (Makin *et al.*, 1999). What has 'cultural capital' (Bourdieu, 1977) in educational settings is experience with books and to a lesser extent computers – not Saturday cartoons, videos, hand-held computer games or popular magazines (Giroux, 1994; Dyson, 1997; Seiter, 1999). This means that for many children there are discontinuities between home and school literacy practices, making it difficult for them to take up school literacies (Hill *et al.*, 1998).

Researchers such as Comber (2000), Graff (2001) and Freiberg (2001) have argued that the dominant book-based literacy practices of the English-speaking middle classes are held up as the norm in schools. Children with diverse literacy experiences are then judged to have deficits which educational settings work to overcome, thus narrowing the range of literacies (Carrington, 2001). These practices marginalise students whose experiences are with languages other than English and with electronic and digital texts. The polarisation of 'high culture'/ 'low culture' (Luke, 1997) also works to exclude popular culture from educational settings and positions many children as outsiders.

Some educators, however, are more attuned to children's family and community literacy practices and interests. All of the educators interviewed in 2001 recognised the significance of popular culture in children's lives and its positive learning potential. This may have been due to an increased focus on multi-literacies in early childhood pedagogy as well as conference presentations, workshops and professional development materials produced as part of the Early Literacy and Social Justice Project (see Jones Diaz *et al.*, 2001).

One educator working with two- and three-year-olds stated that popular culture is 'very prominent' in children's lives – that '60–70 per cent of what they have at home is popular culture'. She commented that the shared interest in popular culture created a 'real camaraderie' amongst the children. Another educator agreed that popular culture has a 'big impact' on children and for many is 'the main part of their lives'.

Where educators are open to broad views of literacy that encompass children's experiences with technologies and popular culture, they are able to connect to children's interests and to validate their strengths. As one educator commented:

> It is interesting when you talk to the children. The children bring so much knowledge we can use if we can tap into it. It's amazing when you ask how much they can tell you. It's good for their language. They can give you lots of descriptive language, lots of detail about whatever it is they are interested in. And that has a powerful impact on their peers.
>
> (Educator, 2001)

Educators interviewed in 2001, although positive about the potential of popular culture for children's learning, raised a number of concerns. These are explored in the following section and compared and contrasted with the views of parents.

Educators' concerns regarding children's engagement with popular media culture

Educators raised similar ideological issues to those of parents, although they did not generally express concerns about consumerism and they were more critical of the stereotypical gender and racial roles available in popular culture than the issue of violence. One of the key ideological tensions reported by educators was the negative portrayal of women and limited male and female roles in popular media culture. Educators commented that children often identify with characters such as Batman, Barbie, and Action Man and that these characters and the associated narratives are frequently the subject of children's play and conversation. These characters were perceived by many educators involved in the study to be 'working to polarise male and female roles' – as one educator put it – and these limited gender roles were frequently reflected in children's play. In particular, popular culture was perceived by many educators to exert a negative influence on boys' identity formation and behaviours, with boys observed engaging in warrior-like hero actions in the playground, or in mock wrestling matches. Whereas middle-class parents were concerned with this type of behaviour as 'violence', educators were more concerned with the gendered identities available to children in the popular media.

Most educators were also concerned about the exclusion or stereotyping of people of colour in children's media and the impact on children's cultural and linguistic identities, particularly for children from diverse backgrounds. Concerns were expressed that mass-produced and globalised popular culture presents limited representation of cultural and linguistic diversity and stereotypical racial images and works to legitimise inequalities. As one educator suggested:

> A lot of the stuff on TV and videos is American. What impact does that have on these kids? It impacts on their language and their culture. They pick up the American sayings from TV. You can look at it in terms of culture. What view of the world are they (Aboriginal children) getting from Disney videos? It's not good if they only get a Disney view of the world.
>
> (Educator, 2001)

The role of popular media culture in promoting violence as the predominant method for solving problems and its influence on boys' identity construction was also raised by some educators. One educator reflected on her views towards popular media culture and recognised that she held differing views depending on the perceived levels of violence. She stated:

> Last year the girls were into Barbie and Hi–5. I thought they were okay. But I say no to *Ninja Turtles*. No *Ninja Turtles*. No *Pokémon*. All that fighting.
>
> (Educator, 2001)

Texts of popular culture do frequently reflect dominant and oppressive discourses of racism, gendered roles, violence and consumerism that limit the possible identities available to children. Due to these concerns, there is much ongoing debate amongst educators about the inclusion of children's popular media culture in educational settings. In 1997, Boyd reported that educators in the United States 'have become increasingly vocal opponents of superhero play' (p. 23). Research conducted for Stage 2 of the Early Literacy and Social Justice Project also found strong resistance to the inclusion of popular culture from many educators (McNaught *et al.*, 2001). Carlsson–Paige and Levin's (1990, 1995) analysis of the reasons educators feel uncomfortable with children's superhero play includes concerns about violence, noise and aggressive behaviours. They argue for the inclusion of adult-mediated superhero play as a way of enabling children to work through issues in their play.

Educators in 2001 had all engaged in critical reflection on their responses to children's popular media culture. They had all moved from positions of banning popular culture and superhero play to positions of integrating it into the curriculum. As one educator stated:

> Banning doesn't work. I don't think there should be censorship. This won't stop them from being interested. . . . If you include it (popular culture) they can work through with it.
>
> (Educator, 2001)

Increased dialogue between home and early childhood educational settings

Increased dialogue and collaborative partnerships between educators, children and families can open up new possibilities for culturally responsive literacy-enriched play that connects to children's interests and expertise. One of the early childhood educational settings involved in the 2001 study incorporated children's popular media culture interests into the curriculum in ways that connected the curriculum to children's lived experiences.

This setting had a group of children (mainly four-year-old boys) who were interested in *Pokémon*. The staff had tried banning *Pokémon* and the associated artefacts (such as cards and toys) but found that this just 'drove the craze underground'. Educators expressed concerns about the equity issues of some children having large numbers of cards and others having none, as well as issues of aggressive behaviours and gendered roles. However, rather than banning the cards, they decided to address the issues by including *Pokémon* in the program. They bought *Pokémon* cards for the centre, included toy catalogues and children's magazines (such as *Disney Magazine* and *K-Zone*) alongside other texts and added birthday cards and wrapping paper featuring *Pokémon* characters to the collage area.

This encouraged the boys who had been observed to be reluctant readers and writers to become actively engaged in literacy experiences. When magazines, books and wrapping paper that related to popular media culture were added to the drawing table, many children initiated extended periods of talking, drawing, cutting and writing that related to the characters and narratives. Most of the children were able to independently read familiar text such as '*Pokémon*: gotta catch 'em all!' and were able to read the names of each of the *Pokémon* characters (even though the print was very small and the text was complex). When *Pokémon* expertise was validated in the setting, other children also began to share their popular culture interests. One girl, for example, expressed her interest in *The Little Mermaid* by repeatedly drawing characters and using them to retell the narrative.

The children who were most interested in the experiences connected to popular media culture were the children (mostly boys) who educators reported were least likely to engage with more traditional print resources. With the addition of popular culture to the literacy materials, these 'reluctant readers and writers' were observed to frequently engage in collaborative experiences where they could draw on their cultural capital to extend their shared understandings and demonstrate their literacy expertise. They looked at magazines, catalogues and *Pokémon* cards together, sharing knowledge and scaffolding each other's reading of the images and text. They talked with each other and shared information about characters and narratives as they cut out, drew and wrote about their favourite popular media characters. They negotiated roles and reenacted and innovated on familiar narratives in dramatic play. They initiated card games using the trading cards, establishing their own rules.

The three- and four-year-old boys were highly interested in drawing, cutting and writing when it connected to their popular culture interests. These were boys who educators reported did not generally show an interest in literacy experiences – and who frequently stated that they 'can't cut' and 'can't write' – yet they created detailed drawings, cut around the images and text on wrapping paper, and engaged in reading and writing of characters' names. The introduction of popular culture texts and artefacts thus acted as a means of including a range of children's experiences in the program and provided a pathway to literacy for many children.

The inclusion of children's popular media culture also opened up dialogue between educators and children about issues of gender and conflict resolution. As one educator reflected:

> Are we prepared to question why we don't like it (popular culture)? It's easier to say 'no'. But we need to think 'what can we learn?' I had zero tolerance in the past to popular culture. I believed that it is not best for children. And that we haven't got time to include popular culture. But really it's easy to add in. You can look at the issues like stereotypes and fighting in the context of children's play, not as an extra thing you have to do. It's better to talk about it.

Early childhood programs such as this one, that connect to children's lived experiences by incorporating children's social worlds and cultural capital, acknowledge children as active agents who process and construct meanings and identities. The inclusion of popular media culture in early childhood educational settings taps into children's interests and pleasures and respects children's agency.

There are dangers, however, in simply including children's popular media culture in the curriculum and expecting children to mediate their own understandings. There is an important role for educators in working with children to understand the relationship between texts and children's social worlds. It is vital that children learn to critique the media and consumer culture and to resist the dominant discourses they embody. Effective critical media pedagogy encourages children to express their pleasure and ideas while at the same time examining multiple perspectives (Alvermann and Heron, 2001).

The integration of children's popular culture narratives and texts in early childhood programs opens up possibilities for dialogue and for educator-mediated critique of a range of texts and discourses. It is essential when engaging in critical literacy that educators do not take away children's pleasure in texts of popular culture nor impose their own views on children (Comber, 1994; Dyson, 1997; Alvermann and Heron, 2001). Educators can work with children's interests to examine the ways that readers are constructed by the dominant culture and construct pathways through the hegemonic discourses presented in a range of texts, including texts of popular culture (Coles and Hall, 2002). Children and educators can critically examine the ways that hegemonic discourses are perpetuated in texts of popular culture, engage in resistant readings and produce counter-hegemonic texts (Marsh and Millard, 2000). Through the collaborative deconstruction of dominant narratives and oppressive practices, educators and children can work towards 'achieving a more egalitarian and inclusive society' (Morrell, 2002: 72).

Conclusion

Research for the Early Literacy and Social Justice Project highlighted the importance of congruence between children's home experiences with literacy and the literacy experiences of the early childhood educational setting (Makin *et al.*, 1999). Coles and Hall (2002) have similarly argued that educators must build links between children's literacy experiences at home and those of the school if we are to foster readers who are able to engage with a range of texts and at the same time have a sense of their own agency. When educators are knowledgeable about children's family and community interests and expertise, they are able to incorporate them into the early childhood program and thereby provide a meaningful program that includes the lived experiences of the child, their family and their community (Arthur *et al.*, 2003).

References

Alvermann, D. and Heron, A. (2001) Literacy identity work: Playing to learn with popular media, *Journal of Adolescent and Adult Literacy*, 45 (2): 118–122.

Anderson, K. and Cavallaro, D. (2002) Parents or pop culture: Children's heroes and role models, *Childhood Education*, Spring, 161–168.

Arthur, L., Beecher, B., Harrison, C. and Morandini, C. (2003) Sharing the lived experiences of children, *Australian Journal of Early Childhood*, 28 (2): 8–13.

Barton, D. and Hamilton, M. (2001) Literacy practices, in D. Barton, M. Hamilton and R. Ivanič (eds) *Situated Literacies: Reading and Writing in Context*. London and New York: Routledge, pp. 7–15.

Bourdieu, P. (1977) *Outline of a Theory of Practice*. Cambridge: Cambridge University Press.

Boyd, B. (1997) Teacher response to superhero play: To ban or not to ban? *Childhood Education*, Fall, pp. 23–28.

Breen, M., Louden, W., Barratt-Pugh, C., Rivalland, J., Rohl, M., Rhydwen, M., Lloyd, S. and Carr, T. (1994) *Literacy in its Place: An Investigation of Literacy Practices in Urban and Rural Communities*. Canberra: Department of Employment, Education and Training.

Buckingham, D. (1993) *Children Talking Television: The Making of Television Literacy*. New York: Falmer.

Buckingham, D. (2000) *After the Death of Childhood.* Cambridge: Polity Press in assoc. with Blackwell Publishers.

Buckingham, D. and Scanlon, M. (2001) Parental pedagogies: An analysis of British 'edutainment' magazines for young children, *Journal of Early Childhood Literacy,* 1 (1): 281–299.

Cairney, T. (2000) Family literacy: Challenges for early education, in J. Hayden (ed.) *Early Childhood Landscapes: Cross national perspectives on empowerment and restraint* (pp. 355–367). New York: Peter Larg.

Carlsson-Paige, N. and Levin, D. (1990) *Who's Calling the Shots? How to Respond Effectively to Children's Fascination with War Play and War Toys.* Philadelphia, PA: New Society Publishers.

Carlsson-Paige, N. and Levin, D. (1995) Can teachers resolve the war-play dilemma? *Young Children,* 50 (3): 62–63.

Carrington, V. (2001) Literacy instruction: A Bourdieuian perspective, in P. Freebody, S. Muspratt and B. Dwyer (eds) *Difference, Silence and Textual Practice: Studies in Critical Literacy.* Cresskill, NJ: Hampton Press, pp. 265–285.

Coles, M. and Hall, C. (2002) Gendered readings: Learning from children's reading choices, *Journal of Research in Reading,* 25 (1): 96–108.

Comber, B. (1994) Critical literacy: An introduction to Australian debates and perspectives, *Journal of Curriculum Studies,* 26 (6): 658–668.

Comber, B. (2000) What *really* counts in early literacy lessons, *Language Arts,* 78 (1): 39–49.

Dahlberg, G., Moss, P. and Pence, A. (1999) *Beyond Quality in Early Childhood Education and Care: Postmodern Perspectives.* London: Falmer Press.

Dyson, A. H. (1997) *Writing Superheroes: Contemporary Childhood, Popular Culture and Classroom Literacy.* New York: Teachers College Press.

Freiberg, J. (2001) Criteria-based assessment in senior high school English: Transcending the textual in search of the magical, in P. Freebody, S. Muspratt and B. Dwyer (eds) *Difference, Silence and Textual Practice: Studies in Critical Literacy.* Cresskill, NJ: Hampton Press, pp. 287–322.

Giroux, H. (1994) *Disturbing Pleasures: Learning Popular Culture.* New York: Routledge.

Giroux, H. (1997) Are Disney movies good for your kids?, in S. Steinberg, J. Kincheloe (eds) *Kinderculture: The Corporate Construction of Childhood.* Boulder, CO: Westview Press, pp. 53–68.

Graff, H. (2001) Literacy's myths and legacies, in P. Freebody, S. Muspratt and B. Dwyer (eds) *Difference, Silence and Textual Practice: Studies in Critical Literacy.* Cresskill, NJ: Hampton Press, pp. 1–29.

Hill, S., Comber, B., Louden, W., Rivalland, J. and Reid, J. (1998) *100 Children Go to School: Connections and Disconnections in Literacy Development in the Year Prior to School and the First Year of School,* Vol. 1. Canberra: DEETYA.

James, A., Jenks, C. and Prout, A. (1998) *Theorizing Childhood.* Canberra: Polity Press.

Jones Diaz, C., Beecher, B., Arthur, L., Ashton, J., Hayden, J., Makin, L., McNaught, M. and Clugston, L. (2001) *Literacies, Communities and Under 5s.* Sydney: NSW Department of Education and Training and NSW Department of Community Services.

Kenway, J. and Bullen, E. (2001) *Consuming Children: Education, Entertainment, Advertising.* Buckingham: Open University Press.

Luke, A. (1993) The social construction of literacy in the primary school, in L. Unsworth (ed.) *Literacy Learning and Teaching*, Melbourne: Macmillan, pp. 3–53.

Luke, C. (1997) Media literacy and cultural studies, in S. Muspratt, A. Luke and P. Freebody (eds) *Constructing Critical Literacies: Teaching and Learning Textual Practice*. Cresskill, NJ: Hampton Press, pp. 19–49.

Luke, C. (1999) Media and cultural studies in Australia, *Journal of Adolescent and Adult Literacy*, 42 (8): 622–626.

Makin, L., Hayden, J., Holland, A., Arthur, L., Beecher, B., Jones Diaz, C. and McNaught, M. (1999) *Mapping Literacy Practices in Early Childhood Services*. Sydney: NSW Department of Education and Training and NSW Department of Community Services.

Malaguzzi, L. (1993) History, ideas and basic philosophy, in C. Edwards, L. Gandini and G. Forman (eds) *The Hundred Languages of Children*. Norwood, NJ: Ablex, pp. 41–89.

Marsh, J. (2000) Teletubby tales: Popular culture in the early years language and literacy curriculum, *Contemporary Issues in Early Childhood*, 1 (2): 119–133.

Marsh, J. and Millard, E. (2000) *Literacy and Popular Culture: Using Children's Culture in the Classroom*. London: Paul Chapman.

McNaught, M., Clugston, L., Arthur, L., Beecher, B., Jones Diaz, C., Ashton, J., Hayden, J. and Makin, L. (2001) *The Early Literacy and Social Justice Project: Final Report*. Sydney: NSW Department of Education and Training and NSW Department of Community Services.

Moll, L., Amanti, C., Neff, D. and Gonzalez, N. (1992) Funds of knowledge for teaching: Using a qualitative approach to connect homes and classrooms, *Theory into Practice*, 31 (2): 132–141.

Morrell, E. (2002) Toward a critical pedagogy of popular culture: Literacy development among urban youth, *Journal of Adolescent and Adult Literacy*, 46 (1): 72–78.

Seiter, E. (1993) *Sold Separately: Children and Parents in Consumer Culture*. New Brunswick, NJ: Rutgers University Press.

Seiter, E. (1999) *Television and New Media Audiences*. Oxford: Clarendon Press.

Tobin, J. (2000) *Good Guys Don't Wear Hats: Children's Talk About the Media*. New York: Teachers College Press.

Urquhart, I. (1996) You see all blood come out: Popular culture and how boys become men, in M. Hilton (ed.) *Potent Fictions: Children's Literacy and the Challenge of Popular Culture*. London: Routledge, pp. 150–184.

Chapter 11

Barbie meets Bob the Builder at the Workstation

Learning to write on screen

Guy Merchant

In ancient Egyptian mythology, the ibis-headed god Thoth was said to be mighty in knowledge and divine speech. He is sometimes described as the inventor of spoken and written language. Alternative versions suggest that the goddess, Seshat, invented writing, leaving Thoth with the responsibility of teaching writing to the human race. Mythology aside, the archeological record shows us how writing was an important social practice in ancient Egyptian culture and how a caste of scribes was instructed in the skill of making glyphs with reed brushes on papyrus scrolls. That was the pervasive technology of the day.

There seems to be little doubt that the new digital technologies of the twenty-first century are challenging the way we think about writing. They are also changing the ways in which we do writing. The mouse on the PC, the touch screen at the cash dispenser (ATM), and the keypad on our cell phone are all writing technologies. These technologies and associated actions such as texting with our thumbs, sending messages on the move, place writing in the new spaces of new times. Digital communication makes new practices possible and makes some existing practices a lot easier.

Writing has a long and intimate relationship with technology, in fact, as Ong (1982) argues, writing *is* technology – in the way that it involves

> the use of tools and other equipment: styli or brushes or pens, carefully prepared surfaces such as paper, animal skins, strips of wood, as well as inks or paints, and much more.
>
> (Ong, 1982: 81–82)

From this perspective it is evident that the digital revolution has provided us with new tools and that recent developments in screen-based technology are leading to some quite fundamental changes in a number of aspects of writing. Lankshear and Knobel (2003) in their exploration of the concept of 'new literacies' describe these as ontological changes – changes which involve new kinds of texts and new kinds of textual practices. They are changes which have major implications for education at all stages. However, although many national educational systems have acknowledged the importance of new technology by designing policy and investing in hardware and training programmes, how professionals develop and use new literacies in the classroom still seems like under-explored territory. While there is a growing literature on innovative work with older students, early encounters with digital literacy are under-researched (Labbo and Reinking, 2003). The question addressed in this chapter is how should early childhood educators respond to digital communication and to the emergence of the new writing?

Before addressing this question, I want to explore some of the defining characteristics of the new writing. These include some quite immediate and concrete phenomena such as the use of new surfaces and media for writing, new tools or devices for written communication, and ways of acting on or using these tools. Of course, there are also well-documented changes in orthographic conventions such as the adoption of new symbols, alternative spellings, and specific words and phrases (Werry, 1996; Shortis, 2001; Merchant, 2001), but these are not central concerns here.

On the surface

The word on screen is a simulacrum of print-type on paper. The writer sees a play of pixels that respond to physical actions in a factitious act of typing. Through processes that most users would be at a loss to explain, digital information is encoded in a form that is read as a scroll and often visually subdivided with page-breaks. These scrolls form texts which we can copy or change, but never touch – at least not in their original form. Their appearance is both virtual and ephemeral.[1] Changes of appearance are easily made, and in most word-processing environments, such as Microsoft Word, fonts can be altered at will with a combination of keystrokes or mouse-clicks, and animated or coloured text is relatively easy to create. We can incorporate or borrow visual and audio material, exploiting the multimodal affordances of the screen (Kress, 2003), copy or change the writing of others and hyperlink within and between documents and machines. Screens can also be a more public surface for writing, making one's work visible to others. Larger screens seem to encourage collaborative work and, of course, without the individuality of handwriting, one person's contribution is hard to distinguish from another's. In order to write on screen, we need more than the hardware and the software. We also need the power to make it all work. Writing is no longer interrupted by running out of paper or ink, but by computer crashes, loss of power and low batteries. In order to use our writing to communicate interactively, we also need connectivity: a signal or a cable. Compared to pen and paper then, the screen is a very different surface for writing.

Writing tools

Currently, there is a proliferation of electronic writing devices, all of which operate, at least in a fundamental way, in more or less the same fashion. They can be categorised as having different forms of portability, from the mobile, palmtop or handheld device, to the slightly more awkward laptop, through to the relatively fixed desktop or satellite TV. Alongside this, there are a number of different ways of acting on these devices. These include touchscreen technology, the stylus, mouse, touchpad, joystick, and keyboard. This array of functional peripherals allows us to write, or to act on screen–writing, by subtle physical manipulation that activates pre-formed letters, words or longer chunks of text. Fingers and thumbs are employed in different ways in using these tools as the labour of writing diversifies beyond the physical demands of pencil control. Furthermore, contemporary writing tools often have multiple functions. The dozen or so buttons on a mobile phone can perform a variety of different actions; like the keys on a keyboard they allow us to select menus, to toggle through options and to scroll up or down screen, as well as to write text. New writing tools change the physical actions necessary for text production. Bomer's close analysis of early literacy workshops shows how young school children interact with a variety of writing tools as they engage in 'valued ways' of producing paper-based texts (Bomer, 2003). This work highlights how the physical routines of handling paper, notebooks, tape-dispensers, scissors and staplers are intimately connected with the production of traditional pieces of writing. When children (or adults) write on screen, they have a very different relationship with material objects.

The writing position

Writing is a physical act and the writing position, or what Bourdieu (1991) calls bodily hexis, describes the physical postures associated with certain kinds of communication. These have been light-heartedly referred to as 'sit up' (desktop), 'lie back' (digital TV) and 'fall over' (mobile phone). But there is a more serious point here. The materiality of new communications technology creates significant ways of holding, gripping and carrying devices as well as physical postures to adopt when using them. As we use new writing tools we are reminded that writing is not just an activity of the mind, but the whole body. As Mackey observes:

> With many of the new media we are changing the role of hands . . . . If the role of our physical interactions with the text is changing we need to be aware of the implications.
>
> (Mackey, 2002: 118)

The particular ways in which we physically orientate ourselves to writing tools are inscribed in the affordances of their design. I sit, looking more or less straight ahead to write on the desktop computer. Both hands type, but occasionally I extend my right hand to cover the mouse, using my forearm and wrist to direct it, my thumb to steady and my first two fingers to press or click. However, quite different positions and actions are deployed when text-messaging or using a cash-dispenser.

In educational contexts, print-orientated practices associated with word-processing and keyboard skills have tended to enjoy a certain privilege over popular thumb-controlled technology (associated with being 'frivolous' – games consoles, joysticks, and more recently with text-messaging). Perhaps this is because finger-typing is more familiar to us, our actions look like typographic practices and they certainly have a closer similarity to book-based literacy.

Beneath the surface

Beneath the surface of writing we can see changes in the roles and functions of writing practices, some resulting from the increased interdependency of communicative modes, and others from ideas of textual authority, publishing and originality. Post-typographic forms work in quite different ways from traditional print texts. As Kress (2003) points out, our reading paths may differ. Not only is it clear that many screen-based texts are non-linear in organisation, but also, Kress argues, the reader's task is 'to establish the order through principles of relevance of the reader's making, and to construct meaning from that' (Kress, 2003: 162). As well as this, writing on screen can involve different processes of composition, publication and distribution (Lankshear and Knobel, 2003) and new forms of interaction. Connectivity and the possibility of rapid response in some media, most notably SMS and e-mail, invokes a completely new style of written communication which has been described as 'interactive written discourse' (Ferrera et al., 1991). In addition to this, the potential for rapid publication and dissemination to a diverse audience has become an important feature of electronic communica-tion, particularly notable in the expanding field of weblogs (see Lankshear and Knobel, 2003).

These and other characteristics of writing on screen illustrate the new possibilities and practices of digital literacy. They challenge us to reconsider writing, to see it as a rapidly changing social practice, in which a wider range of technologies are now at hand. Writing technologies are resources for meaning-making and, in so far as education is concerned with creating liter-ate futures, providing early experience of the new writing is crucial.

Learning to write in a digital environment

So what are the implications of large-scale changes in writing technology for those working in the early years? We may not need a mythology to account for the invention of digital literacy, but just like the ancient Egyptians, we need to educate our young writers so that they have control of the technologies and insight into the social practices in which they are used. We can start by looking at two influential concepts in the professional discourse of early childhood literacy: first, the 'print environment' and second, the idea of 'emergent literacy'.

Most children, at least in the post-industrial West, are surrounded by print texts from a very early age. Early literacy learning, it is argued, involves children, with their carers, parents, or educators in developing an awareness of the salience and significance of print and co-constructing meanings with reference to print. The crucially important learning that this sort of apprenticeship to the literate world develops is often summed up as a recognition that 'print is used to carry meaning'. Over a relatively short period of time the print environment has been transformed by digital technology. Not only have we witnessed the growing importance of the visual image (Kress, 2003), but also ways and uses of writing have developed in new and unexpected ways (Rheingold, 2003). Digital literacy is already a feature of young children's lives and a significant feature of the print environment (Marsh and Thompson, 2001).

Emergent literacy is a term that has gained currency with early years educators as a way of acknowledging young children's early experience and development in literacy. As Riley observes, the term describes

> the earliest phase of understanding about print that enables the child to generate hypotheses about the nature of reading and writing.
>
> (Riley, 1996: 89)

Children's mark-making and early experimentation with writing, previously dismissed as scribble, is therefore seen as an important initial stage through which they develop an understanding of symbolic representation (Clay, 1975). Early years provision in writing now normally provides a range of opportunities for children to engage in exploratory mark-making in relatively unstructured ways or in the context of socio-dramatic role play (Roskos and Christie, 2001). However, relatively little has been written about the use of new writing technologies in this context (see Labbo and Reinking, 2003 for a review). Provision for early experimental writing in the UK is normally paper-based. The screen is the site for early work on ICT skills or for practising attractively produced routines in such areas as shape or letter recognition, rather than for emergent writing, however that is conceived.

In order to explore these themes of early writing and new technology, I now turn to some small-scale research that looks at young children's interactions with new writing tools. This not only shows what knowledge children bring to the act of writing on screen and the different understandings of literacy practices involved, but also underlines the need for new ways of thinking about early literacy development that take in a fuller account of the growing role of new technology on all our lives.

Background

To investigate the place of digital literacy in early years settings, I draw on fieldwork conducted in a children's centre that caters for two- to four-year-olds in a large city in the North of England. The centre operates out of refurbished office space, known as the Workstation, in the Cultural Industries Quarter, less than half a mile from the centre of this urban area. The Workstation (http://www.workstation.org.uk/), is an interesting location because of its close association with creative applications of new technology. Its current list of tenant profiles features 36 businesses, 16 of which make explicit reference to new media and digital technology (Workstation, 2003). So, for example, Dialogue Communications is a successful company in the cellular communications industry, whereas Can Studios specialises in interactive e-learning. Nestled between these businesses is the Workstation Children's Centre – a unit that accommodates 32 children between the ages of six months and five years. The staff at the centre are strongly committed to building on children's interests, and emphasis is placed on creativity and educational provision that is sensitive to cultural diversity (Workstation Children's Centre, 2003). Surprisingly, however, in view of the centre's location, new technology does not have a particularly high profile in the curriculum. A rather tired desktop PC is jammed in a corner of the main classroom next to the writing table. It is, according to the staff, slow and tends to 'crash' if over-used. There is some software, stacked up next to the monitor, and most of this appears to be directed to promoting basic literacy and numeracy skills such as letter and number recognition. This is used, according to the staff, 'when somebody can be bothered to turn it on' – in other words, not on a regular or planned basis.

As part of a technology week, staff provided children with computer keyboards, old mobile phones, and two portable computers as well as various toy versions of these technologies. Bob's Mobile Phone (Vtech), one of three Bob the Builder toy phones currently on the market, acted a catalyst for some of the play activity. This play phone, with pre-recorded messages, is based on the popular children's cartoon series *Bob the Builder*. My First Laptop (IQ Builders), an electronic learning toy with working keyboard and screen, enabled children to rehearse the actions done on the 'real' machines. The equipment was set out on the writing table, located in a base which caters for 18 children between the ages of two and four. During the technology week, visits were made on each morning session. This amounted to approximately 10 hours when daily routines such as registration and story time were accounted for. Observations of the children's interactions at the writing table and their use of the technology were recorded as handwritten field notes, with the author acting as a participant observer. This approach allowed for opportunities to talk with the children and to respond to requests for help. However, being a participant did not involve any conscious attempts to direct the children's activity, although it should be acknowledged that adult presence, interest and even gaze may give implicit messages about the status of an activity in the relatively unstructured environment of the unit.

The children's on-screen writing was saved when it seemed that they had finished, and samples of this are referred to in this chapter. While this provides interesting evidence of young children writing on-screen, it is clearly not a subtle enough approach to capture nuances of the writing process, such as the variations in speed of electronic mark-making, mis-keying (resulting, for instance, in the appearance of a message box on screen) or the interplay of conversation, action and on-screen mark-making. So, the evidence presented here provides important groundwork for a more extensive examination of early on-screen writing. Given the paucity of research this area, such exploratory work is clearly necessary.

Is this for kids?

The children's initial reactions to this marked change in provision could be described as mildly curious. As they came to the writing table, we noted comments like:

Paddy: What's this? . . .
Charlie: How do you turn it on? . . .
Africa: Is this for kids? . . .

From the equipment available, the portable computers attracted the most attention. These were running standard word-processing software, displayed in a large font size. Africa's comment above suggests that she associates the portable computer and perhaps word-processing in particular as adult work and this may go some of the way to accounting for the initial reluctance of some of the children. Generally speaking, the older children were keen to apply their knowledge of writing and to engage in familiar routines. Paddy is a confident and articulate four-year-old who already has considerable control over pencil and paper technology. He was quick to announce that he was 'going to write a sentence' and produced his writing after about five minutes of concentrated independent work (see Figure 11.1).[2]

Paddy, like some of the other four year-olds, performed the kind of literacy activities that were sanctioned in this educational setting. They displayed knowledge of the routines associated with schooled literacies. These children's first attempts at writing on screen tended to be about demonstrating what they already knew (Clay, 1975 calls this the inventory principle) and so a number of these children, with varying degrees of accuracy, wrote their

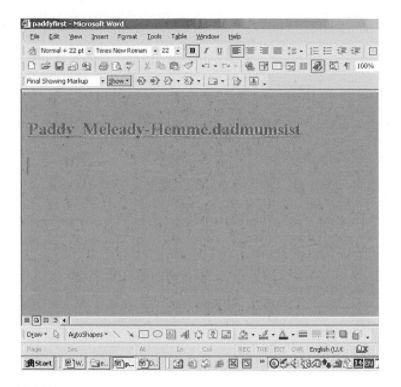

Figure 11.1 Writing your name

own name or laboriously picked out the letters of the alphabet in order. In the process of doing this, their conversation drew on different aspects of their experience of digital literacy. Three themes emerged here. They talked about technology and particularly about the computers they saw or used at home; they talked about what it was like to write on screen; and they commented on or asked for guidance on the act of writing. These categories are illustrated with comments from the children in Table 11.1.

The comments show how these young children are not only aware of the routines and practices of the educational context, but are also drawing on funds of knowledge (Moll *et al.*, 1992) about digital literacy from their lives outside the Workstation. They show familiarity and curiosity about the technology, a growing appreciation of what it is actually like to write on-screen and a developing practical expertise in terms of how keyboard actions influence the appearance of text on-screen. Embedded in this work is an understanding of what Clay (1975) refers to as the sign concept and a clear understanding of the difference between drawing and writing as a form of symbolic representation.

Table 11.1 Talking about digital writing

Commenting on technology	Commenting on the process of writing on-screen	Working out how to write on-screen
M: My daddy's got a computer at home	C: You need to really concentrate when you're typing	P: Oh, I pressed the wrong one
L: We've got little computers	A: This won't work on the Apple	C: Full stop now – I'll need a full stop
C: I've got one at home	M: I'm just trying out writing	L: Where's the L?

Barbie colours

Melody is an unassuming three-year-old who often stands to one side of an activity, rather like an interested onlooker. Initially she appeared to be somewhat over-awed by the idea of working on a laptop computer. Nevertheless, after some time weighing up the situation she decided to introduce herself:

Melody: I've got my Barbie jeans on today.
GM: Oh yes they're good . . . and a matching bag.

[Melody shows the denim bag with its picture of Barbie stitched on]

GM: Would you like to write?

[Melody responds with a nod and pulls up a chair]

Melody: Where's the 'm'?

After being shown the letter M, she continued to write her name, occasionally tilting the screen to get a clearer view. It took her a little while to get used to operating the keyboard – holding her finger down too long on each letter key produced a stream of onscreen text that she was not happy with. Her first attempt to write her name looked something like 'MMMEEEEEEELLLOOODDDYYYY'. On a second attempt she wrote her name accurately, adding 'Barbie' and 'Bob the Builder' to complete her text. Her inventory of words she knows is shown an impressive achievement. The finished work is shown in Figure 11.2.

Melody was interested in the appearance of her writing on the screen. Her initial tilting of the screen demonstrated how she was aware that her actions on the keyboard would be immediately visible. Adjusting the tilt of the screen, she used her hands to orientate the text to her point of view, employing an adjustment of reading position familiar to users of portable computers (see Mackey, 2002 for the use of the hands in reading). Dissatisfaction with her first piece of writing, followed by the question 'Do you know how to get rid of this?' suggests that she is also familiar with the idea of text deletion or opening new files, providing further evidence of a growing sense of control in her digital writing.

Figure 11.2 Melody's inventory

In addition to this, she became aware, from watching others, that she could change the colour of her writing.

Melody: Does it do pink?
GM: Let's have a look.

[I show her how to get a coloured background – she chooses pink]

Melody: Yes . . . what about the writing?
GM: Mmm we can change that too. What colour do you want?
Melody: Pink.

[We try, but, of course, you can't write pink on pink, so we compromise by changing the background.]

What is interesting here is how Melody is keen that her text conveys meaning through its visual appearance as well as through the verbal content of her writing. Here she becomes preoccupied with the affordances of the screen (Kress, 2003). She also makes a personal statement about herself, drawing on her experience of popular culture and incorporating Barbie and then Bob the Builder. This shows engagement in the sort of techno-literacy practices reported in Marsh's study of young children in home settings (Marsh, 2004).

The sign's ready

Melody's digital writing was essentially a solitary activity in which she seemed to be recording what was important to her. Yet at the same time, some of the other children were creating a collaborative narrative around the writing table. This was based on the TV cartoon character of Bob the Builder. The following extract is from Louis' phone call. He was standing at the table with one hand on the keyboard of a portable computer and the other holding a mobile phone to his ear. Wendy is Bob's business partner in the TV series.

Louis: Hi Wendy . . . How you doing? . . .
            The road's not working . . .
            Yes . . . OK . . . Bye then.

[Louis puts the phone down and begins typing furiously with both hands.]

Charlie: I'll do a sign then.

[Now Charlie types quickly too. Nearby a tape is playing 'I am a music man'. Charlie's typing begins to follow the rhythm of the song.]

Charlie: I'm writing about the road. 'It's not fixeded yet.'

[Louis picks up the mobile phone.]

Louis: Hello Charlie . . . Hello Charlie . . .
            Is that Charlie? . . . The sign's ready . . .
            OK bye.

In this sequence, the children are incorporating digital communication into their socio-dramatic role-play in ways that are reminiscent of Hall's accounts of literacy in play (Hall, 1987, 1991). Louis and Charlie improvise a typical *Bob the Builder* scenario using the mobile phone (an object that regularly features in the TV programmes) and their knowledge of the sign–generating possibilities offered by word-processing. Observing this play sequence, I was struck by the way in which the children began to act out everyday literacy practices, combining their knowledge of popular culture with the technology which was provided in order to produce a narrative which was engaging and important to them. Their spontaneous, improvised role-play draws on a shared knowledge of popular cultural texts and incorporates the use of new communications technology in a socially situated context, as was seen in Gillen *et al.*'s observations of role play in Chapter 9 of this book.

Farmer Pickles breaks a leg

Clearly, adult involvement in early digital literacy is likely to take a number of forms. Where children were keen to write their name or display their knowledge of the letters of the alphabet, adults in the proximity were often recruited into the task of locating letters on the keyboard or helping to identify letter sequence (orthography). In the sort of spontaneous role-play described above, there seemed to be little need for adult intervention. However, other play sequences show how adult workers can model and extend children's interactions with digital literacy.

In the following play sequence, the adult capitalises on the children's interest in *Bob the Builder* narratives and takes a leading role. One of the children, Chester, has fallen over and hurt his leg. The educare worker, who is helping a younger child working on a portable computer, comforts Chester and, realising that he is not too upset, diverts his attention by inviting him into a play narrative in which he becomes the character of Farmer Pickles (also from *Bob the Builder*).

Adult: Oh dear . . . It'll be all right . . .

[Chester nods. There are no tears.]

Adult: Poor old Farmer Pickles . . . Let's phone the hospital.

[Chester smiles. Charlie picks up a mobile phone.]

Charlie: Hello . . . Farmer Pickles broken leg.

[Adult holds another mobile phone to her ear.]

Adult: Can you give me your name so I can type it into my computer?

[Charlie looks up at his screen. It says his own name. He begins to read it out.]

Charlie: c . . . h . . . [etc.]

Adult: What's your number?

[Charlie doesn't have any numbers on his screen, but he quickly tucks the phone against his shoulder and types in a string of figures – it looks like it might be his home number – and then reads them out.]

In this play sequence, the adult modelled another social practice familiar to the children. Their knowledge of how hospital accident and emergency systems routinely involve digital literacy provided a template for further socially situated role-play. As we often see in early years settings, other children who were merely observers in this sequence picked up these ideas and the role of hospital reception later proved to be a potent scenario for interaction and collaboration that playfully incorporated new technology.

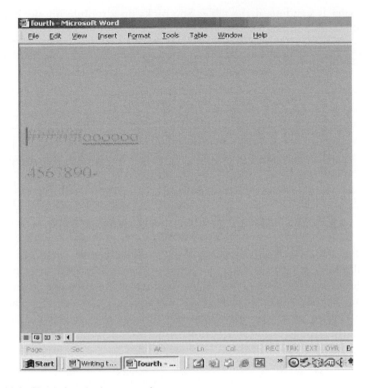

Figure 11.3 Charlie's telephone number

Techi-toddlers

In the sessions observed, the younger children in the unit were more dependent on adult guidance than the older ones. Nonetheless their interactions
with writing technology not only demonstrated their knowledge about digital communication, but also their willingness to explore and to experiment.
Saira is one of the younger children in the base and usually prefers to talk in
single word whispers to those adults whom she is familiar with. In the following extracts from my field notes we see Saira aged two years two months at
the writing table.

1. Saira is sitting on an educare worker's knee. Her hand stretches out to
touch the keyboard of a portable computer. She presses a key with her
outstretched first finger and gazes towards the screen (she's touched the
'enter' key – nothing happens). The educare worker gently guides Saira's
finger. She presses the letter 'l', holding it down and watches a string
of letters rise up on the screen in rapid succession. 'You're writing.' The
adult says.

2. Saira is standing at the table. She picks up a mobile phone, cups it in both hands and begins to press the keys as if sending a message. 'Are you texting?' asks the adult. Saira still doesn't speak but continues to press the keys with her thumbs.

Saira's interactions with the writing technology were typical of the approaches shown by the younger children in this study. They appeared to be less likely to choose writing table activity unless accompanied by a familiar adult worker. It was impossible to tell to what extent this reluctance was caused by the presence of new equipment, an unfamiliar adult or both, and certainly this warrants further investigation. However, on the occasions when younger children were involved, they explored the computers and the phones with interest, and in much the same way that they engage with other activity. Touching keyboards and keypads needed little prompting, although the precision of letter key pressing actions observed in the older children was not so often in evidence. This raises issues about the sort of understandings about writing on screen that children develop over time. Although some of the concepts of print and principles of writing that Clay (1975) observed may still apply, it seems that emergent literacy on screen may need to be subjected to a fresh analysis.

What became clear from these observations was that the younger children needed little assistance, and in fact they sometimes demonstrated quite sophisticated knowledge of how the technology works. So, for example, in pressing the keys of a portable computer, while looking at the screen, Saira shows that quite specific hand actions are likely to result in changes in the screen's appearance. Her handling of the mobile phone is evidence that she is familiar with a basic operational concept associated with this communication tool – repeatedly pressing keys with one's thumbs is what you do. To what extent she knows about this action as written communication is harder to ascertain. Nevertheless, her actions show us what the early stages of digital literacy might look like.

Discussion

In her influential book on writing, Clay (1975) meticulously describes the development of early mark-making. Her theory of writing principles provides a robust account of the understandings that young children develop through early mark-making and emergent writing. Examples of these are the recurring principle (writing consists of shapes and letter strings that are repeated), the generative principle (writing uses signs that are repeated in different combinations) and the sign concept (writing represents something beyond itself). However, some of these principles are clearly characteristics of the paper-based technology that Clay was looking at. So, for instance, the directional principle is a given in most writing on screen: letters are produced from left to right and a new line starts as soon as you reach the margin. Table 11.2

Table 11.2 Clay's (1975) principles and writing on-screen

Clay's principles/ concepts	The principles in practice	Typical kinds of understanding	Writing on-screen
Recurring principle	Letters recur in patterned strings or words	I can repeat what I write	Holding down a key; cutting and pasting
Directional principle	(English) print runs left to right and top to bottom	My writing goes across the page and on to the next line	Word processors use orthodox directional principles
Generating principle	A finite number of symbols are used to generate new meanings	I can use what I know to write new messages	The same on page and screen
Flexibility principle	Writing is made up of shapes that change in particular ways	I can experiment with the shape and size of letters	Experimentation is not usually possible in word processing programs
Inventory principle	Listing the letters or words that are known	These are all the letters/words I know	Lists can be generated in the same way
Contrastive principle	Some letters change their significance if rotated	I can reverse some letters	Word processors orientate letters in an orthodox way
Abbreviation principle	Words can be abbreviated	I can shorten words	The same – although some word processors 'auto-correct'
Copying principle	The essential meaning of writing does not change when repeated	I can copy writing and its meaning is unchanged	The same on page and screen; cutting and pasting makes this easier
Sign concept	Written words can be spoken (and vice versa)	I can represent speech in writing	'Talking' software and voice recognition illustrate the relationship
Space concept	Particular conventions govern the placing of words and the use of space	I can make some choices in using space on the page	Some programs allow for control of design features
Message concept	A written message can be read and understood by others	I can communicate to others through my writing	Generates more varied relationships and interactions in terms of time/place

provides a fuller picture of Clay's writing principles and shows their relationship to digital writing.

Clearly additional principles – those which apply specifically to screen-based writing – could be added to the list. A basic understanding that actions on a keyboard appear on a screen before you seems to point to the impor-tance of knowing where to direct one's gaze (*a gaze principle*). It also seems that an idea of where to apply pressure on a keyboard and for how long are important things to know about. In digital writing, the physical act of letter formation is not important, but other choices take its place. The labour of writing is transferred to letter selection, pressure and duration. This suggests that there are *selection* and *pressure principles*. As children become confident with the way keyboards work, they are frequently drawn into experimen-tation with the rhythms of digital writing. In this study, Charlie's typing, synchronised with the music from a nearby tape recorder, provides a useful illustration of this *rhythmic principle*. In summary, then, the work I have documented in this chapter shows how some of these principles are explored in on–screen text production. Clearly, further work is needed to elaborate the understandings that children develop in screen-based writing.

Young children's work as meaning-producers, characterised in terms of mark-making and emergent writing, regularly takes place in the context of solitary or collaborative play (Hall, 1991; Teale and Suzby, 1986). This neces-sary playful and experimental activity can now be re-examined in the light of new and affordable writing technologies. The work reported here suggests that such a re-examination is most likely to occur when practitioners shift the emphasis from technology to communication. In early years educational settings, such as the one described in this chapter, it often seems that such possibilities are constrained by the largely unarticulated views of adult workers about what sort of technologies are appropriate for young children (Luke and Luke, 2001; Turbill, 2001). The intersection of culturally reproduced schooled literacy practices and curricular structures with official and unofficial guidance construct early writing and ICT in particular ways. I suggest that viewing screen-based technology as a tool for meaning-making and communication changes the way in which it is perceived by adults and used by young children.

Early years practitioners have often been unsure of how to make the best use of new technology in their provision. Approaches which involve creating computer areas that are in some sense distinct from the daily routines and practices of classroom life clearly have their disadvantages. Practitioners would benefit from hearing more about innovatory ways of integrating new tech-nology, such as the ideas of targeted teaching and building thematic connec-tions (Labbo, Sprague, Montero and Font, 2000).

As we have seen, young children inhabit a complex world in which electronic and digital media play an important role (see also Marsh, 2004). The communicative practices to which they are apprenticed include many traditional forms, but these exist side by side with new and rapidly developing practices which blend print, audio and visual media. Responding to these multi-literacies (New London Group, 1996) is a key task for educators in all sectors. Previously, the print environment has been identified as an important influence in the literacy experience of under-fives – here I suggest that we need to extend our view to include the linguistic and non-linguistic representations of the post-typograhic era we are entering. This may mean re-thinking the role played by different semiotic systems in early childhood education, for, after all, the multimodal practices that characterise the new communicative practices of screen-based technology are significant in the lives of children outside the classroom, just as they are significant in the lives of the adult workers they interact with in the classroom.

Acknowledgement

Many thanks to Hannah, the staff and children at the Workstation Children's Centre and also to Cathy Burnett for her helpful comments on an early draft of this chapter.

Notes

1 A record of our digital writing is usually retrievable by those with expert technical knowledge, as several high-profile political scandals have demonstrated.
2 Screen shots reprinted by permission from Microsoft Corporation.

References

Bomer, R. (2003) 'Things that make kids smart: a Vygotskian perspective on tool use in primary literacy classrooms', *Journal of Early Childhood Literacy*, 3 (3): 223–247.
Bourdieu, P. (1991) *Language and Symbolic Power*. Cambridge: Polity Press.
Clay, M. (1975) *What Did I Write?* London: Heinemann Educational.
Ferrara, K., Brunner, H. and Whittemore, G. (1991) 'Interactive written discourse as an emergent register', *Written Communication*, 18 (1): 8–34.
Hall, N. (1987) 'The literate home corner'. In P. Smith (ed.) *Parents and Teachers Together* (pp. 134–144). London: Macmillan.
Hall, N. (1991) 'Play and the emergence of literacy'. In J. F. Christie (ed.) *Play and Early Literacy Development* (pp. 3–25). New York: University of New York Press.
Kress, G. (2003) *Literacy in the New Media Age*. London: Routledge.
Labbo, L. D. and Reinking, D. (2003) 'Computers and early literacy education'. In N. Hall, J. Larson, and J. Marsh (eds) *Handbook of Early Childhood Literacy* (pp. 338–354). London: Sage.
Labbo, L. D., Sprague, L., Montero, M. K., and Font, G. (2000) 'Connecting a computer center to themes, literature, and kindergartners' literacy needs'. *Reading Online*, 4: 1. Available: http://www.readingonline.org/electronic/labbo/, accessed 10 November 2003.
Lankshear, C. and Knobel, M. (2003) *New Literacies: Changing Knowledge and Classroom Learning*. Buckingham: Open University Press.

Luke, A. and Luke, C. (2001) 'Adolescence lost/childhood regained: on early intervention and the emergence of the techno-subject', *Journal of Early Childhood Education*, 1 (1): 91–120.

Mackey, M. (2002) *Literacies across Media: Playing the Text*. London: RoutledgeFalmer.

Marsh, J. (2004) 'The techno-literacy practices of young children', *Journal of Early Childhood Research*, 2 (1): 51–66.

Marsh, J. and Thompson, P. (2001) 'Parental involvement in literacy: using media texts', *Journal of Research in Reading*, 24 (3): 266–278.

Merchant, G. (2001) 'Teenagers in cyberspace: language use and language change in internet chatrooms', *Journal of Research in Reading*, 24 (3): 293–306.

Moll, L., Amanti, C., Neff, D. and Gonzalez, N. (1992) 'Funds of knowledge for teaching: using a qualitative approach to connect homes and classrooms', *Theory into Practice*, 31 (2): 132–141.

New London Group (1996) 'A pedagogy of multi-literacies: designing social futures', *Harvard Educational Review*, 66 (1): 60–92.

Ong, W. J. (1982) *Orality and Literacy: The Technologizing of the Word*. London: Methuen.

Rheingold, H. (2003) *Smart Mobs: The Next Social Revolution*. Cambridge, MA: Perseus Books.

Riley, J. (1996) 'The ability to label letters of the alphabet at school entry: a discussion of its value', *Journal of Research in Reading*, 16 (1): 32–71.

Roskos, K. and Christie, J. (2001) 'Examining the play–literacy interface: a critical review and future directions', *Journal of Early Childhood Literacy*, 1 (1): 40–59.

Shortis, T. (2001) *The Language of ICT*. London: Routledge.

Teale, W. H. and Suzby, E. (eds) (1986) *Emergent Literacy: Writing and Reading*. Norwood, NH: Ablex.

Turbill, J. (2001) 'A researcher goes to school: using new technology in the kindergarten literacy curriculum', *Journal of Early Childhood Literacy*, 1 (3): 255–279.

Werry, C. (1996) 'Linguistic and interactional features of internet relay chat'. In S. C. Herring (ed.) *Computer-Mediated Communication: Linguistic, Social and Cross-cultural Perspectives*. Amsterdam: Benjamins.

Workstation (2003) *Tenant Profiles: 31 July 2003*. Sheffield: Workstation. http://www.workstation.org.uk/, accessed 31 October 2003.

Workstation Children's Centre (2003) *Prospectus: 2003*. Sheffield: Workstation.

Chapter 12

Resistance, power-tricky, and colorless energy

What engagement with everyday popular culture texts can teach us about learning and literacy

Vivian Vasquez

Picture this. It is fifteen minutes before dinnertime. Patricia decides to put this lag time to good use by sitting with her six-year-old son, Kris, at the dining room table to read a series of cards, each with one word written at the center.

Patricia holds up a card with the word 'had' on it.

Kris: h–h–had
Patricia: That's good you're sounding out. [Holds up a card with the word 'after' on it.]
Kris: af–ter
Patricia: Really good sounding out Kris. Read this next one slowly so you don't miss any sounds.

[The phone rings while she is holding up the next card. She continues to hold up the card in one hand while picking up the phone with the other. While she's on the phone Kris takes out a *Pokémon* card from his pocket and begins looking at it.]

Put that card away. That's why you're having trouble keeping up with your reading.

Kris: g—o—ing
Patricia: Excellent.

[In the background the sound of a timer goes off. Kris's mother gets up, opens the oven door and announces that dinner is ready. From the other end of the kitchen she calls out, 'Daddy can finish up with you later'.]

As his mother busies herself with final dinner preparations, Kris turns to me and asks if I would like to see his new *Pokémon* magazine and cards. *Pokémon* is a name given to a popular series of what are called 'pocket monsters', imaginary characters that have various capabilities such as being able to transform into different versions of the same character, and powers, such as using water, electricity, or fire to fend off opponents. These characters live in an alternate reality where they have the ability to evolve by winning battles over one another (Vasquez, 2003a). With its introduction to American television in 1996, *Pokémon* quickly became popular culture material for children in playgrounds, neighborhood streets and schoolyards. It was an imported Japanese cartoon dubbed in English and created in anime style. Anime film was first introduced in the 1960s by master animator Osamu Tezuka who in 1963 produced Japan's first televised anime, *Astro Boy* (Vallen and Thorpe, 2001). At the time, anime was produced by painting images on cels. Celluloid animation is based on a series of frames or cels in which the object is re-drawn in each consecutive cel to depict motion. This was the technique used by all cartoon creators before the dawning of computer animation.

Kris: Look at this (pointing at a chart in the magazine). This says resis-tance, it tells you how much resistance these (pointing at various cartoon characters, known as Pokémon) have to each other and these (pointing to a symbol at the bottom of one of his cards) tells you how much energy you need to do Power Tricky (a gaming strategy particular to *Pokémon*). And this down here (pointing to yet another symbol on another *Pokémon* card) tells you how much energy, like colorless energy, you need to win.

Vivian: How do you know all this about *Pokémon*?

Kris: Actually, my friends and I learn together. We read the trainer maga-zines and make our own cards and watch TV.

In the modern world, language is not the only important communication system. Today, images, artefacts, and many other visual symbols have gained in significance. So it would not be surprising if you have been witness to exchanges similar to those at the opening of this chapter. Children, more so than adults, seem to have an affinity with these new communication systems, as is displayed by Kris in the second exchange and as evidenced by his com-ment regarding where he learned about *Pokémon*, namely through magazines, through conversations with his friends, through creating his own cards and through television. It is therefore not enough to rely on a single cueing system, as was the case in the exchange between Kris and Patricia where phonics was given center stage. In order to best support the literacy learning of children today, we need to understand what literacies they currently learn and use and what participating with such literacies affords them. While talking about everyday literacies, Alvermann and Hong Xu (2003: 147) note that popular culture 'is not something to be shunned, set aside, or kept at a distance'.

Texts for a new millennium

Popular culture texts such as *Pokémon* cards and games have become the kinds of materials that many children 'read', have access to, and participate with as literate beings in the new millennium. For the purposes of this chapter, I will use 'popular culture' to refer to everyday culture where audiences negotiate its consumption (Alvermann and Hong Xu, 2003). *Pokémon* has become such a hot topic for conversation that even John Stossel, a media personality who co-anchors a popular television show in the USA called *20/20*, dedicated a segment to it in which he argued against those who claim that *Pokémon* viewing encourages children to gamble (Vasquez, 2003a). *Pokémon* has even had a turn at being on the cover of *Time* magazine (1999). Pikachu, one of the best-known *Pokémon* characters, was included in Macy's Thanksgiving Day Parade, joining the ranks of Snoopy and Curious George in an American tradition that started in 1927. In November 2001, the Academy of Motion Picture Arts and Sciences sponsored a lecture on Japanese animation (Vasquez, 2003a). Even more interestingly:

> the University of Hawaii Center for Japanese Studies Endowment, in November 2000, sponsored a two-day conference, Pikachu's Global Adventure. The conference involved an international team of professors, lecturers and media scholars from around the world who gathered to discuss the phenomenon Pokémon
>
> (Vasquez, 2003a: 119)

In this chapter, I will highlight opportunities for engaging pleasurable and powerful literacies by looking at three- to eight-year-old children's appropriations of the popular text, *Pokémon*. Specifically, I will show and tell of the literacies children learn and use while participating as a member of a *Pokémon* club, and as they create their own *Pokémon* cards and work with various *Pokémon* texts. My intent is to show what engagement with such popular culture texts can teach us about learning and literacy and to discuss the powerful and creative learning people can bring to the aspects of popular culture with which they choose to identify.

The children whose work I describe were part of a five-year study on literacy development and popular culture that took place at a child care pre-school and before and after school center in a suburb of Toronto, Ontario, Canada. The center is located in a lower-middle-class neighborhood where approximately 50 per cent of the children receive government subsidy. The children are culturally diverse, many of them being first-generation Canadian. For a summary of data sources and analysis, refer to Appendix 1. This study made use of interpretive methods (Bogdan and Biklen, 1992) and data were analyzed inductively.

Show and tell: literate behaviors that come from children's participation and use of popular culture texts

As a former pre-school and elementary school teacher of fourteen years, I ask myself how young children's participation with popular culture texts could inform my own literacy teaching practice and my students' learning. This is, in fact, what is central to this chapter. My intent is not to sell teachers on using popular culture text in the classroom, even though I have been witness to the power in doing so when teachers are able to negotiate interesting and meaningful ways to support their students' cultural and linguistic experiences (Luke, O'Brien and Comber, 1994; O'Brien, 1998; Kavanagh, 1997; Dyson, 1999, 2003; Alverman and Hong Xu, 2003; Carrington, 2003). Further, I am not arguing that everything learned from playing *Pokémon* is good, but that there are a lot of good things we can learn about how best to support children's literacy development by watching children closely as they engage with such texts. My intent, therefore, is to show and tell about the sorts of literate behaviors that come from children's participation and use of popular culture texts such as *Pokémon*. I believe there are some important questions that those of us who work with young children can ask with regard to popular culture texts. The following is a list of such questions that can act as a starting point for this work and which formed the basis for the research questions in this study:

- What motivates children to 'stay in the game' in spite of the increasing complexity of that game? What attracts them to the game in the first place?
- How can we capitalize on the new literacies developed through engagement with everyday popular texts that children encounter during the course of daily life?
- What does it mean for learning to be social? What happens to literacy development in these social spaces?
- What role do multimodal texts and the integration of different symbol systems play in literacy development?

Pokémon texts are just one example of the sort of highly complex literacies that children are appropriating, especially since the dawn of the new millennium and the multi-mediation of texts. Luke (2000) refers to these complex literacies as 'new literacies'. In essence, this chapter is about developing 'new critical literacy' pedagogies and curricula that go beyond debates over basic skills and best methodology, but that are informed by observation and analysis of children's participatory engagement with texts for which they have an affinity and for which they are willing to participate in complex learning situations for a sustained period of time.

Comber (2001) describes critical literacies as involving people using language to exercise power, to enhance everyday life in schools and communities, and to question practices of privilege and injustice. She continues to suggest that often – perhaps usually – critical literacies are negotiated in the more mundane and ordinary aspects of daily life. As such, a critical literacy curriculum needs to be lived. It arises from the social and political conditions that unfold in communities in which we live. Therefore, it cannot be traditionally taught. In other words, as teachers we need to incorporate a critical perspective into our everyday lives with our students in order to find ways to help children understand the social and political issues around them (Vasquez, 2004).[1]

Critical literacies include an ongoing analysis of textual practices: How do particular texts work? What effects do they have? Who has produced the text, under what circumstances, and for which readers? What's missing from this account? How could it be told differently? (Comber, 2001: 1). My experience working with teachers attempting to engage in critical literacy shows me that in many cases, social issues are treated as variables to be added to the existing curriculum. This, rather than using these issues to build curriculum, is done because the topics are associated with cynicism and unpleasurable work. However, critical literacy does not necessarily involve taking a negative stance, rather it includes looking at an issue or topic in different ways, analyzing it and hopefully being able to suggest possibilities for change or improvement.

Popular culture texts: an introduction

I was first introduced to the world of *Pokémon* gaming by my nephew, Curtis (see Figures 12.1 and 12.2), who purchased his first set of cards at age six when he and my husband Andy walked into a corner store in his neighborhood and he noticed familiar television cartoon characters on the packaging of

Figure 12.1 Curtis creating his own *Pokémon* cards

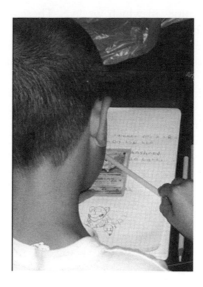

Figure 12.2 Curtis creating his own *Pokémon* cards

Figure 12.3 Pokémon cards created by Curtis

some collector cards. The children I write about in this chapter were from the before and after school center Curtis attended.

I have written previously (Vasquez, 2003a) about Curtis' engagement with *Pokémon* cards, highlighting the literacies Curtis learned and used as he created his own *Pokémon* cards (see Figures 12.3 and 12.4).

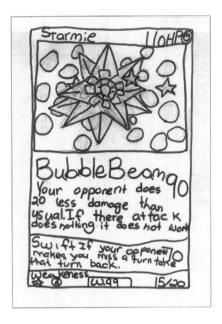

Figure 12.4 Pokémon cards created by Curtis

In particular, I have used Gee's (2003) principles of learning to show that many of the same principles apply to the construction, understanding and design of the *Pokémon* cards. In a study of first-person shooter games, Gee used previously documented research on literacy development regarding important principles of learning to unpack the principles of learning that undergird the playing of computer games (Gee, 2003). In the study, he developed a collection of learning principles, such as *Learning about and coming to appreciate design* and *Design principles are core to the learning experience* (Gee, 2003). I have summarized the intersections between some of Gee's principles of learning and the repertoire of skills children use when designing such cards. Table 12.1 represents this summary and is included here to illustrate specific connections between Gee's principles of learning and the skills used by children in designing their *Pokémon* cards.

Inserting unofficial curriculum

Pokémon has been banned from Curtis' school, so he is able to do this kind of work only at the before and after school center, at home, or while with his neighborhood friends. The kind of work that counts at school is represented in Figure 12.5. It stems from a story starter that he and his classmates were required to use during writing time in his third grade classroom. Upon closer

Table 12.1 Intersections between creating *Pokémon* cards and Gee's Principles of Learning

Principle	
Active, Critical Learning Principle All aspects of the learning environment including the ways in which the semiotic domain is designed and presented are set up to encourage active and critical, not passive, learning.	In order to trade cards successfully players engage in an active, not passive, flurry of decision-making regarding gaps in their card collections along with determining how the value of particular cards would increase the worth of their collection.
Design Principle Learning about and coming to appreciate design and design principles is core to the learning experience.	The children found great pleasure in creating their own cards. To engage in the redesign of cards required an understanding of how the cards were designed in the first place.
Semiotic Principle Learning about and coming to appreciate inter-relations within and across multiple sign systems (images, words, actions, symbols, artifacts, and so forth) as a complex system is core to the learning experience.	While creating their cards, the children drew from and made use of multiple sign systems through engagement with such resources as books and magazines, videos, and the Internet. The children live in Canada and were used to the metric system. The cards made use of the imperial system. While creating their cards, therefore, they made use of a conversion program they found on the internet to convert the Pokémon's weights and heights from imperial to metric measurement.
Committed Learning Principle Learners participate in an extended engagement as extensions of their real-world identities and	The children took on the role of Pokémon trainer as they created and designed their cards. With lots of effort and practice they played out this Poke-world identity for extended periods of time.
Practice Principle The learner gets lots and lots of practice in a context where the practice is not boring.	The sustained time they were able to devote to the task of designing was impressive.
On-Going Learning Principle The distinction between learner and master is vague, since learners, thanks to the operation of the 'Regime of Competence' principle listed below, must, at higher and higher levels, undo their routinized mastery to adapt to new or changed conditions. There are cycles of new learning, automatization, undoing automatization, and new reorganized automatization.	Card manufacturers were very good at sustaining gamers' interest by continuously putting out different versions of the cards. With each new version came another complex set of understandings. With this players were required to continuously adapt to new or changed conditions for trading, collecting and designing.
Situated Meaning Principle The meanings of signs (words, actions, objects, artifacts, symbols, texts, etc.) are situated in embodied experience. Meanings are not general or decontextualized. Whatever generality meanings come to have is discovered bottom up via embodied experiences.	While designing *Pokémon* cards the meaning of signs are situated in the designer's experience as a collector and trader of cards which is contextualized based on who the other trainers are and the corpus of cards that they have on hand.

Intertextual Principle
The learner understands texts as a family ("genre") of related texts and understands any one such text in relation to others in the family, but only after having achieved embodied understandings of some texts. Understanding a group of texts as a family (genre) of texts is a large part of what helps the learner make sense of such texts.

Multimodal principle
Meaning and knowledge is built up through various modalities (images, texts, symbols, interactions, abstract design, sound, etc.), not just words.

Intuitive Knowledge Principle and Affinity Group Principle
Intuitive or tacit knowledge built up in repeated practice and experience, often in association with an affinity group, counts a great deal and is honored. It is not just verbal and conscious knowledge that is rewarded.

Learners constitute an 'affinity group', that is a group that is bonded primarily through shared endeavors, goals, and practices and not shared race, gender, nation, ethnicity, or culture.

Bottom-Up Basic Skills Principle
Basic skills are not learned in isolation or out of context, rather what counts as a basic skill is discovered bottom up by engaging in more and more of the game/domain or game/domains like it. Basic skills are genre elements of a given type of game/domain.

Dispersed Principle
Meaning/knowledge is dispersed in the sense that the learner shares it with others outside the domain/game, some of whom the learner may rarely or never see face-to-face.

Insider Principle
The learner is an 'insider', 'teacher', and 'producer' (not just a 'consumer') able to customize the learning experience and domain/game from the beginning and throughout the experience.

Designing their own cards required the children to frequently engage with a variety of related texts. They knew which magazines to go to for information on the strengths of the various characters and which internet sites could offer them further information, how the magazines and knew/worked in conjunction with the internet sites and other resources to provide them with the information they needed.

It goes without saying that meaning and knowledge underlying the creation of *Pokémon* cards was built up though various modalities and not just printed words.

Curtis and his friends formed what Gee refers to as an affinity group, that is a group bonded through shared endeavors and practices. Knowledge gained through repeated practice and experience carried with it great cultural capital. For example, Curtis became better and better at knowing how to draw the various characters and became 'the' primary resource for neighborhood children who wanted to design their own cards.

The more that Curtis and his friends created their own cards and engaged in the exchange of cards the more they liked it and the more they learned about it. As such this learning always took place in social spaces in particular contexts. The experiences he had with his affinity group provided opportunities for him to take on different roles as 'insider', 'teacher', 'producer' and 'consumer'.

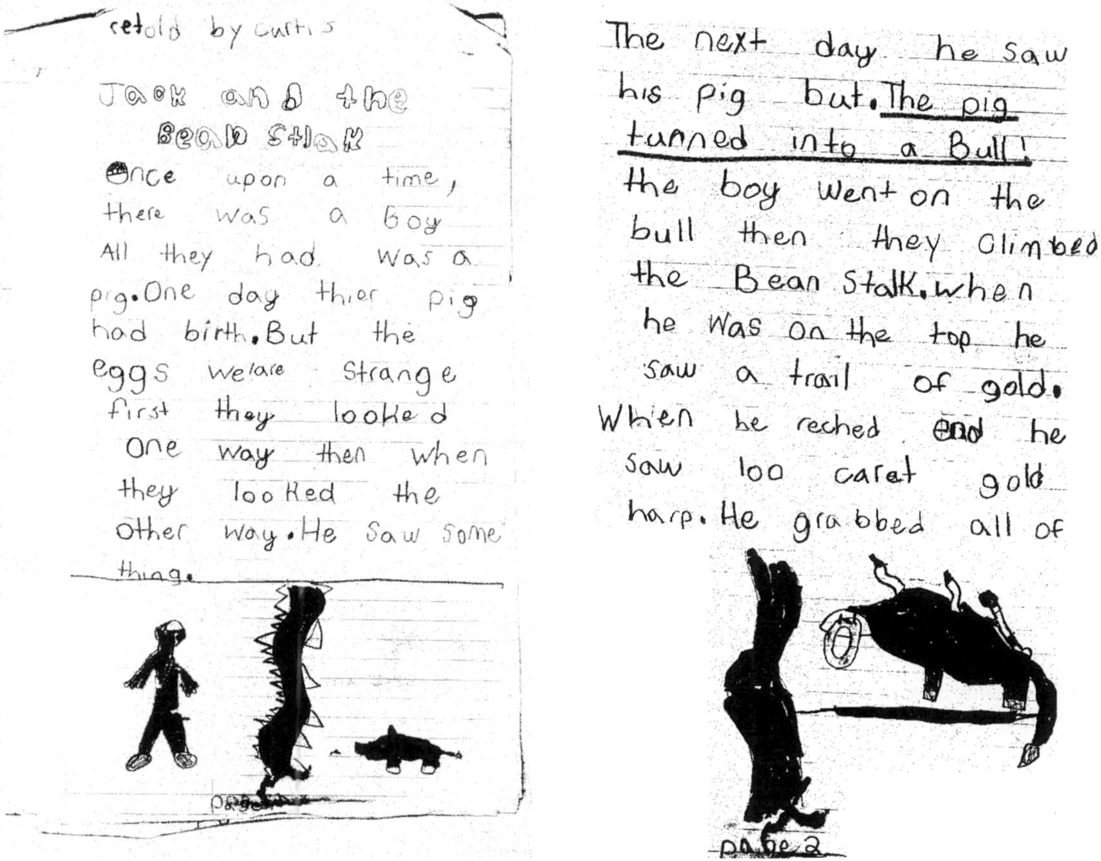

retold by curtis

JooK aNd the
BeaD StloK

Once upon a time,
there was a boy
All they had was a
pig. One day ther pig
had birth. But the
eggs welare strange
first they looked
one way then when
they looKed the
other way. He saw some
thing.

The next day. he saw
his pig - but. The pig
turned into a Bull!
the boy went on the
bull then they climbed
the Bean Stalk, when
he was on the top he
saw a trail of gold.
When he reched end he
saw loo carat gold
harp. He grabbed all of
- page 2

Figure 12.5 A story written by Curtis at school as part of the official curriculum

inspection, however, the ways in which Curtis is able to insert his interest in *Pokémon* into the 'official curriculum' become noticeable, but only to those who know *Pokémon*. The 'O' in 'once upon a time' is not just any 'O'. It is in fact a Pokeball, a cage of sorts used to keep pocket monsters. The Pokeball is also a sign of an impending Pokebattle. The cover of his journal is peppered with pocket monsters. He is able to insert his interests because his teacher is not familiar with 'Poke discourse' or the ways of talking and doing by those familiar with *Pokémon*.

The text Curtis has created is therefore heterogeneous. It contains a combination of 'official' classroom text (assigned genre, assigned format, assigned base topic) and 'unofficial' classroom text (*Pokémon*). His story represents an instance of Bakhtin's heteroglossia, where struggles over difference and different ideologies take place (Bakhtin, 1981). The struggle in this case takes place between the text that Curtis is told to write for class and the text that Curtis wants to write regarding *Pokémon*. Foucault (1982) talks about how language users are both produced by discourse and producers of discourse. Curtis' story reflects how he is forced to comply with creating text assigned by his teacher while at the same time interrupting that text by his insertion of a Pokeball into his story. This interruption of the official classroom text is readily recognizable to his peers but remains invisible to his teacher. As such, the text carries cultural capital in his peer world.

The question we need to ask here is, how can we strike a balance between creating spaces for childhood popular culture discourses in the classroom while at the same time making sure not to co-opt their interests? A growing number of accounts documenting such work with students are appearing in print (Alvermann and Hong Xu, 2003; Comber, 1993; Dyson, 2003; O'Brien, 1998; Luke, O'Brien and Comber, 1994; Vasquez, 2004). In the following section, I outline pedagogical approaches to using *Pokémon* texts which were undertaken with the children at the childcare center. The children were aged between three to eight years old.

Toy packaging as text

The children regularly brought to school toy packages and cut-outs from magazines to share with one another. Capitalizing on this, I asked them to bring in packaging from their *Pokémon* toys. The following exchange took place while a group of children and I were looking across a series of such texts which we spread out on the classroom floor.

Vivian: How many times do you see 'Gotta Catch 'Em All'?[2]
Curtis: You can find 'Gotta Catch 'Em All' in almost all the posters that you find.
Vivian: Any ideas why that might be?
Curtis: Uh, I don't know. I can take a guess though.

Vivian: Okay.
Curtis: Well in the show, the object is to catch all the Pokémon. So maybe that's 'Gotta Catch 'Em All' means you gotta (pause) catch them all.
Vivian: So catching, is that the same or different as collecting?
Emily: It's sort of like collecting cards.
Miguel: Except you're collecting the Pokémon.
Emily: Who wants us to do that?
Miguel: The sellers?
Curtis: Ya, they make the Pokémon for their job.

This brief exchange set the groundwork for later conversations whereby the children and I began to look more closely at the use of words across *Pokémon* texts and how these ideologically position readers. We did an analysis of the texts by bringing to the fore the way that audience is maintained through the consistent use of the phrase 'Gotta Catch 'Em All', as Curtis noted, 'in almost all the posters [author note: referring to toy packaging, posters, magazines and other *Pokémon* related products] you find'. We also brought to the fore the notion of consumerism when Emily asked, 'Who wants us to do that?' and Miguel replied, 'The sellers'.

Vivian: If these posters and pictures didn't have the images of Pokémon on them would you still know that these are Pokémon?
Curtis: Well yes because like I said before 'Gotta Catch 'Em All' is on almost everything.
Miguel: And they have the same kind of thing like they made a *Pokémon* pasta so it's like you 'Gotta Catch 'Em All' except it's you 'Gotta Eat 'Em All'.
Vivian: So the 'Gotta' was the same the ''Em' was the same and the 'All' was the same.
Emily: Right instead you don't say catch. It's eat. You 'Gotta Eat 'Em All'.

In this exchange, the children begin to unpack how the same wording is used in different contexts, playing and eating, to encourage the same 'collecting' behavior. Emily shared later in the conversation that when she and her sister eat *Pokémon* pasta (pasta in the shape of *Pokémon* characters) they check to see which Pokémon they have eaten, with the goal of eating all the different characters.

Vivian: Let's try to find all the words that have to do with catching or collecting. You said it has to do with collecting right?
Curtis: Yeah
Vivian: Okay so let's find all the words that have to do with collecting.
Miguel: Catch . . . best

Vivian:	D'best
Emily:	D'best
Vivian:	What do you think that has to do with collecting? D'best?
Miguel:	Like you gotta get the best or something like that.
Vivian:	And you said the best is . . . ummm . . . what are the three categories?
Curtis:	Rare, common, uncommon
Vivian:	So then the best would be which . . . which one would the best be?
Emily:	Rare.
Vivian:	Let's look at this one to see if there are things that have to do with collecting.
Curtis:	Watch these little creatures grow like magic.
Vivian:	How do we know this is a collecting thing?
Curtis:	Well, it's not really collecting it's just like watching creatures grow like those dinosaurs that grow in water.
Miguel:	But you when you see one grow maybe you want to see all of them grow.
Vivian:	Yeah yeah
Curtis:	Watch those creatures grow. They would be one.
Emily:	After you want one, you might want more.
Vivian:	That's true. Let's find some other words that mean collecting.
Curtis:	Some . . . They . . . Their . . . 25 packs
Vivian:	Any other ones?
Miguel:	10 packs . . . original
Vivian:	You were talking about original before
Curtis:	Uhum.
Vivian:	What about this one?
Curtis:	Collect more Puzzles
Emily:	Again, more more more

This transcript represents qualitative analysis of media texts whereby the children and I began to uncover the symbols and codes used to position viewers in particular ways. By identifying the different ways that the phrase 'Gotta Catch 'Em All' was presented, Curtis, Emily, and Miguel began to recognise how Pokémon were being offered to them in intertextual ways as indicated by the use of such words and phrases as 'D'best', 'original', '25 packs' and by the use of the plural version of merchandise as in 'collect more puzzles' or '25 packs'. These are some of the words and phrases used across *Pokémon* texts that engage the same practice of having to 'catch 'em all'.

During other conversations, we engaged in quantitative analysis, counting and sorting different ways that collecting was represented and then talking about why certain representations were more dominant. For instance, we discovered that a large percentage of the words used to entice collectors fit into a category of words that mean something is rare or uncommon such as 'D'best' or 'original'. Also, the way that words and phrases co-occur or collocate (Fairclough, 1989: 115) as in 'Gotta Catch 'Em All' and 'collect more puzzles' offers a dominant scheme for classifying 'collecting' behavior. The main meaning relations (Fairclough, 1989) being used are synonyms, as in 'catch' and 'collect', and hyponymy, as in the use of 'more' and 'D'best', where the meaning of one word is included in the meaning of another word. Fairclough (1989: 116) suggests that 'a text's choice of wording depends on, and helps create, social relationships between participants'. For instance, the use of 'collecting' vocabulary has experiential value in terms of representing *Pokémon* trainers, who collect *Pokémon* cards.

Quantitative analysis, semiotic analysis and sociological analysis

The kind of analysis outlined above lends itself to semiotic analysis, the study of signs, symbols and signification systems. This semiotic inquiry can then lead, for example, to analyzing the use of color as semiotic shorthand to produce gendered texts. For instance, the creators of *Pokémon* claim that these creatures are not gendered, yet there are clearly recognizable features that lead children to assign gender orientations to particular characters. The following are some comments from the children with whom I worked when I asked them if Pokémon were male or female.

Vivian: Are Pokémon male or female? Are they boys or girls?
Emily: Clefairy could be a girl.
Julia: Sometimes Pikachu could be a girl but sometimes Pikachu could be a boy.
Eric: Pikachu sucks. Bulbasaur I think is a boy.

When I asked Emily why Clefairy could be a girl, she told me that first of all Clefairy sounds like a girl 'but mostly she's a girl because she doesn't look like a boy'. She classified the Pokémon gender not from the semiotic information she had available, but with the semiotic information that is missing, claiming that Clefairy did not look like a boy and therefore must be a girl. Her second comment is directly tied to a conversation she had previously with Eric and Ryan who were busy sorting Pokémon according to whom they liked and didn't like. Clefairy was one of the Pokémon that, according to Eric, 'sucks'. When I asked the boys what they meant, they basically used the same rationale that Emily did, claiming that if Clefairy were a boy, its characteristics would be consistent with other 'boy' Pokémon, e.g. it would be a boy color like blue or green instead of pink, which is a girl color. In Emily's schema, if Clefairy were a boy, then it probably would not have fit into the 'sucks' category. In the boys' schema, if Clefairy were more like the other 'boy' Pokémon, based on its appearance, then it too would be male. When I asked Julia why Pikachu was sometimes a girl and at other times a boy, she referred me to the cartoon. In the cartoon, Pikachu is often seen being cuddled and hugged by Ash, Pikachu's trainer. When in battle, however, Pikachu is quick to shoot off lightning bolts to take down his opponents. Pikachu therefore has both 'girl' and 'boy' qualities. It is not surprising, therefore, that when I asked the children for their favorite Pokémon, it was the girls and younger children who chose Pikachu. (For further accounts of highly gendered discourses of early childhood refer to Carrington, 2003; Davies, 1989; McNaughton, 1997; McNaughton and Hughes, 2001; Vasquez, 2003b; Yelland, 1998).

Developing highly complex, new literacy pedagogies

Pokémon texts are just one example of the sort of highly complex literacies that children face today. In essence, this chapter has been about developing 'new literacy' pedagogies and curricula beyond debates over basic skills and best methodology. Rather, these new literacy pedagogies should be informed by observation and analysis of children's participatory engagement with texts for which they have an affinity and for which they are willing to participate in complex learning situations for a sustained period of time. Through engagement with such texts, young children participate in an open pedagogy where print text is not privileged over all other texts, especially those that stem from the children's everyday lives. Rather, it becomes one of many symbol systems used as a generative multimodal tool for cultivating different forms of literate behaviors beyond those traditionally associated with literacy, such as reading and writing. This supports the idea that participating in children's culture is based on an acknowledgement of a broad range of literacies. In this open pedagogy, where learning is not pre-determined but generated − based on a functional need to continue to learn to play the game better − children thrive as literate beings, continuously seeking out more knowledge and willingly taking up the challenge of participating in a game that grows in complexity and difficulty over time.

Notes

1 For more on the negotiation of critical literacies refer to Comber, 2001; Comber and Simpson, 2001; Vasquez, 2001a, 2001b, 2003b, 2004.
2 'Gotta catch 'em all' is a phrase from the *Pokémon* rap that is at the beginning and end of the *Pokémon* cartoons.

References

Alvermann, D. E. and Hong Xu, S. (2003) Children's everyday literacies: intersections of popular culture and language arts instruction. *Language Arts*, 81 (2): 145−154.
Bakhtin, M. (1981) Discourse in the novel. In M. Holquist (ed.) *The Dialogic Imagination: Four Essays by M. Bakhtin* (pp. 259−422). Austin: University of Texas Press.

Bogdan, R. C. and Biklen, S. K. (1992) *Qualitative Research for Education* (2nd ed.). Boston: Allyn & Bacon.

Carrington, V. (2003) I'm in a bad mood. Let's go shopping: interactive dolls, consumer culture and a 'glocalized' model of literacy. *Journal of Early Childhood Literacy*, 3 (1): 83–98.

Comber, B. (1993) Classroom explorations in critical literacy. *Australian Journal of Language and Literacy*, 16 (1): 73–83.

Comber, B. (2001) Critical inquiry or safe literacies: Who's allowed to ask which questions? In S. Boran and B. Comber (eds) *Critiquing Whole Language and Classroom Inquiry*. Urbana, IL: National Council of Teachers of English.

Comber, B. and Simpson, A. (2001) *Negotiating Critical Literacies in Classrooms*. Mahwah, NJ: Lawrence Erlbaum Associates.

Davies, B. (1989) *Frogs and Snails and Feminist Tales: Preschool Children and Gender*. Sydney: Allen and Unwin.

Dyson, A. H. (1999) Coach Bombay's kids learn to write: children's appropriations of media material for school literacy. *Research in the Teaching of English*, 33 (4): 367–401.

Dyson, A. H. (2003) Popular literacies and the 'all' children: rethinking literacy development for contemporary childhoods. *Language Arts*, 81 (2): 100–109.

Fairclough, N. (1989) *Language and Power*. London: Longman.

Foucault, M. (1982) *The Archeology of Knowledge*. New York: Pantheon Books.

Gee, J. P. (2003) *What Video Games Have To Teach Us About Learning And Literacy*. Cambridge: Palgrave.

Kavanagh, K. (1997) *Texts on television: School literacies through viewing in the first years of school*. Adelaide: Department for Education and Children's Services, South Australia.

Luke, A. (1998) Getting over method: literacy teaching as work in new times. *Language Arts*, 75: 305–313.

Luke, A. (2000) Critical literacy in Australia: a matter of context and standpoint. *Journal of Adolescent and Adult Literacy*, 43 (5): 448–461.

Luke, A., O'Brien, J. and Comber, B. (1994) Making community texts objects of study. *Australian Journal of Language and Literacy*, 17 (2): 139–149.

MacNaughton, G. (1997) Who's got the power? Rethinking gender equity strategies in early childhood. *International Journal of Early Years Education*, 5 (1): 57–66.

MacNaughton, G. and Hughes, P. (2001) Fractured or manufactured: gendered identity and culture in the early years. In S. Grieshaber and G. Cannella (eds) *Diversity in Early Childhood*. New York: Teachers College Press.

O'Brien, J. (1998) Experts in Smurfland. In M. Knobel and A. Healy (ed.) *Critical Literacy in the Primary Classroom*. Newton, New South Wales: Primary English Teaching Association.

Vallen, M. and Thorpe, J. (2001) A night at the Academy: anime comes of age. The Black Moon. Accessed at: http://www.theblackmoon.com/Academy/academy.htm.

Vasquez, V. (2001a) Classroom inquiry into the incidental unfolding of social justice issues: seeking out possibilities in the lives of learners. In B. Comber and S. Cakmac (eds) *Critiquing Whole Language and Classroom Inquiry* (pp. 200–215). Urbana, IL: National Council of Teachers of English.

Vasquez, V. (2001b) Negotiating critical literacies in elementary classrooms. In B. Comber and A. Simpson (eds) *Critical Literacy at Elementary Sites* (pp. 55–66). Mahwah, NJ: Lawrence Erlbaum Associates.

Vasquez, V. (2003a) What *Pokémon* can teach us about learning and literacy. *Language Arts*, 81 (2): 118–125.

Vasquez, V. (2003b) *Getting Beyond I Like the Book: Creating Spaces for Critical Literacy in K–6 Classrooms*. Newark, DE: International Reading Association.

Vasquez, V. (2004) *Negotiating Critical Literacies with Young Children*. New Jersey: Lawrence Erlbaum Associates.

Yelland, N. (ed.) (1998) *Gender in Early Childhood*. London: Routledge.

APPENDIX I   DATA SOURCES AND ANALYSIS

Type of data	Source	Analyzed for:
Interview	Focal students	Student perspective
	Other students	Teacher perspective
	Classroom teacher	Teacher perspective
	Center director	Administrator perspective
	Parent	Parent/home perspective
Observation	Literacy lessons	Literacy opportunities and literate
	Small group work	behaviors
	Shadowing focal students	Children's participation with popular culture texts
		Discourse on popular culture texts
		Children's participation with multi-mediated texts
Print documents	Children's work	Nature of children's work with
	Popular culture texts	everyday, popular culture and media
	Media texts	texts
Audio recording	Focus students during	Literacy opportunities and literate
	small group work	behaviors
		Children's participation with popular culture texts
		Discourse on popular culture texts

Note: The focal students are those featured in this chapter.

Chapter 13

Behind the scenes

Making movies in early years classrooms

Helen Nixon and Barbara Comber

I'm on really dangerous ground in a way that people are saying . . . because people just think 'She's just holding up the camera, kids just holding a camera. That's all'.

(Helen Grant, March 2003)

I had one mum, she actually came in and she was quite angry about the whole thing and said 'First of all, if you're going to be doing this sort of thing in the classroom, can you send some flash cards home so we can do some real work at home?'

(Andrew Lord, January 2003)

Introduction

In recent times, early years classrooms have increasingly been dominated by an insistence on literacy. Internationally, this move is marked by programs incorporating a 'literacy block' or a 'literacy hour', (some of which are government or system mandated), designed to deliver centralised benchmarks. Literacy education policy and standards-based assessments are now key matters for the state. In some respects literacy (or at least reading) has always been the province of early childhood educators. Along with inducting children into the world of school, their major role was to teach children to read. However, the new demand for all children to perform at pre-specified literacy standards has arguably produced extra anxiety amongst parents and professionals alike. This task of course – namely making sure all children measure up against the benchmarks – is a different accomplishment for teachers and children in poor and linguistically and culturally diverse communities than it is for affluent middle-class English-speaking communities where some children begin school already having met the initial benchmarks for literacy. It is not that meeting proper literacy benchmarks is not an achievable or laudable goal, but that the educational pathway by which such performance is met may need to remain open to negotiation in local sites. In our view what constitutes 'proper literacy' (Lankshear and Lawler, 1988) also needs to remain up for scrutiny as repertoires of literate practices are expanding in terms of the media, modes and languages required for living in an increasingly globalised world (Kellner, 2000; Luke and Luke, 2001; New London Group, 1996).

Historically, teachers have an odd relationship with television and film (Buckingham, 1993; Buckingham and Sefton-Green, 1994; Dyson, 1993, 1997; Kavanagh, 2003; Marsh, 2000). Television, movies and other elements of popular culture marketed for children are frequently seen as being in competition with traditional print literacy or even as simply bad for children. International literacy education professional associations still include 'Turn off the TV' weeks as part of their strategies to enhance literacy levels. Television and film are often set up in opposition to children's literature. Somewhat ironically, new information and communications technologies (ICTs) are being promoted as 'learning technologies' and being brought into primary schools, while television and film continue to be relegated to popular culture and are often excluded. However, some teachers have long known the power of the popular and the potential of the screen in bringing children to school learning and literacies. In this chapter we draw extensively on the work of two South Australian primary school teachers, Helen Grant and Andrew Lord, who, as we see in their comments quoted above, are only too aware of the political tensions about incorporating film-making into the early literacy classroom.

Helen Grant has been teaching in state primary schools for twenty-six years. Her long-term interests in media and cultural studies combined with her expertise in language, especially through her role as an ESL (English as a Second Language) teacher, have been brought together into a powerful pedagogical mix. Her recent work brings together insights from systemic functional linguistics, media studies and critical literacy. In her current role as an English as a Second Language teacher, Grant takes classes from early childhood to Grade 7. She works in mainstream classrooms as well as withdrawing groups of ESL children for intensive language work. The school has a strong 'New Arrivals Program' for children who have recently arrived in Australia and Grant has been given 'an open brief' in terms of the ways she works to build students' linguistic and literate repertoires. A major priority is film-making and she has now built an extended body of work with children in this and her previous school.

Andrew Lord is an early childhood classroom teacher in a school in the southern suburb on the outskirts of the capital city. The area is predominantly working-class with young families attracted by comparatively cheaper land and home packages. Andrew has been teaching for 25 years. He has a strong commitment to maintaining 'play' in early childhood, and an interest in ICTs and the media. Andrew works with a wide definition of literacy in his classroom program and curriculum. Like Grant, Lord is interested in taking on ambitious projects with his class of five- and six-year-old children. We refer here only to selected instances of their work, but it is important to emphasise that the examples we discuss are not one-off; rather, these teachers build a classroom corpus of artefacts, shared memories and public perform-ances across the school year. It is these wider cultural practices in which children participate as members of the classroom community.

Grant and Lord are part of a South Australian teacher community heavily influenced in the 1980s by the work of well-known educator Garth Boomer. Two of Boomer's key ideas were (1) language across the curriculum and (2) negotiating the curriculum (see Green, 1988b, 1999). In the projects which we draw on and describe in this chapter, these themes underpin a number of the teachers' pedagogical approaches. Both teachers demonstrate a strong commitment to the principles of negotiating with students and building language work and play into the curriculum, and both have also taken up more recent moves to multiliteracies (New London Group, 1996) and incor-porating information and communications technologies (ICTs) into the cur-riculum. In other words, these are teachers who cumulatively build their professional practices with direct engagement with a range of theory and principled decision-making. We met Grant and Lord through two different projects that called for the serious involvement of 'teacher-researchers'. In both of these projects, Grant and Lord were involved in making short films either with teachers or with students. Grant joined a teacher-researcher net-work investigating teaching and assessing inclusive literacies in diverse com-munities and Lord was part of a project exploring information technology, literacy and educational disadvantage. We outline a little of Lord's and Grant's professional histories here as we believe it is important to understand not only what the teachers did and their effects, but also how they came to be approaching literacy curriculum and pedagogy in the ways that they do. We are interested in the knowledges, dispositions, expertise and politics that allow teachers to design productive and critical literacies. From our perspect-ive, Lord and Grant take up positions as 'cultural workers' (Freire, 1998) in seriously grappling with the politics of everyday life and children's diverse representational resources.

Both Grant and Lord contest developmental discourses that position young children as incompetent or as unready for complex literate practices (Reid and Comber, 2002; Baker and Freebody, 1993). They do not accept normat-ive models of literacy development that take it for granted that text analysis and production are for older children. Instead, they assume that young chil-dren can and should express serious ideas, engage in cultural analysis and produce significant multimedia artefacts. Indeed, they position young chil-dren as researchers of language and culture, as we will see. While they take children seriously and hold very high expectations for what is possible, they also make the time for pleasure, play and humour. How they do this work and what it accomplishes is the focus of this chapter.

Teachers and students as film-makers: Where's the literacy in that?

While there is considerable rhetoric about multiliteracies, there is less evidence of complex and critical multiliteracies in practice (Comber *et al.*, 2002; Comber, 2003). Like Lord and Grant, we have a commitment to imagining and sustaining school literacies which are simultaneously pleasurable and powerful. Part or our research agenda is to document and analyse the innovative work of teachers who are informed by an overt politics of social justice and a socio-cultural theory of literacy. The dominance of minimalist approaches to literacy in some government policy (Luke *et al.*, 1999) threatens to dampen teacher motivation and risk-taking. In these times, it becomes crucial to identify and support approaches that go beyond the basics and accomplish demonstrable and significant learning.

Grant has incorporated film-making into her role as an ESL teacher and her body of work is more extensive than we can explore here. For the purposes of this chapter we consider two films made with five- to seven-year-old children – *Aussie Slang* (2002) and *Wave Cultures* (2003). *Aussie Slang* is an eight-minute film made in a documentary style. Five-year-old children work with Grant to interview teachers across their school. The film begins with stills of children's illustrated drawings titled 'Aussie' and 'Fair go'. We hear two children speak accompanying each slide. The first says 'Aussie means Australian' and the second says 'fair go means being fair'. The full title of the film appears: *Aussie Slang: Under investigation by 5-year-old Australians*. We see the faces of two young children who say in unison to camera: 'this film is about Australian slang'. We then begin to see a repeated scenario in which children hold a microphone up to adult informants in their school and ask pre-prepared, pre-rehearsed questions about their knowledge of slang. The children are positioned as investigative journalists exploring a social phenomenon, namely types, uses and lexical items of Australian slang. In the process of interviewing, the children discover that a number of their teachers are bilingual and speak English as a second language. These teachers know some Aussie slang but explain some of the difficulties they had learning some of it. The children begin to explore whether other languages have their own slang by asking teachers whether they know any slang in their first language. As the film progresses, children illustrate and rehearse the slang words and phrases they have been told. Where slang terms are in languages other than English, they are subtitled. In this section of the film, children's spoken voices are heard as voice-over to still images of their annotated drawings in a demonstration of their newly developing vocabularies and understandings, which by then apply to a range of languages, not only Australian English. The film concludes with a performance of 'slang' to camera from a selection of our young film-makers, this time speaking directly to the audience as they play with their expanded vocabularies. The final image is of the original two young interviewers who say 'oo roo' (goodbye in Aussie slang) and wave to the viewer.

We invited Grant to tell us what was important in the process of making this film.

> This was a topic on Australia – and I was working with the teacher-librarian and the class teacher, and we planned together our term's work of one afternoon a week. We divided the class into three groups, and I took my ESL students. We focused on a different area that we wanted under that heading, and so we decided to do . . . to tie in with us, I thought that would be good to look at language, and then when you think about language, it's not just one language but slang, and then not just slang but whose slang, because we talked about that too. I mean even with the children, their language – a lot of the things that I actually showed them in books – they didn't use, a lot of those words they don't know because they don't use them. You know the historical Australian slang like 'cobber' and Aboriginal English like 'deadly', all that kind of stuff – children don't use that. So we then thought about asking other people in the school too. Children virtually asked the questions: 'Do you know any Australian slang? And what is your favourite?' So they took the role of interviewers.
>
> (Helen Grant, March 2003)

Apart from the obvious pleasure children have interviewing, filming and performing with a camera, the project of making *Aussie Slang* involved a range of curricular and wider cultural knowledges, as we discuss below. Importantly, as Grant emphasises, the film is 'there forever'. It becomes part of the historical record in the school archives. As a collectively produced artefact it represents the work of individuals within a class or group. She explains further:

> Just making the film is like creating a little bit of history and I like to keep everything I do. I keep a copy in the library so they've got it for future. When those children graduate there's a film made when they were five.
>
> (Helen Grant, March 2003)

The second film produced by Helen Grant and a class of five-year-old children, which we discuss here, is *Wave Cultures*. In this project Grant responded to a circulated invitation for a local film-makers award (which is part of South Australia's biennial Come-Out Festival of youth arts). The theme for the year was 'waves' and children were invited to treat the theme in any way they wished. This short film simply shows the children, who speak 13 different languages, moving across a wall and making a greeting in their own language. English subtitles are provided. Like many of Grant's co-productions with children, both these films emphasise linguistic and cultural diversity.

The film *Super Sausage* (2002) was made in a very different context. Andrew Lord's student population was largely Anglo-Australian working-class and the film was made with the whole class. Andrew explains to us how the idea for the movie was generated:

> Yeah, the big movie in the second term holidays was *Spiderman*, not that many kids were to see it because it was rated MA or something or other. A couple of kids had been to see it and they had all seen the MacDonald's tie-in or whatever it was, so they were all very Spiderman-mad. They'd seen us make a movie in that we'd documented the zoo last term and they knew we could do big stuff.

> Making the movie was actually my suggestion but it was based on the idea that this is something that they would enjoy so it was me reading the classroom I guess, but they're keen on super heroes, we've made a movie, we've got some stuff on video and they're excited about the whole thing, let's do something big and make a movie, and I guess that came out of the experience the year before of we did the Christmas play where we gave the whole term over to doing the Christmas play at the end of the year, and once again we had the whole campus come and see our Christmas play and that got pretty big, so I'd had the experience of doing something big in drama before, so the whole thing said 'We'll go ahead with this' and so we got the idea of making a movie, and super heroes seemed to be the thing to be because it was in the air at the time.

(Andrew Lord, January 2003)

The movie itself was based on the traditional superhero genre, but is more of a spoof than serious imitation. This 30-minute film opens with a two-minute title and credits sequence which begins as follows:

Screen 1:	Spence [school name] Productions
Screen 2:	A Room 4 Film
Screen 3:	Super Sausage
Screen 4:	Starring
Screen 6:	Brenda, Dane, Ryan and Adity
Screen 7:	as the Snag of Steel
Screen 8:	Jake
Screen 9:	as Dr Vincent van Nasty
Screen 10:	Laura
Screen 11:	as Belle Lovely
Screen 12:	Rhys

Screen 13:   as The Old Toymaker
Screen 14:   Amy
Screen 15:   as the Fairy Godmother
Screen 16:   with

Subsequent screens repeat a pattern of listing several students' names followed by a screen that reads 'with' or 'featuring' or 'special appearances by' and 'crew'. The final screen reads: 'no sausages were harmed in the making of this picture'. This opening two-minute sequence achieves several objectives. First, expectations of the genre of the film are established by listing its main characters as superhero, super villain, old toymaker, fairy godmother and beautiful girl. Secondly, students in the class are named and the film is established as a collective effort. Thirdly, the excessive nature of the credits – emphasised further by the accompanying music, change of background for every screen and the final note that no sausages were harmed – anticipates the parodic or send-up nature of what is to come, and also highlights the pleasures that we imagine children took in first producing and subsequently watching the film. It was clear from what Lord told us that he too had great fun making the film, as did he and the parents when watching it with the children. Making *Super Sausage* provided a safe space in which students and teacher could together enjoy what Grace and Tobin (1998) describe as the 'collective transgressive pleasures' of satire, parody and social laughter to be found in classroom video production.

The main sequences of the film are indicated by its section titles which appear on the screen: 'Once there was an Old Toymaker', 'Meanwhile in a gloomy Castle', 'Meanwhile in the Big City', 'And they fell in love', 'A trip to the Classiest Restaurant in Town', 'Later . . .'. The story opens with an old toymaker who is so poor he cannot afford real sausages but must instead eat wooden ones that he carves himself. While asleep he is visited by a fairy godmother who grants him his wish and sends him 'the best sausage in the world'. Super Sausage – mostly represented by a brown paper hanging puppet – turns out to be part hero, part anti-hero. He flees from being eaten and travels to the city to help people in superhero style (but is mostly rebuffed). There he meets and falls in love with Belle Lovely. Together – in a fantastic sequence which anticipates a 'barbeque of terror' using 'tongs of horror', 'onions of creepiness', and 'fork of scary stuff' – they save the world from Vincent van Nasty and his vampire rissoles. When they realise at the end that they cannot be together because, as Belle Lovely notes, 'you are a sausage and I am a girl', the fairy godmother returns and grants Super Sausage his wish to be with Belle forever by changing her into a sausage too. One of Lord's strategies is to teach the children that they can play with conventions and turn them on their head. Thus traditional fairy-tale expectations associated with happy endings are confounded. The frog/sausage is not turned into a handsome prince. Rather, in an ironic send-up – which Lord acknowledged is 'pinched from *Shrek*' – in order to be with her hero, the heroine is turned into a sausage.

Building complex 3D literate repertoires

> I view literacy as an active, cross-curricular process where children build systems of knowledge by engaging in personally purposeful language tasks using these to refine existing knowledge and then using that refined knowledge as a jumping off point for new learning . . . I think that an awful lot of what passes for 'literacy' in this day and age is actually 'language skills'. And that, it seems to me is the big failing of the 'literacy block' – it just isn't literacy. It's learning letters of the alphabet and word families and spelling demons and sight words and editing skills (and all of these are important things) but it isn't literacy in that the only purpose this stuff seems to have is so that kids can perform party tricks – 'Write ten words that rhyme with orange'. Why would you want to do that? So I suppose my 'jargon free, plain language' definition of literacy would be something like 'Literacy is what happens when an individual chooses to use the language skills they have for a purpose'.
>
> (Andrew Lord, March 2003)

> Five-year-olds made little overhead puppets on the overhead projector, made from cellophane. It was the activity to retell *The Three Little Pigs*. And then we used a different medium – digital photography – to retell the story. We used little masks, and we all went out in the playground, and they had to choose a location for each part of the story. We had each shot drawn on a story map, so they'd know the plan. Two children organised the actors – a stage manager and a director. So they gave orders, like: 'We have to go into the cubby next'. So all the class would follow, with a couple playing around in the bark chips, and so on. I just try any way I can to manage a class group. Now those images can be published in a book, and children may want to write about them, or make an audio tape, or even try another medium like film to record another version of the story.
>
> (Helen Grant, March 2003)

As we see above, Lord contests what he sees as limited skills-based approaches to language as not being literacy at all and, in preparing a presentation for his peers, he arrives at his own definition of literacy which foregrounds purpose. In answer to our questions about where the literacy is in her film-making program, Grant describes the complex activities, negotiation and decision-making involved in learning to make even a simple film based on a familiar story. Lord and Grant have strong understandings of what a socio-cultural approach to multiliteracies requires of them in designing an early childhood literacy curriculum. They refuse simplistic models of literacy and instead build a curriculum around the negotiation and construction of complex texts which draw on existing cultural and linguistic resources, everyday knowledges and objects, and induct children into new repertoires of practices.

Theories of literacy learning that begin from a socio-cultural perspective have been important in educators' arguments against the narrowing down of the literacy curriculum to de-contextualised activities that focus merely on code-breaking. They provide instead a strong rationale for a curriculum that aims to develop sophisticated repertoires of literacy practices. These repertoires include decoding skills, but these skills are understood to be learned and used in the service of authentic meaning-making for the kinds of 'real' purposes Lord refers to above. According to this view, literacy is the making of socially recognisable meanings using available material technologies. People learn to use literacy in the course of their social interactions and when they need to get things done in everyday life. They use the range of material technologies available to them to make these meanings, whether these be pen and paper, digital still cameras, or computer software and desktop computers. Grant's and Lord's teaching begins from the assumption that, as is the case for adults, children also have genuine purposes for reading and writing or making films, and the cultural artefacts they produce will have real consequences in the world. Cameras and audio tape recorders are some of the many material technologies these teachers encourage their children to use in the process of developing repertoires of literacy practices that include complex and sophisticated literacies.

At least two models of literacy and literacy learning that are popular among teachers in the Australian context begin from the assumption that literacy is a socio-cultural practice, and argue that all children today need to develop repertoires of sophisticated literacy practices. The first is the four resources model developed by Peter Freebody and Allan Luke (Freebody and Luke, 1990; Luke and Freebody, 1999). The second is the 3D model developed by Bill Green (Durrant and Green, 2000; Green, 1988a), where the three dimensions of literacy learning are the operational, cultural and critical. Both models have many elements in common (Durrant and Green, 2000). Here we use Green's 3D model to illustrate how Grant's and Lord's film-making curriculum encompasses all three dimensions. Although the operational, cultural and critical dimensions of literacy are in practice developed simultaneously, for the purposes of clarity we will separate them here and discuss each in turn using illustrations from Grant's and Lord's curriculum practice.

Film-making and the cultural dimensions of literacy learning

Often in practice it is the cultural dimension that is foregrounded in curriculum work. According to Green's (1988a) original formulation of the 3D model, the cultural dimension refers to learning the culture and literacies associated with the disciplines or learning areas of the curriculum – in this case the learning area of language arts, English/literacy or media education. Within schooling, it is part of the *culture* of the English/literacy or media classroom for children to practice and learn a variety of means of self-expression, communication and semiotic representation. Film-making is just one of many means which can be explored in the curriculum.

Film-making is also understood by Grant and Lord as being 'cultural' in other senses. First, it assists them to make language and culture the object of study in their classrooms (Luke, Comber and Grant, 2003). For example, in Grant's classroom cultural diversity is used as a resource for learning as students' languages and cultures are explicitly made the subject of inquiry. Grant explains that she always begins by asking students two questions: 'Why are you making this film?' and 'Who is going to watch this?' For her, the children's films are not artificial exercises or dry runs. Rather, they have a purpose – the reason why they are being made – and they have an intended audience – the people who are going to watch them. Grant uses these questions to challenge her students to think about what they are producing from these perspectives. As a teacher she therefore foregrounds the authentic and public nature of their films at the same time as she draws on her students' own cultural concerns, questions and interests as important and necessary starting points for their production of new cultural texts.

Because she works with ESL students, many of the films made by Grant's class set out to represent and celebrate the cultural diversity of the classroom in symbolic and artistic form. Learning more about each other's histories, languages and cultures, and sharing this knowledge with others in their immediate and wider communities, drives student engagement and participation. At the same time as they participate in the cultural practice of collaborative film-making, Grant's students also necessarily practice their developing understandings of their new and common language, which is standard Australian English.

Similarly, the making of the film *Super Sausage* also began with students' immediate interests. The topic had a life among Lord's students because, as he says, movies of superheroes were something that was 'in the air' at the time. Children in his class were interested in and talking about the *Spiderman* movie even if they had not actually seen it. It had entered popular discourse and children's cultural lives through cross-media promotions and fast-food product tie-ins. But in what sense is this a 'real' context for learning? For Lord, even though the superhero genre is fantasy, it is also 'real' in young children's lives in the same way that play is real. As he says, play is real to children because it is about situations which children 'deem to be real'. The richness of young children's language during imaginative play is an important part of their cultural lives and is therefore a worthy subject of attention, whether during classroom time devoted to oral storytelling, or classroom time devoted to scripting and producing a narrative film based on a fairy-tale or fantasy.

A second point about cultural dimension of literacy learning in these classrooms is that the film texts not only arise from but also are inserted back into their cultural lives. Film products are the vehicle by which the new knowledge generated in the classroom is circulated within the school and wider community. Children know that the films will be seen and discussed by others. Thus there is an authentic purpose for the film-making that is closely related to students' own experiences.

The aim of *Aussie Slang* was to investigate the concept of 'slang' as evidenced in the different languages spoken by members of the school community. The film drew on children's and teachers' understandings of slang terms in Australian English, but also on individuals' knowledge of slang terms in a number of other languages including Arabic, Serbian and Khmer. The making of *Wave Cultures* required the group of children from 13 different countries to talk about how to wave, as well as what a wave signified, in their culture, whether this was hello or goodbye or something else. These film texts in turn were shown to a wider school community audience and also became potential resources for other language and literacy lessons in future classrooms. Similarly, *Super Sausage* was always intended to be screened for the wider school community. From the beginning it had an implied audience and a planned public outcome. It was envisaged as a crafted artefact designed to bring entertainment and pleasure, and a showcase for students' learning in relation to literacy and other learning areas. As students were well aware, *Super Sausage* would eventually take its place in a film archive alongside such films as the documentary of a project in which students recreated the experience of a working zoo.

Thus student-produced cultural artefacts are deliberately positioned within the public arena where they can be experienced and responded to by a range of audiences. Children's production of and participation in what Lord calls 'big events' are important to both teachers, who work with children to enter film competitions associated with youth arts festivals or to screen their films for audiences of teachers, parents and peers. In Lord's view, 'the world premiere of *Super Sausage*' was as important to the curriculum as its production.

Finally, a key philosophical and political principle for Grant and Lord is that they assist children to engage with the full range of cultural practices that they are studying. In the case of film-making, this means that at the same time as they produce films with the children, the teachers provide opportunities for children to organise and attend film screenings, to participate in lunch-time film clubs, and to establish and borrow from a library of student-produced films. Over time, students produce a body of work that is reproduced to send home for families to enjoy but which also enters the official archive of the school. Grant is now also receiving some small film-making sponsorships from local businesses and responding to wider inquiries about her students' films by making them available for sale to the public at a small cost. In this way her students do not merely 'pretend' to be film-makers.

Rather, they witness and participate in the full range of practices associated with film appreciation and with the funding, production and distribution of films.

Thus both teachers are working with children to build particular cultural dispositions in relation to inquiry, media-making and the arts. In the process their students are developing cultural capital of value within the wider social arena. While this is a common goal of schooling, the difference here is that rather than beginning from the canon of 'great' English literature or other valorised cultural artefacts, Grant and Lord consciously begin from and work with the popular, the pleasurable and the everyday.

Film-making and the operational dimensions of literacy learning

Each time a film is made, the operational dimensions addressed by the curriculum will vary. In the *Aussie Slang* project, Grant's children learned at least three operational dimensions of film-making: making a storyboard, framing a shot, and making meaning by incorporating still graphics – their scanned drawings – into live action footage. In the shorter film *Wave Cultures*, made very quickly with a group of five year-old new arrivals to Australia, the operational dimensions were more limited. As Grant expressed it, for that film no editing was needed, only jump cuts:

> They set the camera up and the tripod outside, with a nice background – we looked at the background which is a mural at the school – and the kids walked across and went 'hello' and 'goodbye' waving in their in their first language . . . it was just a matter of setting the shot up and getting children to press the button, press it on, press it off, so they could see through the LCD what was on and what was off, and each little snippet, that was the action, and I get somebody in the class to be stage manager, floor manager, and they say: 'Quiet on the set. Action.' And then film.
>
> (Helen Grant, March 2003)

Grant explained that with this same group she was looking at colour and projection using cellophane and an overhead projector, adding that 'those five-year-olds can tell you what a silhouette projection is and what transparent is. They know it. They know those two words because that's what we're doing in media.'

In the *Super Sausage* project Lord's students explored several operational aspects of film-making as they learned to:

- design and make sets
- scan their artwork
- frame a picture through the LCD of a digital video camera

- film a sequence against a fixed location
- film a sequence incorporating movement by using a makeshift dolly
- use a computer for digital editing
- transfer sequences of the film from digitised to analogue form so that it could be reviewed on a normal video cassette recorder.

In both classrooms, teachers deliberately and systematically taught their students new vocabulary and inducted them into new semiotic practices associated with film–based image-making. Such operational skills are useful in their own right, and are transferable to other times, places and projects. Moreover, teachers assisted children to develop their skills in being able to use these practices for their own purposes. They introduced children to an embodied understanding that such texts are crafted cultural constructs that can be used for specific purposes and ends.

So far, we have described some of the operational dimensions of film-making that Grant and Lord made explicit in the classroom and gave their students practice in using. At the same time, behind the scenes both teachers also encouraged students to practice the operational dimensions of more traditional early years literacy learning. Much of the language work in both teachers' classrooms focused on talk; it was conducted through talk, and was often about talk. Each film project began with narrative storytelling and oral story-boarding which was eventually translated on to paper with adult assistance.

In Grant's case, as students learned medium-specific vocabularies, written glossaries of film-making terms were made for future reference. Media terms introduced to children included 'LCD', 'framing', 'background' and 'foreground'. The topic Australian slang also provided a rich stimulus for learning new language as well as questioning language as children played with phrases such as 'bloke' (man), 'can it' (be quiet), 'have a cuppa' (have a cup of tea), 'spot on' (exactly) and 'kerfuffle' (fuss). In Lord's classroom, jokes and other plays on language were exploited for their own sake and as potential material for the *Super Sausage* film script. Some of these such as 'barbeque of terror' and 'tongs of nervousness' were first introduced by Lord, but the students added others and enthusiastically took up Lord's invitation to use a thesaurus to explore alternative linguistic constructions and in the process expanded their vocabularies.

Many other kinds of learning took place as well. In Lord's classroom, the kind of play that children of this age engage in as a matter of course took on another function. The children learned about the semiotic potential of objects (Kress, 1996). They saw how their play, toys and dress-ups could take on another function and become props and part of the plot in the film. At the same time, they talked about the conventional meanings associated with symbols like spiders when they are filmed in webs in the corners of dark and dusty castles or flower petals when they are thrown over the heads of a happy couple like Belle Lovely and Super Sausage, filmed running in slow motion towards each other.

The critical dimensions of literacy learning in these projects

Grant's and Lord's curriculum addressed the critical dimension of literacy learning in several ways. Both teachers emphasise action and doing. Their students are encouraged to act on the world by generating questions and collecting information, and by discussing and analysing their findings and their drafts as they go about making their films. Both teachers deliberately exploit children's linguistic and cultural resources. Both teachers position students as actors and agents in and on their worlds and places the films they make into the wider world for public scrutiny. Finally, both teachers encourage children to question who uses what kinds of language and images with what kinds of effects.

In the *Super Sausage* project, Lord's class deliberately played with references to other films. They used various kinds of music and other cultural references to produce a film that was fun to make and enjoyable to watch for a wide audience. Noting that much of his students' experience of older media forms and artefacts had been mediated through television programs like *The Simpsons*, Lord encouraged children to be similarly playful with catch phrases and conventions familiar from popular film and television. This led to little touches such as the referencing on screen of one of the songs sung by the class as being 'available now from selected record stores', and the note at the end of the film assuring viewers that 'No sausage was harmed in the making of this picture'. While Lord originally took the lead on such occasions, he noted that once the children were given licence to talk about things they were familiar with from other media they engaged in quite a lot of discussion about stereotypes and clichés and the intertextual referencing used to signify things like the horror or romance genres. Lord noted that:

> A lot of that was me saying it, but when I said it they went 'Oh yeah, we know what that means'. Obviously the kids aren't going to come up with playing the organ [to signify horror] straight away, but when we did it they said 'Oh yeah, we've seen things . . .'

> The beginning was a pinch from *Pinocchio*, and we watched *Pinocchio*, and then by the time we came to the end of it, the kids were fairly well tuned into it by that stage and were saying 'Oh yeah, we could do this . . . like the ending [was a pinch from] *Shrek*, so they were coming up with ideas. Or that part where Belle says 'Untie him or the rissole gets it'. I mean there was none of that when we started out, it was one of those things that 'How could we make them . . . ?' I think she had the knife and somebody said [in that] movie there she said 'Untie him'. And

taking him off to jail . . . one of the kids was cluey enough to say 'At least we can make the sequel now. He's still alive so he can be in the next one', *The Return of Dr van Nasty*.

(Andrew Lord, March 2003)

Thus the teacher gives students permission to articulate and examine their emerging understandings about text construction and deconstruction, both of which are important elements of critical literacy practice.

Documentary films made by Grant's students were also fun to make and watch, but at the same time, were often intended to make a difference to how audiences think about the subject of the films and the issues they raised. They incorporated a critical dimension in that they challenged the ways that social diversity is often masked or silenced in dominant cultural forms such as newspapers or history textbooks. In some cases, her students used their films to redress the absence of appropriate or up-to-date material about particular cultures and histories. For example, when a group of older students found that available printed material on Sudan was out of date, they drew on interviews with local community members as alternative resources for one film. Similarly, when making a film about Afghani settlement in Australia, another group of children investigated inscriptions on Afghani graves in local cemeteries and collected old photographs from members of the local Afghani community. The film *Aussie Slang* addressed the critical dimension of literacy learning by foregrounding issues of class and race. It explicitly raised the question 'What is *Aussie* about Aussie slang?' As Grant explained, 'it's not just "historical" language in that it is forever changing, and the slang depends on who uses it and which group you belong to'. In this way, the film foregrounded questions of social positioning and social difference and contested the homogenising and universalising tendencies of discourses of nationalism which continue to circulate in the Australian media despite the social diversity of the Australian population.

Working with multiple languages and multiple media, Grant and Lord construct rich opportunities for their young students to play and learn. Their classroom practices illustrate ways in which it is possible for teachers of even very young children to integrate all three of the operational, cultural and critical dimensions of literacy learning into the curriculum.

Happily ever after?

In respecting and learning from these teachers, we do not romanticise their work or the media artefacts they produced with the children. As Andrew Lord emphasised, 'It's not as easy as it looks'. While we may wish that classrooms were media-labs (Thomson and Comber, 2003), the schools where Grant and Lord work are not Hollywood or Bollywood, and their media resources are slim. Apart from the limits of human, technological and material resources, in addition these teachers dealt with ongoing tensions, of a practical and political nature, as they continued to try to make the space for complex critical literacies in early childhood classrooms. They spoke about the need to be aware of ethical matters concerning people's values and safety, as well as the more mundane issues of classroom management.

Not surprisingly, children sometimes wanted to make films which were violent, films which perpetuated gender inequalities, and films which may be interpreted as maintaining cultural stereotypes. These are complex issues which have faced teachers with respect to children's writing and reading for some time (e.g. see Dyson, 1993; Gilbert, 1989; Lensmire, 1994). However, they become even more prominent when children are engaged in producing film text as decisions about positioning and representation, scripts and plots, are immediately confronting and have potentially long-term consequences. Both Grant and Lord grappled with children's desires to depict violence. In regard to *Super Sausage* Lord set the ground rules by saying that 'there won't be any fights and no-one is going to die'. In Grant's situation, working with refugee children on temporary visas, she had additional factors to consider about which stories could be told, whose faces could be shown, which music could be played, and so on. Again both teachers incorporated these complex issues into their teaching, explicitly drawing children's attention to the possible consequences and interpretations which may result from their decisions. Children were being inducted into critical dispositions which required them to anticipate the effects of their textual practices. In addition, the children's products needed to be read as school-produced cultural artefacts. Both teachers needed to anticipate how the children's films might be viewed by their colleagues, school leaders and parents.

Along with these important concerns are the everyday complexities of managing the work of making films with large groups, indeed whole classes, of young children. Both teachers refer to occasional difficulties with supervising children who were misbehaving while at the same time directing the films. In fact in 2003, Lord reported that he postponed his big project until the fourth term when he felt that the particular class was ready to handle the levels of self-control required to successfully bring off such an undertaking. Behind the scenes there is all the management required of all teachers. In adding film-making to the curriculum, the teachers added to their labour (organising talent releases, supervising the use of expensive equipment, ensuring permission to leave the school grounds, and so on). However, in adding film-making to the curriculum, Grant and Lord also make available complex repertoires of literate and language practices such that young children can begin to understand first hand what it means to frame a picture, invent and script characters, and tell a story using images and dialogue and sound. They are engaged from the beginning in exploring language choices, questions of representation, and the semiotic potential of everyday objects.

We believe that it is important to closely document the work of early childhood teachers who are managing to design and accomplish complex literacy curricula with young children. Such teachers defy moves which reduce teaching to a series of routine actions and techniques. They contest some forms of developmentalism which result in infantalisation of the curriculum. They demonstrate powerfully that literacy teaching is always political, always cultural, always social, and potentially about positioning even very young people as analysts, producers and designers. While we write about these teachers here, our bigger project is to work with teachers to document their own work. Many forms of documentation are needed, accounts authored by teachers themselves, co-authored with researchers, across multiple media and in many different outlets. One of the most difficult parts of teachers' work is professional isolation and loneliness. This can lead to cynicism, burnout and anti-intellectualism. Grant and Lord resist such trends. These are teachers who go out on a limb in times when it may easier to teach by the book. If we think about teachers' work as cultural, then collaborating with this workforce to closely study and document practice is crucial to the status and the health of the profession.

References

Baker, C. and Freebody, P. (1993) The crediting of literate competence in classroom talk, *Australian Journal of Language and Literacy*, 16 (4): 279–294.

Buckingham, D. (1993) *Children Talking Television: The Making of Television Literacy*. London: Falmer Press.

Buckingham, D. and Sefton-Green, J. (1994) *Cultural Studies Goes to School: Reading and Teaching Popular Media*. London: Taylor & Francis.

Comber, B. (2003) Critical literacy: What does it look like in the early years? In N. Hall, J. Larson and J. Marsh (eds) *Handbook of Early Childhood Literacy*. London, New Dehli, Thousand Oaks, CA: Sage.

Comber, B., Badger, L., Barnett, J., Nixon, H. and Pitt, J. (2002) Literacy after the early years: a longitudinal study, *Australian Journal of Language and Literacy*, 25 (2): 9–23.

Durrant, C. and Green, B. (2000) Literacy and the new technologies in school education: meeting the l(IT)eracy challenge?, *Australian Journal of Language and Literacy*, 23 (2): 89–108.

Dyson, A. H. (1993) *Social Worlds of Children Learning to Write in an Urban Primary School*. New York: Teachers College Press.

Dyson, A. H. (1997) *Writing Superheroes: Contemporary Childhood, Popular Culture and Classroom Literacy*. New York and London: Teachers College Press.

Freebody, P. and Luke, A. (1990) 'Literacies' programs: debates and demands in cultural context, *Prospect*, 5 (3): 7–16.

Freire, P. (1998) *Teachers as cultural workers*. Boulder, CO: Westview Press.

Gilbert, P. (1989) Student text as pedagogical text. In S. De Castell, A. Luke and C. Luke (eds) *Language authority and criticism: Readings on the school textbook* (pp. 195–202). London: Falmer Press.

Grace, D. and Tobin, J. (1998) Butt jokes and mean-teacher parodies: video production in the elementary classroom. In D. Buckingham (ed.) *Teaching Popular Culture:
Beyond Radical Pedagogy* (pp. 42–62). London: UCL Press.

Green, B. (1988a) Subject-specific literacy and school learning: a focus on writing.
Australian Journal of Education, 32 (2): 156–179.

Green, B. (ed.) (1988b) *Metaphors and Meanings: Essays on English Teaching by Garth
Boomer*. Adelaide: AATE.

Green, B. (ed.) (1999) *Designs on Learning: Essays on Curriculum and Teaching by Garth
Boomer*. Adelaide: AATE.

Kavanagh, K. (2003) Old technologies and learning to be literate, *Australian Journal of
Language and Literacy*, 26 (1): 39–52.

Kellner, D. (2000) New technologies/new literacies: reconstructing education for the
new millennium, *Teaching Education*, 11 (3): 245–265.

Kress, G. (1996) Writing and learning to write. In D. Olson and N. Torrance (eds)
*The Handbook of Education and Human Development: New Models of Learning, Teaching
and Schooling* (pp. 225–256). Cambridge and Oxford: Blackwell.

Lankshear, C. and Lawler, M. (1988) *Literacy, Schooling and Revolution*, London:
Routledge/Falmer.

Lensmire, T. (1994) *When Children Write: Critical Revisions of the Writing Workshop*.
New York: Teachers College Press.

Luke, A. and Freebody, P. (1999) A map of possible practices: further notes on the
four resources model, *Practically Primary*, 4 (2): 5–8.

Luke, A. and Luke, C. (2001) Adolescence lost/childhood regained: on early intervention and the emergence of the techno-subject, *Journal of Early Childhood Literacy*,
1 (1): 91–120.

Luke, A., Comber, B. and Grant, H. (2003) Critical literacies and cultural studies. In
G. Bull and M. Anstey (eds) *The Literacy Lexicon* (pp. 17–35), 2nd Edition. Prentice-
Hall, Melbourne.

Luke, A., Lingard, R., Green, B. and Comber, B. (1999) The abuses of literacy. In
J. Marshall (ed.) *Educational Policy* (pp. 763–788). London: Edward Elgar.

Marsh, J. (2000) 'But I want to fly too!': Girls and superhero play in the infant classroom, *Gender and Education*, 12 (2): 209–220.

New London Group (1996) A pedagogy of multiliteracies: designing social futures,
Harvard Educational Review, 66 (1): 60–92.

Reid, J. and Comber, B. (2002) Theoretical perspectives in early literacy education:
Implications for practice. In L. Makin and C. Jones Diaz (eds) *Literacies in Early
Childhood: Challenging Views, Challenging Practice* (15–34). Sydney: Maclennan +
Petty.

Thomson, P. and Comber, B. (2003) Deficient 'disadvantaged students' or media-
savvy meaning makers? Engaging new metaphors for redesigning classrooms and
pedagogies, *McGill Journal of Education*, 38 (2): 305–328.

Afterword

Jackie Marsh

As the chapters in the this book attest, the world of early childhood literacy is in transition. This is a result of a complex interplay of factors which include increased use of digital technologies, globalisation and its attendant economic, political and social effects and the contested nature of childhood itself. In recent years, we have seen the emergence of aspects of childhood that have hitherto been negligible, such as the child as consumer, and child as agent. The boundaries between various age groups are blurring, with the use of terms such as 'tweenager' to signal early acquisition of adolescent interests, or the phenomena of 'kiddult' fiction in which certain book titles are marketed to both adults and children. This is a world in which there are few certainties and in which little should be taken for granted.

In Part 1 of this book, the dynamic nature of contemporary childhoods was emphasised and, in looking forward, the need to focus on the complexity of children's literacy practices is paramount. Traditional early childhood schooling has tended to focus on normalised versions of childhood in which developmentally appropriate practice can be neatly packaged for children who enjoy linear developmental trajectories. From early mark-making, to representations of known letters, through to standardised spelling; those early steps to literacy have, until recently, appeared to be straightforward and ultimately knowable. The chapters in Part 1, however, suggested otherwise. Not only are children's developmental journeys anything but linear (Dyson, 2002), they are shaped by diverse cultural, social, political and economic contexts and constantly responsive to technological innovations. This means that any analysis of young children's early language and literacy development needs to be cognisant of wider social practices and to attend to the rich divesity of children's experiences. Not to do so is, as the chapters in Part 1 reminded us, to limit our own understanding and to restrict the intellectual, cultural and social lifeworlds of young children.

Hitherto, research in the field of early childhood literacy has focused almost entirely on print on paper and, in doing so, has privileged particular modes of communication. There has been an over-emphasis on research into early mark-making, the reading of (canonical) story books and the teaching and learning of phonics. This narrow vision means that there is much yet to be learnt about how children encode, decode and make meaning using a wider range of modes of communication. The chapters in Part 2 of this book have offered meaningful accounts of children's engagement with a range of media and have contributed to an understanding of the affordances of these different modes. There is, obviously, much more work to be done in this field, but these chapters have thrown some light onto the complex, multimodal textual worlds of young children in contemporary societies. Only by deepening our understanding of children's interactions with a range of technologies can we begin to work our how best to support their growing understanding and development. This, as the chapters in Part 2 reminded us, requires observant, informed researchers and educators who respect children's choices and responses and who reflect carefully on the adult's role in this dynamic.

Such reflection on development and learning in a new media age is the hallmark of transformative teachers and, in Part 3, the work of insightful and sensitive educators was shared in order to develop further informed communities of practice in the field of early childhood techno-literacy. This work is, in many ways, just beginning, but it also draws on many years of excellent practice in relation to early childhood education. It is important to remember that, although we are in the midst of profound changes in communication and technology, some aspects of young children's literacy lives remain unchanged and many of the skills, knowledge and understandings developed by educators in the past continue to be essential to current and future schooling. However, there do need to be urgent and fundamental shifts in practice if the 'toddler netizens' (Luke, 1999) who populate early childhood settings across the globe are to be offered curricula and pedagogy which build appropriately upon their expertise and which prepare them for a future in which competence in the analysis and creation of multimodal texts is crucial. This should be an immediate concern for pre- and in-service teacher education but, unfortunately, in many countries around the world we see a frozen impotence in the face of these major and fast-moving cultural changes. For some, this communicational paradigm shift has created anxiety and uncertainty; lack of guidance from policy-makers in terms of future curricula direction has increased the level of risk felt by individual teachers and, in the blame culture of the 'Risikogesellschaft' (Beck, 1998), few early years educators feel prepared to chance the introduction of untried and untested pedagogies.

Although the chapters throughout this book are not intended to provide a blueprint for early years literacy curricula which offer children access to meaningful and relevant engagement in multimodal practices, they do raise key theoretical and empirical issues for consideration and they provide glimpses of pedagogy and curricula which reflect twenty-first-century concerns. However, this work is not to suggest that attention to contemporary communicative practices will address all of the difficulties faced by children as they journey along the road to literacy competence. Continued lack of equity in relation to cultural, economic and social capital will ensure that that does not happen (Bourdieu and Wacquant, 1992). Nevertheless, it is important to remember, as Paulo Freire notes:

> If education cannot do everything, there is something fundamental that it can do. In other words, if education is not the key to social transformation, neither is it simply meant to reproduce the dominant ideology.
>
> (Freire, 2001: 110)

Although early childhood education cannot change deeply embedded political, economic and social injustices, it can challenge them and an important step in this direction is to offer children opportunities to develop further their critical capacities with regard to multimodal text analysis and production. Literacy curricula which continue to emphasise the 'basics', which persist in privileging the written word above all else, which focus almost entirely on the page rather than the screen, and which base this work on a monolithic canon of texts, are steeped in dominant ideologies that reflect traditional concerns (Luke and Luke, 2001). The chapters in this book have provided a challenge to this prevailing attention to outmoded forms of communication in early childhood education and have offered alternative ideological and sociological analyses of children's contemporary literacy lives that can provide a platform for the development of culturally relevant curricula and pedagogy.

References

Beck, U. (1998) *Risk Society*. London: Sage.

Bourdieu, P. and Wacquant, L. J. D. (1992) *An Invitation to Reflexive Sociology*. Cambridge: Polity Press.

Dyson, A. H. (2002) *Brothers and Sisters Learn to Write: Popular Literacies in Childhood and School Cultures*. New York: Teachers College Press.

Freire, P. (2001) *Pedagogy of Freedom: Ethics, Democracy and Civic Courage*. Oxford: Rowan & Littlefield.

Luke, C. (1999) What next? Toddler netizens, Playstation thumb, techno-literacies, *Contemporary Issues in Early Childhood*, 1 (1): 95–100.

Luke, A. and Luke, C. (2001) Adolescence lost/childhood regained: on early intervention and the emergence of the techno-subject, *Journal of Early Childhood Literacy*, 1 (1): 91–120.

Index